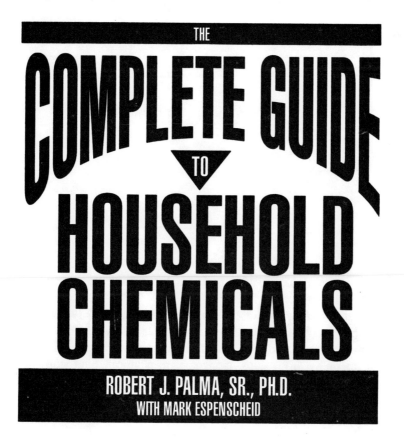

THE COMPLETE GUIDE TO HOUSEHOLD CHEMICALS

ROBERT J. PALMA, SR., PH.D.
WITH MARK ESPENSCHEID

Prometheus Books

59 John Glenn Drive
Amherst, NewYork 14228-2197

CHABOT COLLEGE LIBRARY

To the memories of the men who
loved and nurtured us—our fathers.

Published 1995 by Prometheus Books

99 98 97 96 95   5 4 3 2 1

Library of Congress Cataloging-in-Publication Data

Palma, Robert J., 1940–
    The complete guide to household chemicals / by Robert J. Palma,
Sr. with Mark Espenscheid.
        p.   cm.
    Includes bibliographical references and index.
    ISBN 0-87975-794-9 (cloth)
    1. Home economics. 2. Consumer education. 3. Household supplies.
I. Espenscheid, Mark. II. Title.
TX158.P24   1994
640—dc20   94-21778
                                                            CIP

Printed in the United States of America on acid-free paper.

Contents

Author's Note

Throughout this book we make every effort to caution readers that the chemical reactions either discussed or alluded to herein can be dangerous, and that all chemicals should be handled with extreme caution and under the *direct* supervision of a trained professional. Neither we nor the publisher warrant that the instructions and formulas in this book are completely free of risk or hazard.

We do not endorse any products discussed herein, and our occasional use of trade names should not be taken to imply that we consider them superior to generic products. Trade names—for example, Spic 'n' Span® rather than "all-purpose cleaner"—are used in those instances where we believe readers are more familiar with a popular trade name than with a generic name or description.

Our recommendations regarding the efficacy, use, cost, and appropriate handling of chemical compounds and commercial products mentioned in this book are based upon firsthand data we collected through observation, in laboratories, or as the result of chemical or related literature.

With respect to medications, whether of the over-the-counter variety or prescription drugs, readers must not change the type, dosage, or any particulars of these medications without first seeking the expert advice of their physician, dentist, pharmacist, or other healthcare professional.

To the best of our knowlege, the information in the text, notes, appendices, and glossary is correct. We solicited dentists, physicians, pharmacists, additional healthcare professionals, and other chemists in developing certain parts of this book and in editing segments of the final draft.

Introduction

Ours is a world filled with chemicals: the products and substances derived from chemicals, by-products of chemical compounds, chemical waste, and so on. Chemicals destroy many of the bacteria and viruses that are responsible for illness and death; various chemical mixtures help alleviate pain; and some have even changed the way humans reproduce as a species. Medications, synthetic materials for clothing, modern housing materials, fuels to aid transportation, fertilizers and pesticides, personal hygiene and cosmetic products, and nutritional supplements are just a few of the areas that benefit from the powerful role chemicals play in our daily lives.

The use of chemicals is not without its hazards as well: certain chemicals and chemical mixtures can be dangerous if mishandled. Our air, water, and soil may be rendered unsafe due to the misuse of chemicals. While it is true that many television, radio, and printed reports point out the negative effects of misused chemicals, it is also equally true that many of the products we use and rely upon are the result of inventive chemistry—in fact, we would be hard pressed to do without them (e.g., plastics, rubber, cosmetics, cleaners, disinfectants, pesticides, and the like).

The overwhelming majority of us are not chemists, and for that reason we cringe at the thought of ever being able to understand the broad array of chemical compounds we use and depend on every day. This mysterious realm of chemistry seems so baffling and complex that most people feel helpless and inept when the subject comes up. Though we are often confused by (or simply ignorant of) the world of chemicals around us, it's hard not to be frustrated, angered, and

11

intimidated by the flood of claims and counterclaims pressed by environmentalists, consumer protection groups, and medical studies on the one hand, and chemical companies, pharmaceutical firms, and related manufacturers on the other. In addition, countless times each day we are inundated with words and images announcing that one or another product is new, improved, makes clothes softer or whiter, is fat and/or cholesterol free, or some such claim. How are we to unravel these messages to decide what is best for us and for our environment?

It may seem that we will never make sense of it all, but if we really want to understand the fascinating world of chemicals in our midst, it just takes a little effort. It took time and a lot of serious thought but today more and more people feel comfortable asking questions of their medical providers. At first the idea of questioning the methods and practices of healthcare providers was a scary prospect, but we learned to do it and most would agree that we are far better for having taken the initiative. Similarly, most of us are not at all sure what goes on under the hood of a car, but with a little help from consumer programs on television and radio and the "how-to" columns in local newspapers we have learned how to ask intelligent questions about repairing, maintaining, and purchasing a vehicle.

With the dawn of consumerism in the late 1970s, a growing number of people have now become more comfortable delving into the content and composition of products that affect their lives. This is particularly the case when shopping for food. Years ago, most people never paid much attention to the content of packaged foods and beverages, but probes by consumer groups and federal agencies like the Food and Drug Administration (FDA), an increased concern for gaining control over what we eat and drink, and the simple economic need to learn the value of comparison shopping found many more people reading product labels for nutrition information and to determine the presence of dyes, additives, and the like.

Now that consumer awareness is more acute in the supermarket, the drug store, and elsewhere in the marketplace, it is time to tackle another major hurdle—the pervasive fear and ignorance of household chemicals and how they affect your life. The more you know about detergents, toothpaste, cough medicines, floor waxes, lawn care products, and other items around the house, the better prepared you will be to assess the dangers of chemicals when they are mentioned in the news; the more selective you will be in choosing products for your home; and the more careful you will be in using, storing, and disposing of chemicals. Your health and safety, your piece of mind, and your wallet will benefit from the information in this book.

We hope to inform and enlighten the uninitiated while increasing the comfort level of people who know next to nothing about the content of the products they use each day. That being the case, simplicity is the key: this book is designed to make life easier for you. Prepared for the curious consumer who has no formal knowledge of ordinary chemicals and their properties, this volume discusses what we take to be some common questions raised about household chemicals. We attempt to answer these questions in a simple and straightforward manner. Our approach is to "walk" you through your home with the goal of explaining the ordinary chemicals found there. Rest assured, you have no reason to feel intimidated, self-conscious, or uneasy. *This is not a chemistry book,* but rather a book about chemicals you are likely to encounter in and around the house. It is offered as a helpful guide for those who want to learn a bit more about the products all of us buy and use every day. Some brand names of chemical products are used because you are more familiar with them than the chemical names, but there are similar products on the market that have the same formulation and/or effects. For example, sodium lauryl sulfate is the cleansing agent found in most toothpastes, shampoos, soaps for personal hygiene, and in some laundry detergents. Just check a few labels in the supermarket the next time you shop. What, you say, detergents in my toothpaste?! Yes, but there is no need for alarm, once the concept of a detergent becomes clear.

Reading a product label need not be intimidating or overwhelming. We will show you how simple it can be. The primary key to using our guide is an open mind and a willingness to learn and have fun. It is our hope that after reading this book you will save money by making better choices while shopping and by being a wiser, more safety-conscious consumer.

Did you know that Americans spend about $15 billion each year on soaps, detergents, bleaches, fabric softeners, waxes, and polishes? If automotive products and items for personal hygiene are added, the amount of money spent (about $36.5 billion) would exceed the gross national product of Peru. In other words, there is a lot of money to be made attracting consumers to specific products for personal or home use. Another purpose of this book, then, is to enlighten you about how manufacturers encourage you to buy one product over another.

We also hope to prevent readers from being harmed when using or disposing of common chemicals.

In the language of today's more computer literate society, this book is intended to be "user friendly." Although there are many long and complicated chemical names used throughout our discussion, it is not necessary to memorize any of them. This is simply the language chemists use; it should not be viewed as a mystery. You may not be able to pronounce many of them, but since they appear on every sort of product label, you must at least try to understand what these chemicals actually do. Remember the sodium lauryl sulfate we mentioned above? Well, it proved to be a rather long name for a basic cleaning agent—a detergent.

In planning this book we "walk you through your home," helping you to better understand the chemistry involved in items found in the laundry room, the kitchen, the bathroom (both inside and outside the medicine cabinet), the living room, the bar, your car and the garage, and the back yard. Environmental concerns are addressed when they arise in each part of the home, rather than attempting to place them in a separate chapter. Words that are used quite frequently are listed with their definitions in a glossary at the back of the book.

Each chapter relates to a specific section of your home. Although there will inevitably be some overlapping of the discussion, we have tried our best to keep each chapter as self-contained as possible. This way, if you wish, you can focus on just those areas of the house and the specific products that interest you most. Consumer products are reformulated every few years and you should be aware that many of these alterations are simply "marketing changes," which often leave the public with the impression that some new and miraculous results will occur. An example is Bayer's analgesic tablets: they are now sold in three different blends, each of which purportedly has a unique formulation. Actually, the chemicals used are not novel or they would attempt to patent each one.

*   *   *

We would like to acknowledge Steven L. Mitchell of Prometheus Books for inspiring us to write this book. His fertile and imaginative mind fueled our nebulous concept of a book for consumers.

Finally, we must point out that we wrote this book for our own satisfaction, since we, too, are consumers. Many thanks to all our present and former students for their encouragement and advice.

1

Before We Get Started

Various complex terms on product labels might seem rather formidable. As most consumers are now aware, when reading the list of ingredients on a product label, the chemical present in the greatest amount is usually listed first, followed by the chemical in the second greatest amount, and so on. The exception to this ordering on labels is sometimes found in cosmetic preparations or pharmaceuticals. In these cases, the pharmaceutical that is responsible for achieving the physiological action (for example, the skin softener in a hand lotion) is listed separately. The antibacterial preparation called Phisohex®, for example, contains only 3 percent hexachlorophene, which is the antibacterial agent. Certain products, such as some toothpastes, only list their active ingredients—in this case sodium or stannous fluoride (stannous being another name for tin).

In some cases product labels can appear alarming, that is if you forget to consider the amount of the substance present. One artificial sweetener lists silicon dioxide as the fourth or fifth ingredient. Silicon dioxide is purified sand! However, it is present in extremely minute quantities and serves as a drying agent to prevent caking. Nearly all liquid bleaches, brand names or otherwise, contain 5 percent hypochlorite, (the bleaching agent). Other liquid bleaches found in the supermarket also contain the same percentage of hypochlorite. Here is a good chance to save money by purchasing a store brand rather than the higher-priced brand name product.

Some pharmaceutical products use an outdated naming system that is no longer accepted by the American Chemical Society. If you can't locate the name of an ingredient, we recommend the *Merck*

*Index.** An example of this naming confusion is the compound ethyl caprylate, used in synthetic fruit flavors. Three correct names for this compound are: octanoic acid ethyl ester, ethyl octanoate, and ethyl octylate, all three of which are listed in the *Merck Index* and cross indexed along with the crude name—ethyl caprylate. Pharmaceuticals are covered in greater detail in the *Physician's Desk Reference* (PDR) or the *Physician's Desk Reference for Nonprescription Drugs.*† Two other excellent books are the *Complete Guide to Prescription and Nonprescription Drugs* by H. W. Griffith, M.D.,‡ and the *Essential Guide to Nonprescription Drugs,* edited by D. R. Zimmerman.**

Nevertheless, some content formulations still list nothing more than the active ingredient. For more information on the chemical composition of a specific product you can always call or write the manufacturer's consumer representative. They are very willing to give any nonproprietary information that you might desire. (See Appendix 4 for a list of toll free numbers.) Proprietary material on a chemical compound or a chemical mixture is information protected by a patent or copyright.

Various of the terms used on labels seem somewhat confusing because they are so long, with many syllables. Chemists use a series of prefixes and suffixes along with formulas for the particular compounds. The prefixes indicate the number of atoms of the same element in the compound: mono = one, di = two, tri = three, tetra = four, penta = five, hexa = six, hepta = seven, octa = eight, non = nine, and dec = ten.

There are two very common combustion products produced from burning fossil fuels. One is carbon *mono*xide, a very toxic gas; the other is carbon *di*oxide, a less noxious gas. The chemist would have used the formulas for each: CO has one carbon atom and only one oxygen atom; therefore it must be *carbon monoxide.* CO_2 has only one carbon atom and two oxygen atoms. The correct name for CCl_4

---

*Published by Merck & Co. of Rahway, New Jersey (1990). This reference volume can be found in most libraries. It lists the correct names for common compounds, some of their physical properties, and the common use for each compound.

†Both of which are published by the Medical Economics Company Inc., Oradell, New Jersey.

‡Published by the Body Press/Perigee of Tucson, Arizona

**Published by Harper and Row, New York.

is carbon tetrachloride. The main constituent of gasoline is the compound octane. Gasoline is comprised of simple compounds having only carbon and hydrogen atoms. The formula for octane is C_8H_{18}. Since this compound contains only carbon and hydrogen, the number of hydrogen atoms need not be listed.

There are some other commonly used prefixes such as *poly* and *hypo*. Poly indicates there is more than one atom per molecule, though it is rather ambiguous since it doesn't indicate how many more than one. Hypo refers to the lowest number of oxygen atoms in a formula. Let's look at some common formulas for chlorine-oxygen compounds. Sodium chloride (NaCl) is the simplest combination and needs no further discussion. NaHClO is named sodium hypochlorite since it has only one oxygen atom, while $NaClO_2$ is named sodium chlorite, $NaClO_3$ is named sodium chlorate, and $NaClO_4$ is called sodium perchlorate.

Are you totally confused? Well, don't feel bad since most chemistry majors can't figure this out either. The naming of chemical compounds can be done using a strict system. Unfortunately there are so many compounds having old-fashioned, obsolete names or a combination of the old and new naming systems that the reader can't help but be confused. Vinegar, for example, contains 5 percent acetic acid; however, the correct name for acetic acid is ethanoic acid. The correct name for muriatic acid (used in pools and cleansing metals) is actually called hydrochloric acid.

Suffixes are even more confusing and the reader should try to ignore them whenever possible. Common suffixes include: *ite, ide, ate,* and *ic.* It would take a great deal of time to explain them, and this is not one of the major purposes of our discussion. Nevertheless, you should try to familiarize yourself with the names of the basic chemical elements. There is no need to memorize them, since they are listed in Appendix 1. You can refer to them as the need presents itself.

CALCULATING COST PER UNIT

Placed on many supermarket shelves, near the item you are considering, will be a label marked UNIT COST. This means that the amount of the product in fluid ounces, pounds, or ounces by weight has been divided into the total cost of the item. An example might be a 16 fluid ounce container of juice that costs $0.68. It will have a unit cost of $0.68/16 or $0.04 per fluid ounce. This is how much it costs per ounce for this brand of juice. By comparing the unit cost of various brands, you can determine how high the unit cost of your choice will be. You don't have to be a scientist or a mathematician to determine unit cost. Whip out that inexpensive pocket calculator (we recommend solar powered models since they cost the same but don't require batteries), punch in the cost in dollars (say $1.28), hit the divide button, punch in the weight or volume (say 8.4 fluid ounces), and then press the equal (=) button. Give it a try. The answer is $0.15 per fluid ounce. Supermarkets are becoming increasingly aware of cost-conscious consumers; some chain stores are even placing calculators on their shopping carts.

An item's unit cost is very important once you have selected a particular product. The same brand name product may be available in different sizes. For example, a store may market a particular brand of dog food in three sizes: a one-pound bag for $0.85, a five-pound bag for $4.05, and a twenty-five-pound bag for $18.50. Which of these bags has the lowest cost per unit? The one-pound bag has a unit cost of $0.85 per pound; the five-pound bag has a unit cost of $0.81 per pound; and the twenty-five-pound bag has a unit cost of $0.74 per pound. In this example, as in most cases, the larger-sized bag has a much lower cost per unit price. *Beware,* not all larger-sized products are less expensive. For example, a generic hand lotion (not protected by a trademark designation and exactly the same as other compounds or products in its classification) in a one-half quart size may sell for $1.37 while a one-quart size of the same brand sells for $2.73. However, both of these sizes have the same per unit cost of $2.73. Some manufacturers realize that many people buy larger sizes to save money. Knowing this, they sometimes don't give discounts for larger sizes. Use your common sense when making these comparison purchases. Buying a fifty-pound bag of potatoes because of the significantly lower cost per unit may be wasteful if you are only able to use a few pounds a week.

Increasingly, we are becoming a metric country and will soon join the rest of the world in using metric units for size, weight, and volume. The use and conversion of "American" units to their metric equivalents is shown is Appendix 2. All you need to know in reading labels are the milligram (mg) and kilogram (kg) units of weight in the metric system (2.2 pounds = 1 kilogram). The liter and milliliter (ml) are units of volume (1 liter = 1,000 ml). The unit of length in the metric system is the meter (m). A meter is slightly longer than a yard. You will see prefixes used with these metric units: m = milli or one-thousandth, d = deci or one-tenth, c = centi or one hundredth, kilo = 1,000 (the basic metric unit).

2

Let's Start in the Laundry Room

While in the laundry room, items of interest that most often come to mind are detergents, liquid and dry bleach, laundry soaps, whiteners/brighteners, fabric softeners, prewash treatments, starches and fabric sizing, hard or soft water, water softeners, and water treatments, to name just a few.

One important term in laundry room chemistry will surface again later when we discuss hair and skincare products—namely, pH. So many manufacturers' advertisements tout that their products are "pH balanced," but what does this mean? The pH scale runs from 0.00 to 14.00. Acidic substances have a pH value of 0.0–6.8. Here are some examples of acidic compounds: gastric acid has a pH of 1.0, muriatic acid has a pH of 1.0, citrus juices range in pH from 4.0 to 6.5. Common alkaline substances are at the high end of the pH spectrum and include: sodium carbonate (washing soda) with a pH of 12.0, and sodium bicarbonate which has a pH of 8.0. We will discuss pH more in later chapters. Keep in mind that if the pH is less than 7.0, the compound is acidic; if it is greater than 7.0, then the compound is considered basic or alkaline. If the pH for a particular product is very close to 7.0, the the solution is near neutral, meaning that it is neither acidic nor basic. The table on page 24 lists other examples.

Q. What does adding sodium carbonate (washing soda) do to change the pH of the water, the detergent, and the items being washed? Why should it matter if the pH level is increased?

THE pH SCALE AND SOME COMMON ACIDS AND BASES

pH	Acid or Base	Example
0–2	Strong Acid	nitric, sulfuric, and hydrochloric acids
3–7	Weak Acid	urine (uric acid), citrus juice (citric acid), vinegar (acetic acid), carbonated beverages, tomatoes, milk (lactic acid), saliva
7	Neutral	pure water, blood*, eggs*
7–9	Slightly Basic (Alkaline)	baking soda, detergents, shampoos, antacids, chlorine bleach
9–14	Strongly Basic (Alkaline)	washing soda, hair remover, ammonia, sodium hydroxide, milk of magnesia

*actually, they are barely basic

A. Sodium carbonate is a basic or alkaline powder generally premixed with detergents or added separately to the wash water. The pH level of the wash water and the clothing therefore increases markedly. High pH is essential for proper functioning of the detergent.

DETERGENTS, SOAPS, AND MORE

Q. What are phosphate detergents?

A. They are simply detergents that use phosphate instead of washing soda to increase the pH of the wash water. They are also more effective than washing soda-type detergents because phosphates can sequester (or tie up) certain metal salts found in hard water and convert the hard water into soft water. A common name for phosphates found in detergents is sodium tripolyphosphate (STPP), which is both inexpensive and not toxic for humans.

Q. If detergents that use STPP are so effective, safe, and inexpensive, why are they banned or limited in certain cities or towns?

A. Some areas have very low levels of phosphates in their rivers and lakes: this is the natural and normal state for these waterways! As phosphates enter these areas from washing machine waste water (as well as farming runoff), they fertilize aquatic weeds and blue-green algae. As these organisms grow, they deplete the oxygen content of the water, thereby killing certain fish and causing foul odors from the growth of undesirable bacteria that do not need oxygen to live (also called anaerobic bacteria). Nearly all of the effected regions in our country have either banned or limited the amount of phosphate permitted in detergents sold in their areas. Read a few labels on detergent boxes to determine if your area has restricted or completely banned phosphates.

Q. Are there any safe substitutes for phosphates in washing products?

A. Sodium carbonate was, and still is, the most common substitute for phosphates. It is inexpensive but it can cause rashes and/ or irritation if the wash water or the chemical in its powdered form comes in contact with your skin. Other substitutes are being tested now.

Q. Is there anything else present in laundry detergents?

A. Detergents can also contain brighteners, bleaches, perfume, anti-redeposition agents, enzymes, surfactants, and chemicals to prevent washing machine damage. *Optical brighteners* are dyes deposited on clothing so they can transmit to the human eye that portion of light which is normally invisible—the ultraviolet rays. Contrary to the claims of some manufacturers, clothes cannot be made "whiter than white," but they can appear to be so. *Antiredeposition agents* coat the clothing with a cotton-like substance called carboxymetacellulose, which prevents the dirt that has been washed off from redepositing on clothes during the wash cycle. The agent is then removed during the rinse cycle.

Detergents have a difficult time breaking down and removing protein substances such as egg, milk products, and blood. The *enzymes* in detergents are present to break down protein substances so they can be removed by the detergent. *Dry bleaches,* such as sodium perborate, are added to bleach out some stains. They are present in small amounts in detergent and usually can't tackle those large "tough" stains. It should be pointed out here that the bleaching agents in laundry detergents do not have to remove a stain to be effective. Changing the color of the stain will serve the same purpose.

The most important component in detergent is the *surfactant* or the basic detergent. This is the chemical in the detergent mixture that actually does the job of removing the dirt.

Q. How does a surfactant clean?

A. The most widely used surfactant is named linear alkydbenzene sulfonate, or LAS. Surfactants have two main functions. First, they reduce the surface tension that water experiences when it comes in contact with the clothing. This allows the wash water to penetrate more deeply into your clothes. Have you ever seen chemically treated fabrics act impervious to water? The surface tension of the treated fabric is so high that water runs off. (No wonder people put fabric guard on sofas, chairs, and carpets.) The formation of beads of water on a freshly polished car is another example of high surface tension. But in order for clothes to be cleaned, the surface of the fabric must be "wet" for the water to penetrate. Surfactants decrease the surface tension of the clothes so they can get wet.

The second function of surfactants is to remove dirt. Since such things as dirt, oil, and grease are insoluble in water—in other words, they don't dissolve—this is a difficult task. Somehow, the surfactant must not only remove the dirt but render it soluble, too. The surfactant molecule has one end that dissolves in oil, grease, and dirt, and another end that is soluble in water. The oil/grease-soluble end dissolves the dirt on the clothing. As the clothes are agitated, the water-soluble end of the surfactant moves the entire molecule, along with the dirt, off the clothes and into the wash water.

Q. Why do detergents and soaps have such a difficult time cleaning in "hard water"? And by the way, what exactly is hard water?

A. Hard water is any water that contains high concentrations of calcium, magnesium, or iron salts. Many people have experienced hard water as having an iron taste or a reddish cast, but the water can be clear, odorless, and taste quite good, yet be "hard."

If you are concerned about your tap water, contact your municipal water supplier. For the many people who depend on wells for their water, here are a few hints you might use to determine if your water is hard: heavy scaling in boilers, a light brown color to the water (iron), the need to use excessive amounts of detergent in the laundry, difficulty getting soaps or shampoos to lather, and the ability of the water to rinse soap off very quickly. Try this test. Wash your hands with soap and rinse them off with distilled water. Repeat the process with your tap water. If the water from the faucet rinses off as slow as the test with distilled water, then you probably have soft rather than hard water. An accurate determination of the degree of hardness in your water can be done for about $15.00 by a testing laboratory.

The problem with hard water is that the minerals present react with soaps or detergents thus blocking them from cleaning, which means that the amount of soap or detergent required for cleaning must increase significantly.

Q. Is there anything I can do to soften my water? Is hard water safe to drink?

A. Hard water is generally quite safe to drink. It is the same as the expensive mineral water that some people enjoy. The only caution is if the water is slightly colored. This usually means high concentrations of iron are present, and some people experience gastric problems with high iron levels.

Fortunately, hard water can be "softened." Water softeners come in various sizes and types. You can purchase either a whole-house water softening unit or a small, localized unit for under the sink or in the laundry room. If your water tastes fine then all you would need is a unit connected to your washing machine. These units are either *ion exchange* or *reverse osmosis* types. The ion exchange type contains tiny, densely packed beads which have sodium salt attached to each bead. As the hard water enters the bead column, the calcium, magnesium, and iron salts "push" the sodium off the column and replace it. The water leaving the column is very low in calcium, magnesium, and iron and very high in sodium. Since sodium ions are exchanged for calcium, magnesium, and iron ions, the process is called ion exchange. It is not necessary for you to understand ions at this point. However, ions are simply electrically charged atoms. Metals form positive ions, and nonmetals form negatively charged ions. When the salt sodium chloride dissolves in water a positive sodium ion and a negatively charged chloride ion are formed.

Reverse osmosis units act somewhat like a filter in that they allow water to pass and prevent the movement of just about everything else. Pressure is needed to force the water through the unit. Some units can even run on tap water pressure. Since reverse osmosis units are rather expensive, those who are considering a purchase are urged to read *Is Your Water Safe to Drink?** The book is a bit difficult for the layperson to read, but the section on reverse osmosis filters is well written.

Q. Even though my water supply may not be hard, would it help in cleaning my clothes if I added a water softener?

A. Since nearly all detergents have water softeners (check the label), don't waste your money purchasing additional softeners unless your water is very hard.

Q. What difference, if any, is there between laundry soaps and laundry detergents?

A. Detergents clean clothes somewhat better than soaps in hard water. (However, they are milder. We will explain this in greater detail shortly.) Soaps are made from cooking animal fat (stearates) and sodium hydroxide with salt. Detergents are prepared from a synthetic surfactant-linear alkylsulfonate (LAS) and other agents.

Q. Are there any detergents that work well in hard water?

A. The presence of water softeners (sequestering agents that render calcium, magnesium, and iron inactive) in the detergent mix indicate which detergents work best. Read a few labels and de-

---

*Consumers Reports Books of Mt. Vernon, New York (1988) pages 216–26.

termine the product that puts water softeners highest on the list of ingredients. Probably, this will be the one that works best in hard water.

Q. Wouldn't the use of laundry soaps be preferred over detergents? Some manufacturers state that their soaps are even 99.44 percent pure.

A. No soap is actually 99.44 percent pure: trapped air alone can account for 1 to 2 percent of its weight. Additives such as fragrance, softeners, and other chemicals can amount to 5 to 20 percent of a soap's weight. Laundry soaps are quite mild and are therefore used for washing baby clothing. Soap reacts with hard water to form an insoluble, unreactive form of soap that is deactivated and unable to clean. It will coat the clothing to some extent with a gray "scum."

Q. Why don't detergents react with the same magnesium and calcium in hard water as soaps do? Why are detergents better for cleaning than laundry soaps?

A. Detergents do react with calcium and magnesium. However, they react to form a soluble compound that is easily removed in the rinse cycle. Soaps form an insoluble compound that clings or sticks to the clothing during all wash cycles.

Q. What is the difference between Sal soda, washing soda, and sodium carbonate?

A. They are all the same compound, which is used to increase the pH level of the wash water. This compound is found in detergents and many household cleaners.

Q. Why are certain cleaning agents referred to as "soap"?

A: According to a popular theory, in the Sapo hills near Rome, many sacrificial altars were built on potash-rich soil (potassium hydroxide is a strong base). When animals or humans were sacrificed as burnt offerings, the fat dripped on to the ground and reacted with the potash to form what we now refer to as crude soap. Like most discoveries, the use of this crude soap was determined by accident.

Q. Why do some detergents foam better than others?

A. Many consumers associate foam with increased detergent power. Foam has little, if any, relationship to the ability of a detergent to clean clothing. The main function of foam is to take up and hold particles of soil, thereby preventing them from redepositing on clothing.

Q. What is meant by biodegradable detergents?

A: Biodegradable materials can break down in water through the action of naturally occurring microorganisms. All modern detergents are biodegradable because the surfactant molecule is linear (straight). Prior to 1966, crooked or branched surfactants were used and, due to the shape of the molecule, they could not be "eaten" by the microorganisms. The concentration of surfactant increased in our waterways and some beaches and sidewalks of lakeside towns became thick with suds.

Q. What is a "builder"? I saw the term once in reference to laundry detergents.

A. Builders are additives that increase the ability of a surfactant to clean. Water softeners, pH adjusters, bleaches, and the like are all builders. An interesting builder in detergents is sodium carboxymethylcellulose. (What a mouthful!) Its function is to prevent dirt particles from getting back on our clothes during the wash. Imagine a white shirt with a black sooty spot. If you washed it with a detergent that lacked a redeposition agent, the soot would be dissolved but would tend to form a uniform grey color all over the shirt.

Q. Are detergents especially designed for fine washables worth the expense?

A. Not really. For the most part, commercial laundry detergents were too harsh for fine washables, so manufacturers created less caustic detergents. In the majority of cases liquid dish washing soaps are mild enough and just as safe for fine washables. The only thing that liquid dish washing soap lacks is a fabric whitener, but a small amount of bluing (for extra whiteness) will do the trick for a fraction of the cost.*

Q. Wait a minute. I'm supposed to add *bluing* to help make my wash *white*?

A. It does sound odd, we know. However, while bluing agent solutions are colored blue, their function is to screen out light rays that give white clothing a yellow cast.

Q. I heard that some detergents have a lot of "filler" just to increase the weight of the detergent so the manufacturer can charge more. Is that true?

A. Fillers do add bulk to the detergent and help it produce a free-flowing powder. An inert substance such as sodium sulfate is commonly added and may constitute 50 percent of the weight of a detergent. We don't think companies add filler to increase profits, especially when you consider that concentrated detergents and liquid detergents are taking a larger market share than ever.

A word of caution! Liquid detergents contain no filler at all, thus they are very concentrated; consumers should be cautious in handling them.

Q. If there are just a few basic chemical compounds in a laundry detergent, then why are there so many detergents on the market? Aren't they all basically the same?

A. The Procter and Gamble Company produces eight laundry detergents and a laundry soap. If you don't believe us, go to your supermarket and read the detergent labels. Most detergents are formulated in nearly the same way. For this reason, we recommend that you to try the least expensive detergent that gives you the desired results.

Q. Are liquid detergents superior to dry detergents?

---

*Always test an inconspicuous part of a garment before trying a new cleaning method.

A. They may be more convenient to use but they clean no better than dry detergents. Since they are more concentrated than the dry detergents, less of the liquid variety is needed. However, when you calculate the cost per load, you will find that they are similar. To calculate the cost per load you will first have to determine the measuring unit used for a load (cups, fluid ounces, or even scoops). Next you will need to determine the number of these measuring units in the container. Once you have done this, divide the number of measuring units in the box into its price. This yields the cost per measuring unit (cents per cup, cents per fluid ounce, or cents per scoop). Multiplying this figure times the recommended amount per load gives the cost per load. The cost per load is much more useful than the cost per unit. More concentrated detergents have a higher cost-per-fluid-ounce value and might seem very expensive until the cost per load is taken into account.

Let's illustrate this with a dry detergent. The cost is $2.30 for 61 dry ounces or 1.75 kilograms. The manufacturer recommends the use of ¾ cup for a load. The problem is obvious. The recommended amount is in cups and the price is based on weight. The simplist solution is to use a measuring cup, pour out the box and determine the number of cups in a box. You can do the same with scoops. Let's assume the box had about 7.5 cups. The cost per measuring unit is $2.30 ÷ 7.5 = $0.31 per cup. The cost per load would be $0.31 per cup × ¾ cup per load = $0.23 per load. As you can see, there really is a difference!

Q. Why are certain laundry detergents supposedly better at cleaning clothes in cold water?

A. We have never seen any evidence to prove this to be true. Let's read some detergent labels and see. The largest selling "cold water" detergent is Cheer®, which is produced by Procter and Gamble. This company also produces Tide®, which is not touted as a "cold water" detergent. The ingredients for their liquid detergent Cheer® are: cleaning agents (anionic and nonionic surfactants), enzymes, water softener, dispensing aid (propylene glycol), buffering agents, water, stabilizing agents, soil suspending agent, color-protecting agent, colorant, and perfume. And these are the Tide®

ingredients: cleaning agents (anionic and nonionic surfactants), enzymes, water softeners, dispensing aids (probably propylene glycol), buffering agents, water, stabilizing agents, soil suspending agent, fabric whiteners, colorant, and perfume.

The only difference in the ingredients is that Cheer® has a color-protecting agent and Tide® has a fabric whitener. Frankly, the only compound that could change the effectiveness of a detergent in cold water is the amount of surfactant. Most liquid detergents are already about 46 to 58 percent surfactant.

BLEACH

Q. Since you pointed out that most detergents have a dry bleach added, why would I need to add additional bleach?

A. The amount of bleach added to detergents is quite small and is easily overtaxed by badly stained clothing.

Q. What is "all fabric bleach"?

A. These are the dry or liquid bleaches that use sodium perborate. To be an "all fabric bleach" it should be able to remove stains with equal ease from cotton, wool, silk, and synthetics.

Q. What chemicals are present in dry bleaches?

A. The list of ingredients for a popular dry bleach is as follows: peroxygen bleaching agent (sodium perborate), protease (an enzyme that breaks down protein), sequestering agent (water softener), bluing agent (the dye that absorbs yellow light so whites won't appear dingy), fabric brighteners (fluorescent dyes), and perfume.

Q. Is there a difference in bleaching ability between dry and liquid bleach?

A. Bleaches do not remove stains but rather convert them to an invisible form. The chemical name for this process is called *oxidation*. The sodium perborate of dry bleach is converted to hydrogen peroxide, which breaks down further to liberate oxygen gas that oxidizes or bleaches. Liquid bleaches contain sodium hypochlorite, which liberates chlorine gas to oxidize or bleach stains. Chlorine is a much more powerful bleaching agent than oxygen. Considering the types of oxidation agents in these forms of bleach, the liquid is more powerful than the dry.

Q. I have noticed that several cleaning agents containing bleach caution against mixing them with ammonia. What's going on?

A. Whenever liquid bleach comes in contact with ammonia, the toxic gas chloramine is formed. Many scouring cleansers such as Comet® contain calcium hypochlorite as a bleaching agent. When calcium hypochlorite reacts with ammonia, chloramine gas is given off.

SAFETY TIPS WHEN USING LIQUID BLEACH

If bleach gets on your skin, in your eyes, or on any part of your body, rinse the area immediately with large amounts of water and ventilate the effected area. If bleach is spilled on the floor, ventilate the room immediately and mop with vinegar later.

PRESOAKS, PRETREATMENTS, AND OTHER STAIN REMOVERS

Q. There are so many pretreating products: sprays, liquids that are squirted on stains, solids that are rubbed on, and presoaks. What are the differences among these products? Do they really work on "ground-in" stains?

A. Presoaks are similar to dry or liquid detergents in their formulation. It only makes sense that if a fabric is placed in contact with a mild detergent prior to regular washing, the clothing will be cleaner. Think of it this way: rubbing, spraying, or squirting a detergent mixture on the stain gives much longer contact time with the stain. It also allows you to place a very high concentration of detergent on the stain (much more than what it receives in the washing machine).

Pretreating products are formulated much the same from brand to brand in that they contain surfactant, enzymes, and bleach. The stick or solid forms seem to be most effective for ground-in stains because the chemicals are pressed deeply into the stain. Pretreating products are only useful when conventional detergents consistently fail to remove certain stains. You can avoid the high cost of pretreatment chemicals by rubbing some liquid detergent (or a paste made from dry detergent) on the stains. Several of the leading liquid detergent manufacturers already advertise this approach. Some readers will remember the old Wisk® commercials that suggested rubbing the product on shirts to remove "ring around the collar."

We don't use commercial presoaks. Instead, we keep a bar of the ugly green-brown Fels Naptha soap in the laundry room. We moisten it and rub it on any stains. It has never failed (even the ball point ink stains in shirt pockets come out). A two-inch thick bar seems to last forever and it's very inexpensive.

Q. Now there are pretreating chemicals that claim you can wait several days before washing the clothes. How can they work after so many days?

A. Pretreating chemicals work within 5 to 20 minutes of their application and then they are done. Five days later no further changes can occur. In other words, the pretreatment process does not change or reverse itself with time. In our opinion, this marketing ploy is just a sales gimmick.

Q. There are all sorts of unconventional methods for removing stains from clothing. Do any of them actually work? If so, how?

A. Some of the most common home stain removers are: water, club soda, and ammonia. Warm water will remove nearly any water-soluble stain if applied before the stain "sets." Fresh blood or urine stains can be removed with cold water (warm or hot water sets these types of stains). Club soda or any other carbonated liquid can remove several types stains because the soda is slightly acidic and the bubbling action removes debris by mechanical action. Ammonia is a basic solution that neutralizes acid stains such as perspiration or antiperspirants. The table on page 36 lists some additional simple chemicals that can be used to remove spots and stains. This is a compendium of safe and effective methods that work as well as commercial pretreatments. *Again, we caution you to test an inconspicuous portion of the fabric first.*

COMMON STAIN REMOVERS
FOUND AROUND THE HOUSE

Stain	Remover
Airplane cement	Acetone or toluene
Asphalt (Tar)	Naptha
Blood	Hydrogen peroxide or cold water
Berry, fruit	Hydrogen peroxide
Grass	Liquid bleach* or alcohol
Lipstick	Alcohol or cellusolve
Mustard	Liquid bleach* or alcohol
Nail polish	Acetone (nail polish remover)
Perspiration	Ammonia or alcohol
Rust or ink	Alcohol or oxalic acid
Scorched clothes	Hydrogen peroxide
Soft drinks	Liquid bleach*

---

*diluted in water

Q. There is a commerical about a laundry detergent whose manufacturer says that it's able to get out dirt, grass, and blood stains because "most stains are protein stains" and the product can remove such stains. Then I see them put several drops of the liquid detergent on a nasty stain—sometimes they will write the product name in the detergent—and in a short time it's gone. Can you explain this?

A. First, let us point out that most stains are *not* protein stains; instead, they are usually dirt or grease. Most detergents have enzymes formulated in them to help remove protein stains, which are indeed difficult to remove, especially after they have "set." The experiment referred to can also be done with nearly any other liquid detergent that contains enzymes. Again, this is

Madison Avenue at its best! The fact that the stain beneath the product's name disappeared is simply because that portion reacted. There's no mystery here.

Q. You have referred to certain kinds of stains "setting." What does that mean?

A. When a stain first occurs, it has minimal contact with heat or moisture. Therefore, it can be removed easily. After some time, atmospheric oxygen has an opportunity to oxidize or change the nature of the substances into a different form that is more resistant to breakdown. Moisture helps to keep a stain soluble. But after a period of time the moisture evaporates, leaving the stain vulnerable to oxygen.

Q. Years ago there were infomercials for what appears to be an extraordinary cleaning product. A small container of concentrated cleaner was supposed to get out what I always thought were impossible stains. The commercial shows a fabric being stained with inks, dyes, motor oil, and the like. A little of the material from the tube is placed into a big bowl of water (it seems to dissolve into a clear solution) and then the stained fabric is placed in the bowl, swished a bit, and, presto, the stain is gone. How can this be?

A. We know the television advertisement to which you refer. Notice that it is only on television or in catalog ads. The name for this product is trademarked but the ingredient mixture cannot possibly have any patent and therefore an identical Canadian product has been available in American supermarkets for about four years. There is no American or Canadian product that couldn't do as well, if mixed in the proper amounts. The product has had no real competition because it is no more than a mixture of detergent, bleach, and a whole lot of marketing and, in our opinion, some rather questionable experiments because we have not yet been able to reproduce them.

FABRIC SOFTENERS

Q. What are fabric softeners made from?

A. They are prepared from compounds called *cationic surfactants* or *resins*. These are remarkably similar to some common detergents. Cationic surfactants carry a positive charge; have a strong attraction for wet, negatively charged fabrics; and form a uniform layer on the surface of the fabric. Early in their history fabric softeners were added during the rinse cycle and "softened" or removed the excess negative charge on the clothing, which was responsible for the scratchiness and rough feeling some clothes have. It also removed "static cling." Fabric softeners added as sheets in the dryer have a thermosetting resin (a resin released by heat) that deposits a waxy coating on clothes, leaving them soft and at the same time neutralizing the negative charge.

Q. Which of these two forms is the best?

A. We have seen a few studies under uncontrolled conditions which indicate that dryer sheets work best. Since the final testing was subjective—feels smoother, less cling, more volume—it is difficult to draw a firm conclusion. The view seems to be that since clothing is usually rather soft when washed with today's detergents, and since most of the "cling" is produced in the dryer, softening after all the cleaning processes are done should result in a softer fabric.

Q. So often I hear about this or that fabric softener being the best at removing static cling. What is static cling and how do these laundry products remove it?

A. In simple terms, static cling is nothing more than electrical charges on clothing. These little charges flow in a circuit, much like batteries supplying energy to a flashlight. Fabric dryer sheets seem to work slightly better than liquid fabric softeners in reducing static cling, but the difference is quite small.

Q. Often we see commercials about fabric softeners that help clothes "fluff up" thicker than some competitor's brand. They show stacks of towels that have been softened with their brand and the stack is higher and looks thicker than the other brand. Is there anything to such claims?

A. We have seen such commercials. Any of the leading fabric softeners will "fluff up" clothes equally well.

Q. The laundry detergent industry, in its attempt to sway us from one brand to another, spends a lot of time and money telling us about built-in bleaches and/or softeners. Do these really work as well as adding separate bleach and softening products during the washing or rinse cycle?

A. We have already discussed the use of premixed dry bleaches and have shown that they are not quite as effective as when bleach is added separately. Just as detergents premixed with bleaches preclude us from controlling bleach concentrations according to need, the same is true for fabric softeners premixed with detergent. Some items—towels and cottons especially—require a greater amount of fabric softener than is present during the rinse cycle. In addition, detergent/softener mixes nearly neutralize themselves during the wash cycle.

FABRICS AND FIBERS

Q. What is the difference between natural and synthetic fibers?

A. The chemical difference is simple: natural fibers are those made from natural sources—cotton, wool, linen, and silk. Cotton is a natural cellulose fiber obtained from the boll of the cotton plant. Whether alone or in blends, it is the most commonly used textile fabric throughout our world. Wool is obtained from sheep and is probably the best fiber for cold weather use because of the yarn's fit when knitted. Linen is obtained from the flax plant in mixtures of various thicknesses, which tend to cling together forming long sheets. Silk comes from the raw gum of the silkworm cocoon. It gives a fine, linear, smooth, and shiny fabric that is susceptible to damage by sunlight and perspiration. Synthetics are made from fibers produced artificially from common chemicals. In some ways they are superior and in other ways inferior to natural fibers. Usually, blends of natural and synthetic fibers produce an optimum product (e.g., cotton and polyester).

Some of the more common synthetic fibers are: Orlon®, Creslan®, Spandex®, nylon, Acrilan®, Fortrel®, and Dacron® polyester. The capitalized names indicate that these are trade names.

Q. Wouldn't we be better off just using 100 percent pure natural fibers instead of the synthetics?

A. Currently, 75 percent of the fibers used for clothing are synthetic, the rest being natural. It is doubtful that we would want to give up the superior qualities of synthetics in order to dedicate so much land for cotton and wool production.

Q. What does it mean for clothing to be "colorfast?

A. Colorfast clothing is prepared with dyes that will not run or bleed onto other parts of the clothing or other clothing in the wash. Most colored clothing made in the United States is colorfast (though not all). Clothing from Pakistan and India is usually not colorfast.

Q. Why do some types of fabrics shrink when dried in a dryer, while others retain their shape?

A. Most natural and synthetic fibers don't retain their shape after laundering. It is the addition of thermosetting plastics (which permanently change their shape upon heating), that allows some fabrics to retain their original shape, even when heated.

Q. Our clothing is produced from all sorts of synthetic fibers: Dacron®, nylon, Orlon®, Spandex®, Dacron® polyester, Acrilan®, and others. Is there really that much difference in their various compositions?

A. The chemical composition of synthetics are slightly different, but the resulting physical properties are significantly different. There are only about five different synthetic fibers used in the manufacturing of clothing. Generally, synthetic fibers are blended with wool, cotton, or another synthetic material. Some of the fabrics with different tradenames are made with identical fibers. Orlon®, Dacron®, Creslan®, and Zefran® are all polyacrylonitride fibers but their physical properties are slightly different. Polyacrylonitride fabrics have "wool like" properties and are easy to care for. These fibers are frequently substituted or blended with wool. Acrylic fibers (polyarylonitrile) are stronger and softer than wool and provide more warmth without being so bulky. Spandex® is a polyurethane plastic that is usually added to wool, cotton, silk, or nylon to increase the stretch and recovery properties (ability to return to its original shape) of the other fabric. Polyamides (nylon) are the strongest synthetic fibers, but they yellow in the sunlight and their use in clothing is somewhat limited. Polyester fabrics are the most popular for use in clothing and are sold under the tradenames of Dacron®, Fortrel®, and Vycron®. Polyester does not shrink or stretch, and when creases or pleats are placed in at the factory, they retain their shape indefinitely. While polyester fabrics are usually blended with cotton, some suits or pants are 100 percent polyester. Polyolefins (Herculon®, Polycreast®, and the like) are very light fabrics used for extreme abrasion situations such as blankets, upholstery, and indoor-outdoor carpeting (Astroturf®).

Q. Why do permanent press fabrics hold their shape when washed and dried?

A. Permanent press fabrics are made from either 100 percent synthetic fiber or natural fiber with enough plastic blended in to achieve the desired properties. Permanent press clothing does not change its shape when heated in a dryer; it remains ridged up to the melting point. In order for it to change shape, the temperature required is much higher than the melting point. Most synthetic fibers do not wrinkle or lose their shape after laundering, while natural fibers (e.g., cotton or wool) do shrink. The reason is that synthetic fibers are plastic and very dense. Natural fibers, such as cotton, are not very dense. They contain some very weak bonds (the attractive forces that hold atoms together in molecules). These weak bonds help to keep the cotton strands connected to each other, which results in a fabric that has a very low density. The term "low density" simply means that there are large empty spaces in the cotton framework. When water is "mopped up" by cotton cloths, the empty spaces are filled up with water. Unfortunately, it is this porous framework, that can release water when heated, which also causes cotton to shrink in a clothes dryer.

Q. Are all synthetic fabrics "permanent press" by definition?

A. In order for a fabric to be "permanent press" it *must* contain some synthetic fiber blended in the yarn. For example, while most natural fibers wrinkle easily, they are very soft and warm. The addition of about 20 to 40 percent polyester results in a yarn that is warm and soft and also wrinkle resistant.

Q. Can the permanent press nature of clothes be changed or ruined by ironing them?

A. Absolutely not. The thermosetting reaction that caused the fabric to lose its "memory" for change cannot be reversed by simply reheating it.

IRONING

Q. When shopping for ironing products, I notice there is spray starch and spray sizing. Is there any difference between them?

A. Most companies produce both a spray starch and a spray sizing for ironing. Starch is made from corn and is, therefore, a mixture of natural products (amylose and amylopectin) which polymerize when heated to form a stiff, rigid surface. Polymerization is the reaction of small molecules called monomers—in this case amylose and amylopectin—to form a huge complex molecule called a polymer. This molecule is long and stiff. Starch gives clothes a stiff and sharp appearance. However, it tends to feel a bit heavier than sizing and can cause the iron to stick.

Sizing is made from cotton (sodium carboxymetacellulose), and polymerizes in a manner similar to starch. However, sizing is much lighter (on the clothing) than starch and hardly ever sticks or leaves a shiny appearance.

Q. Does it matter if I use tap water or distilled water for my steam iron?

A. You should always use distilled water if possible: it contains very little dissolved minerals. Tap water usually has dissolved minerals, which, over time, can clog the iron.

Q. **After using my steam iron a number of times, I notice a cloudy film on the side of the see-through water compartment. What is this? How can I get rid of it?**

A. When water is vaporized in the iron, any minerals present in the water are not vaporized, and remain trapped inside the iron as an insoluble white residue. This is especially noticeable if you have "hard water." The residue consists of magnesium and calcium carbonates. Since these are basic or alkaline compounds, they will react and dissolve in an acid substance such as white vinegar. It is not surprising that people use vinegar or similar acids to clean coffee pots, coffee makers, vaporizers, and other appliances that heat water.

LAUNDRY ROOM HAZARDS

Q. **Aren't there various types of chemical hazards and environmental risks present in the average laundry room?**

A. Frankly, we can't think of one environmental risk, if the chemicals in the laundry are used in a normal manner. Certainly there are numerous chemical hazards for adults and children of which everyone should be aware.

As we have said, liquid bleach, or sodium hypochlorite, can damage the skin temporarily, but it can cause lasting damage to the eyes, mucous membranes (in the lips, nose, and throat, etc.), and the stomach. Containers of liquid bleach should be stored well out of the reach of children. In fact, it is a good idea to put all laundry chemicals out of their reach, even sprays! Detergents are also very caustic substances and should not be allowed to come in contact with wet skin. This is especially true for "phosphate-free" bleaches, where very alkaline sodium carbonate (washing soda) is used to replace phosphates. Don't forget, liquid detergents are just as hazardous as dry ones. Dry bleaches, liquid fabric softeners, and prewashes are all skin irritants and should be used with caution even by adults.

The best first aid treatment for any laundry room chemical spilled on the skin or mucousal surfaces is to FLUSH IT IMMEDIATELY WITH AS MUCH WATER AS POSSIBLE!

Afterward, call your local hospital or physician for follow-up treatment. Laundry chemicals are very nasty things and should not be treated in a cavalier fashion.

3

Beyond the Medicine Cabinet

We differentiate between common chemicals found in the bathroom —those that are not often found in the medicine cabinet—and what are called over-the-counter (OTC) pharmaceuticals, which are normally found in the medicine chest. Some of the items of primary interest in this section are cleaners, disinfectants, soaps for personal hygiene, shampoos and conditioners, detergent bars, and specialty soaps.

If you check the labels of items found in your bathroom, many will probably claim to be "new and improved" or have a "new and improved formula." Do these words really mean anything? Most of the time such phrases simply mean that the manufacturer has modified the formula ever so slightly, just enough that the claim can be made. Take these claims with a huge grain of salt and a healthy dose of skepticism, since often they are mere advertising gimmickry. One of the mildest, yet most effective bathroom surface cleansers is a product called Bon Ami®. It is a mild abrasive whose basic formula has not changed since the product's inception. If something works for you and it fits your needs, why change? "New and improved" doesn't always mean better. Bear this in mind when purchasing products for the bathroom. Sometimes the old tried and true products are far superior to anything new or to products that claim to be improved.

Many of the items that you purchase for cleaning in the bathroom are really simple variations of common chemical formulas. Baking soda, liquid bleach, dry bleach, rubbing alcohol, hydrogen peroxide, and other simple chemicals have been used in the formulas of many cleaning products. Baking soda can be used as a toothpaste, a deodorizer, an antacid, an abrasive, and as a douche, among other things. Rubbing alcohol cleans; disinfects; lowers the temperature of the skin when applied; and, when mixed with other compounds, serves as one of the most versatile agents in the bathroom. Hydrogen peroxide not only bleaches but cleans wounds and scrapes, disinfects, and (in the correct proportion) serves as a rather effective mouthwash. It even whitens teeth! *Caution: hydrogen peroxide can be used to clean the mouth or as an oral dentifrice, but* do not *ingest or consume it.* In this chapter we have provided some simple formulas for you to try. They are safe and we have found them to be inexpensive and very effective. You can save quite a bit of money by using them and even have a little fun. You will find these formulas sprinkled through the chapter.

Now, let's get started by looking at the cleaning products we often use in the bathroom.

BATHROOM CLEANERS

Basic Surface Cleaners

Q. What is the composition of products that clean grout and bathroom tile?

A. Both products generally contain sodium hypochlorite (what amounts to diluted laundry bleach) and/or calcium hypochlorite and a detergent. Sodium and calcium hypochlorite react in the same way, except that sodium hypochlorite is a bit stronger. You can make a very inexpensive tile/grout cleaner by mixing two parts liquid laundry bleach with ½ part of any phosphate-based liquid floor cleaner, 3 parts isopropyl alcohol, and 4½ parts of water. Two tablespoons of dry Spic 'n' Span® or other dry phosphate cleaner can be substituted for the liquid floor cleaner. Place the solution in a used plastic pump sprayer.*

When mixing this grout and tile cleaner, remember our cautions about handling liquid bleach; and isopropyl alcohol is

---

*Be sure to thoroughly clean the pump sprayer before filling it with this solution. Better still, buy an unused pump sprayer just to be extra safe.

flammable, so be careful not to have this ingredient anywhere near open flames or heating elements. Check the label of the liquid floor cleaner to be sure that it is phosphate based.

Q. **A number of bathroom cleaning products claim to remove the soap scum build-up or grayish-brown mildew that often forms between tiles. Can these products do this? Will your recipe do this?**

A. Removing soap scum build-up and mildew stains is not a difficult task! Ammonia or phosphate cleaners easily remove soap scum build up. Mildew can be killed by applying liquid bleach.

Q. **Are anti-mildew cleaners for the bathroom worth the extra cost?**

A. Most of these types of cleaners contain inexpensive bleach. Just take the cap off any container and notice that the odor is quite strong. Bleach is the most effective means of destroying mold. We recommend using diluted laundry bleach rather than these fancy cleaners.

Q. **What about bathtub cleaners? There are so many foaming, bubbling, fascinating items to choose from. How is anyone to know which is (are) the best?**

A. Spray cleaners are much too expensive. For the most part they contain a disinfectant with a long chemical name. Disinfectants kill bacteria, which simply reappear within a few hours. Diluted laundry bleach cleans and actually disinfects better, and it is much more economical. The formula we provided for grout and tile cleaner will work as well as any commercial bathtub cleaner. It may not froth and foam, but it has the same cleaning ability. For those who hate the smell of bleach—and who doesn't—there are scented bleaches on the market that are less offensive to the nose, and they are comparably priced. Also, as with any strong cleaning agent, protect your hands with gloves if you have sensitive skin. Bleach, diluted or otherwise, can dry out your skin. It's also wise to clean in a well-ventilated room.

Q. And what of glass cleaners? Is there any real difference between the various brand name products and the more generic types found in the supermarket?

A. The key ingredients in glass cleaners are ammonia to remove fats and grease, and alcohol to dissolve other materials. We suggest mixing two parts of ordinary isopropyl alcohol (available at the supermarket and called rubbing alcohol) with one part ammonia and seven parts water. This homemade cleaner works as well as any commercial cleaner and is a real money saver! The ammonia and alcohol evaporate as you wipe the grease and other material off. To create a glass cleaner formula that works a little better on grease, add a few drops of liquid dish washing soap to the above mixture.

Q. Many floor and bathroom cleaners contain a disinfectant. But you've just said that even with disinfection the bacteria reappear. Are you saying we don't need these cleaners?

A. While they do kill bacteria, their effectiveness doesn't last long. Yet, bacterial build-up should be prevented. With proper cleaning using soaps and/or detergents on a regular basis, this shouldn't occur. Typically, these cleaners contain a surfactant, or a soap. Ethyl alcohol, triethylene glycol, and dimethyl benezene ammonium chloride are common antibacterial agents in these cleaners.

   Pine oil mixed with alcohol, or unmixed, is also an excellent antibacterial agent. We believe that pine oil preparations made with alcohol and water are not only terrific antibacterials, but great cleaners and inexpensive as well. The combination of alcohol, pine oil, and water is a money-saving combination.

Q. What is the difference between disinfectants, antibacterial agents, and antiseptics?

A. Glad you asked! Antiseptics and antibacterial agents are the same in that they kill *some* bacteria and, to some extent, prevent the growth of new bacteria. Antiseptics are generally applied to the body, while antibacterial agents can be applied to any surface. Disinfectants not only kill *all* bacteria but viruses as well; they are usually too harsh to be applied to the skin.

Q. Are scouring powders that contain bleach and abrasives safe for the bathroom surfaces and for those who use them?

A. Many of the scouring cleansers we find in our homes contain bleach and strong abrasives. Disposable plastic gloves are recommended to prevent your hands from being scratched by the abrasives and irritated by the bleach. Many abrasive cleansers contain aluminum oxide or silicon oxide. These abrasives are not suitable for many surfaces, because they might scratch. High-gloss surfaces such as stainless steel or Formica® might be damaged by using strong abrasives. *Be aware that aluminum oxide has a rating of eleven on the Moh's hardness scale, whereas a diamond is assigned a value of fifteen and talc has a value of one.*

You should also be wary of the dry bleach in various cleansers. *If the label states that your cleanser contains calcium hypochlorite and/or sodium hypochlorite, then you must be sure that you do not mix it with liquid ammonia or any product that contains ammoniated salts.* An ammoniated salt is listed on the label as "ammonium." An example would be ammonium chloride. *Any ammoniated salt will react with either calcium or sodium hypochlorite in solution to form a poisonous gas, in the same manner as ammonia (in solution). Treat ammoniated salts with the same care as as liquid ammonia.* (See page 34 for the safe handling of hypochlorite salts and liquid bleach.)

Toilet Bowl Cleaners

Q. How do toilet bowls come to have those ugly rings that we have to clean?

A. Toilet bowls can accumulate calcium and magnesium carbonate from hard water. Dirt usually becomes embedded in this scale. The key is to remove this basic scale with something acidic and safe. Oxalic acid (from the pharmacy or supermarket) is very inexpensive and safe. It comes as either flakes or powder. Simply shake it in and let it react (foam).

Q. There are so many toilet bowl cleaners on the market: crystals that bubble and foam when placed in the bowl, and liquids whose manufacturers claim they do a better job of cleaning and dis-

infecting because they can be squeezed onto the side of the bowl and can reach under the rim to get all those "hard to reach places" where awful germs can linger. Are these products no more effective than the oxalic acid crystals you recommend?

A. Rest assured, if you want bubbling, then the oxalic acid crystals will react with any scale by bubbling up a storm. The bathroom cleaners in the bent containers are not only novel but quite ingenuous. Why not just purchase a similarly shaped container and refill it with a saturated solution of oxalic acid that contains about four drops of liquid floor cleaner per quart?

Q. **What of those drop-in tablets or the specially packaged items designed to be placed in the water tank to release their cleaning solution with every flush? Won't these save time and trouble cleaning the bowl? How do they work?**

A. These items are designed primarily to *keep* the bowl clean rather than to clean a dirty bowl. Hard water scale and imbedded debris will have to be removed eventually. These products just delay the need to do so. The ingredients are not listed on most of their containers, so we did a bit of "chemical sleuthing." From the warnings on various labels, we were able to deduce that nearly all of them contained a solid, strong, chlorine-type bleaching agent. One brand listed an "organic chlorine compound" and another listed a "quat." Our best guess is that they contain quaternary ammonium chlorides, which are solid, strong, and excellent bleaches or disinfectants and are called cationic surfactants—so they have cleaning properties, too.

Q. **I don't know about you, but my kids often flush all sorts of "things" down the toilet. If I use one of these continuous cleaning products, is there any risk of dangerous chemical reactions if something else is mixed with it?**

A. We can't think of anything that a responsible parent would give a child to play with (and inevitably put in his/her mouth) that would be dangerous when mixed with the continuous cleaner. Of course, we are not suggesting that a child should grab his toy and continue playing. All objects should be washed thoroughly before the child is permitted to handle them again.

Q. **If one of these concentrated tablets is used in the toilet tank, is there any risk of damaging the toilet fixtures? And what, if any, danger does the cleaning agent pose to a pet that often mistakes an open toilet for its water dish?**

A. Some tablets can cause heavy scaling on the metal surfaces in the toilet tank. One particular brand is so caustic, it clogs up our neighbor's tank about twice a year. The strength of the chemicals in the toilet bowl water approaches that of one-quarter strength liquid laundry bleach. Those who have nomadic animals looking for an oasis shouldn't use continuous cleaning toilet bowl cleaners.

Q. **Many toilet bowl cleaners are very concentrated and powerful, considering the reaction I see when they are first put in. I'm worried about what I might be doing to the environment. Should I be concerned?**

A. We will never have a pristine environment again. What we have now is a consensus on what is an acceptable amount of filth in our environment. The federal government, through its Environmental Protection Agency (EPA), guarantees a minimum degree of safety to our environment throughout the nation. Waste water in cities comes from all sources: drain sewers, toilet bowls, dishwashers, rain water run off, industrial effluent, and the like. It is treated with rather sophisticated technology to clean up the water. The discharge from these sewage treatment plants is monitored for chemical concentrations that are unsafe for discharge into rivers and lakes. Toilet bowl discharge is a minuscule amount of pollutant, even if you and your four hundred neighbors use half a dozen different products among you and all of you flushed at the same time.

Drain Cleaners

Q. **How do commercial drain cleaners work?**

A. There are acidic and basic drain cleaners. Most of the liquid drain cleaners are just concentrated sulfuric acid. *This is one of the most hazardous chemicals used in the home and, as such, should be used with extreme caution!* These thick, syrupy liquids are more dense than water and in nearly undiluted (full strength) form they sink to the level of the obstruction that is plugging the drain. If the obstruction is organic (hair, soap, or the like), the drain cleaner will vigorously attack the material and render it soluble by dissolving it. Unfortunately, sulfuric acid will also attack some metals. It reacts with the clog and/or the water to give off quite a bit of heat and, if used improperly, it can crack porcelain bowls.

Basic drain cleaners contain the strong base sodium hydroxide, which reacts with grease to convert it to soluble soap, much like sodium hydroxide sprays react with baked-on grease in oven cleaners. Aluminum pellets are also present because they react with the sodium hydroxide to form a gas. This gas aids in unclogging the drain by mechanically moving the mass. This reaction also gives off quite a bit of heat and may crack porcelain bowls and loosen metal plumbing fixtures.

WARNING!

Drain cleaners are some of the most dangerous chemicals people have in their homes, besides prescription drugs. Splashing strong acids or bases on the skin or in the eyes is very dangerous. If you do spill these chemicals on yourself, flush the affected area with lots of running water. Then remove or even cut away any clothing that might have been contaminated. Swallowing drain cleaners may be fatal. In the event of ingestion DO NOT INDUCE VOMITING! Go to the hospital immediately, or call 911 or your local poison hotline.

Mixing drain cleaners with any other household chemical may also prove to be fatal. Strong acids and strong bases are very reactive. Mixing drain cleaner with laundry bleach, for example, can produce toxic gases. If you are in doubt about the commercial products you are using, always call the manufacturer's Consumer Relations Department and ask before mixing household chemicals. Many consumer product representatives have toll-free numbers to call if you have any question about their products (see Appendix 4).

Q. Many drain cleaners containing crystal sodium hydroxide as the active ingredient claim to be safe on metal or plastic pipes. They also claim to be safe in cesspools and septic tanks. How can this be true?

A. By the time the drain cleaner reaches the cesspools or septic tanks it is so diluted that it is often harmless. But while these cleaners are working on a drain clog they do concentrate in specific areas where deterioration to some types of piping can occur. We advise that you consult a plumber if you have additional questions.

Q. Some drain cleaners use pressure to clean out plugged up areas. What chemicals are present in these cleaners?

A. Chemicals under extreme pressure are very dangerous. For this reason, pressurized drain cleaners contain no chemicals. They work through the sheer force that is designed to push the clog away, much like plunging action does.

Q. There are some newer drain cleaners out on the market now. The label indicates that they contain enzyme cultures and surfactants. From what I understand, these cleaners are supposed to remove the "gunky" deposits that build up in pipes. How do they work? Are they more effective than the sodium hydroxide- or sulfuric acid-type drain cleaner?

A. The enzyme cultures attack organic material in the plugged-up region and break them down into a soluble form that can be washed away with the surfactant. While they are much safer to use than the conventional drain cleaners, they may not be effective on certain materials.

SOAPS

Q. Is there a difference among soaps used for personal hygiene?

A. Soft soaps, solid bar soaps, and solid detergent bars are all used for personal hygiene. Soft or liquid soaps aren't any more effective than bar soaps but are considerably more expensive. All soaps are made from sodium or ammonium hydroxide and one or more of the following: tallow (animal fat), coconut oil (lauric acid), palm oil (oleic acid), olive oil (oleic acid), cottonseed oil (linoleic acid), or isethionic acid (a completely synthetic source). Ammonium hydroxide is used to obtain a soft or liquid soap, while sodium hydroxide reacts to form firm bar soap.

All soaps list the main cleaning ingredient first. Here are some examples: Dove® soap (sodium cocoyl isethionate [from isethionic acid], sodium tallowate [from tallow]; Lever 2000® is basically the same as Dove®; Palmolive®, Irish Spring®, Dial®, and Coast® soaps (sodium tallowate, sodium cocoate [from coconut oil], or sodium palm kernelate from the oil of palm kernels). All four brands specify either sodium tallowate or sodium palm kernelate. It all depends on what is in stock at the time. They can have skin conditioners, perfumes, antibacterial agents, and other agents that aren't of much use. Castille soaps (e.g., Kirk's®) contain no additives at all and are not irritating. They also are the best lathering bar soaps in hard water and nearly as good as detergent bars in their cleaning ability.

Q. What is tallow?

A. It is the mixture obtained by passing steam through animal fat. The light (less heavy) portion of tallow is called stearic acid. The sodium salt of stearic acid, called sodium stearate, is in plain bar soap but it's called sodium tallowate. Coconut oil is more unsaturated and produces a higher-quality soap than tallow. It's not important that you understand the difference between saturated and unsaturated at this point. Just remember that oils are unsaturated and solids are saturated. Shaving bar soap is prepared from potassium soap (soap made from potassium hydroxide rather than sodium hydroxide) and extra unreacted stearic acid. This gives it a slow-drying lather and a liquid soap that foams easily.

Q. What do you mean by *detergent* bars? Is it the same type of soap we use in the laundry?

A. We certainly don't mean laundry detergent, because that would be harsh and irritating to your skin. The detergent used in personal hygiene bars is much milder. Some examples are: sodium alkyd benzene sulfonate, sodium cocoglyceryl, and sodium cocoglyceryl sulfonate (found in Zest® bars). The benzene in these detergents is converted to a noncarcinogenic. Another example of conversion of a harmful chemical into a safe form is in the formation of soap. Sodium hydroxide, which is very caustic, reacts with tallow to form sodium tallowate (soap).

Detergent bars do have advantages over soap bars in that they don't react with minerals in the water like soap does when insoluble precipitates form (soap film or soap scum). When Zest® was first introduced, it cleaned very well but tended to leave the skin dry. The addition of moisturizers solved this problem.

Q. Are different antibacterial agents used in bar soaps and detergent bars?

A. For a reason that eludes us, they all use triclocarban.

Q. Can you explain the purpose of all those other ingredients in our soaps and detergents?

A. Coconut oil, palm kernel oil, and lauric acid are added to enhance lathering. Sodium chloride adjusts the firmness of the bar. Ether sulfonates help very soft water rinse off the soap. Glycerine keeps the bar moist. Titanium dioxide makes the bars white, and chromium oxide makes them green. Other colors are obtained by mixing in federally approved dyes. Di- or tetrasodium EDTA stabilizes the bars by removing minerals. Butylhydroxytoluene (BHT) is an antioxidant (thus keeping fats and oils from oxidizing and turning rancid). Trisodium phosphate is an extra wetting agent that allows the water to penetrate, and triclocarban kills bacteria. Perfumes, of course, make the soap smell nice.

Q. Wait! I've read some bar soap labels and they had some other ingredients.

A. Don't be confused. Different chemicals can have the same effect. Most of the large manufacturers produce different soaps with slightly different formulas and names. For example, most companies produce a regular and a deodorant bar. The regular bar would not list triclocarban, but the deodorant bar would. The largest soap and detergent manufacturer in the world is the Procter and Gamble Company of Cincinnati, Ohio. It sells Ivory®, Coast®, Kirk's®, Lava®, and Zest® bars. Each is slightly different than the others and are most suitable under the conditions in which they are used. If you're not sure about your bar soap or liquid soap, call the company's toll-free number and its representatives will be happy to tell you what their soap/detergent bars will do.

Q. I've always wondered: what makes Ivory® soap float? Is it because it is 99.44 percent pure?

A. Purity has nothing to do with floating. In 1930 an employee of the Procter Soap Company fell asleep and let the mixing machine run too long. This caused air to be accidentally mixed with the soap, and that's what allowed it to float! One of the chemists at the Procter Soap Company sensed that this accident could be put to commercial use. By the way, the employee who fell asleep was not fired. For more information on the history and use of Ivory® soap, please contact the Consumer Aid Department of Procter and Gamble Company.

Q. Are detergent bars more effective than soap bars?

A. Detergent bars have an advantage over soap bars because they don't react as much with the minerals present in hard water to form insoluble precipitates. They don't leave the dreaded "soap scum" that soap bars deposit around sinks, in tubs, and on shower tile.

Q. I know all sorts of people who have sensitive or allergic skin. They often buy special soaps. Aren't products like Neutrogena® and Alpha Keri® the purest and safest soaps available?

A. Just about any good soap is as good as these two soaps. It's not the basic soap that causes skin irritations but rather all the *extra added ingredients* introduced to help market them. These are the true culprits. In our opinion, these special soaps are far too expensive. Try the generic store brands!

Q. I noticed a generic soap on the shelf next to the Neutrogena®
at a store: the generic contained glycerine. What is that and what
does it do?

A. Neutrogena® soap also contains glycerine (glycerin). It is a poly
(many) alcohol used as an emollient (softener), a humectant
(moisturizer), and a demulcent (smoothing agent).*

CLEANSING CREAMS

Q. What's in cleansing cream? Is this the same as cold cream?

A. Cleansing creams are usually referred to as cold creams. Probably
the most popular cleansing cream, Noxema Skin Cream®, has
these ingredients: camphor, phenol, clove oil, menthol, linseed
oil, water, stearic acid, soybean oil, eucalyptus oil, calcium hydroxide, and ammonium hydroxide. The camphor, clove oil, and
eucalyptus oil are important for odor. Menthol is a slight antibacterial agent and an astringent, stearic acid allows penetration
through the skin, linseed oil is an emollient (softening agent),
phenol is a strong antibacterial agent, and the hydroxides present
increase the pH. We don't know why soybean oil is in there.

For those with sensitive skin, the manufacturer has a fragrance
free formulation as well.

Q. Like shampoos and deodorants, are cleansing creams pH balanced?

A. Yes, they are brought close to the natural pH of the skin, which
is between pH 5 and pH 8. Some brands are slightly more alkaline
(greater than 8) to ensure proper solubility and reactivity of the
components on and into the skin.

Q. Some of the creams or lotions seem to be very oily or greasy
while others absorb fast into the skin. Why is that? Does it depend
on each person's skin type?

---

*We thought you'd be interested to know that the very same glycerine
is a by-product in the production of soaps and is used in glues and tobaccos
to keep them from drying too fast.

A. Absorption of these creams or lotions has little to do with skin type. If the skin is either dry or oily, it makes little difference. Creams that are easily absorbed into the skin usually incorporate lots of stearic acid, which facilitates transportation of components into the skin. These are usually referred to as "vanishing creams." Other "cold creams" use much more lanolin, petrolatum (what most people call petroleum jelly), and mineral oil and leave a sealant (greasy feeling) on the skin.

Q. **Besides removing dirt and (for women) makeup from the face, another reason for cleansing the skin is the removal of excess oil. This oil and the acne that often results from its presence has sprouted a whole industry to respond to this concern. Can you discuss the various acne preparations and their chemical content?**

A. We would be delighted to, but our discussion must wait until chapter 4 when we delve into the many products referred to as *medications.* Unlike these products, soaps and cleansing creams fall into the category of cosmetics. As you'll come to learn, the restrictions on the content of a cosmetic are significantly less than those governing medications.

Q. **Whether the climate is hot or cold, dry or wet, much is made of the need for hand and body lotions and creams. What's in them and how do they work? Are some really better than others, or are they all pretty much the same?**

A. People who have sensitive skin need year-round protection, especially in the winter. Ideally, a lotion should moisturize the skin, heal any damage, and protect skin from further damage. In our opinion, the very best at this task is Vaseline Intensive Care® lotion or a generic equivalent. The existence of a number of generic equivalent products indicates that the original is probably very good, approaching the status of a benchmark. Vaseline Intensive Care® lotion contains water, glycerine (emollient and healant), stearic acid (to help penetrate the skin), glycerol stearate (moisturizer), mineral oil (protectant), lanolin (natural wax replacement), and petrolatum jelly (to seal off the skin). Perhaps one might consider Vaseline Intensive Care—Dermatologic Formula®. It is about 40 to 50 percent petrolatum and mineral oil. If you have very dry skin, consider this or generic equivalents (the petrolatum oil and mineral oils should be listed first, before water or any other component).

We have an inexpensive formula that might help you. Take two or three parts inexpensive skin lotion and add two parts of mineral oil (found at the supermarket), and mix (with some heating if needed), then add five to six parts of petrolatum oil. This latter step will require some heating so the petrolatum will melt and dissolve. Now mix thoroughly and allow to cool.

SHAVING CREAMS

Q. What's in shaving cream? Again, are all shaving creams basically the same?

A. Shaving creams are all basically the same in that they contain water, stearic acid, triethanolamine and sodium lauryl sulfate (soap), and menthol (a cooling agent and mild antibacterial). Some also contain such questionable items as aloe vera, sorbitol (a sweetener), and various other products. One way you can tell if a shaving cream (or most other common products) are unique is by the price. Shaving creams are by and large priced very competitively, even the store brands. That tells you they have nothing new to sell.

Q. Is there any difference between the standard shaving creams that burst forth from the can in a huge gush of foam and those which emit a small ribbon of colored gel in your palm and then transform into a foam when applied to the face (or to a woman's leg)?

A. The leading "colored gel"-type shaving creams contain: palmitic acid, triethanolamine, "fatty acid esters," alcohol, and aloe vera gel as the major ingredients. The two leading conventional shaving creams, which supply a rich foam from a canister, contain stearic acid (in place of palmitic acid), triethanolamine, laureth–23 (in place of "fatty acid esters"), and the surfactant sodium lauryl sulfate (in place of lauryl alcohol and aloe vera gel). Both types of saving creams offer compounds that serve the same basic function, i.e., they lubricate, moisturize, penetrate the hair shafts and skin, and cleanse the skin (surfactants). Therefore, one should receive similar results from either type of shaving cream. The gel-type creams must be rubbed into the beard or skin, and this extra contact with the hair is beneficial.

Q. Some of the gel-type shaving creams, and even a few of the creams in cans, have a formula that imitates the heated cream that barbers were known for using when giving a shave. How can the manufacturers recreate that sensation of heat?

A. The sensation of heat on the skin is easily obtained by various compounds that increase the circulation of blood in the area applied. Most of the "sore muscle liniments or creams" contain irritants such as methyl salicitate or salicylic acid, which leave a pleasant, warm feeling. Some shaving creams use these irritants for the same purpose. If you want a hot shave, you still have to visit your barber.

HAIR PRODUCTS

Shampoos

The chemistry of shampoos is much like that of cosmetics: it is often dictated by marketing and economics. If all automobiles had exactly the same configuration and were equally efficient and appealing, how could the manufacturers sell their particular brands? Everything in shampoos must be somewhat different so various companies can make claims for superior performance or appeal. The truth is that there is not much difference in the multitude of these products on the market today. Save your money and purchase store brands or those on sale. If you read the list of ingredients on the containers of store brand shampoos, you will find that they are exactly the same as most brand name shampoos. The detergent lauryl sulfonate, or another form of lauryl sulfate, is used in over 90 percent of the shampoos manufactured today.

Q. All right, so they may have the same or similar types of ingredients, but doesn't it matter what proportion these chemicals are in? Maybe the better shampoos have more of the right ingredients, whereas the less expensive brands have more of the filler-type ingredients.

Is there any truth to this? Could this be why people stay with a brand name for years and are reluctant to try something new?

A. We'd prefer you didn't use the term "better shampoo." The *best* shampoo for you is a very subjective choice. Remember, store brands are usually placed right next to the brand-name shampoo, sometimes with the note "compare to brand X." Well, go ahead and compare the ingredients of the two. Remember, the amount of ingredients present are listed in decreasing order. If you really want a surprise, copy the ingredients in a brand like White Rain's® shampoos for dry, salon, regular, and oily hair. (Gillette shampoos were chosen only because the company was eager to provide the ingredients in their products.) Do you see any big differences? Did you know that brand name companies produce shampoo for generic companies? Most large brand name companies (for example, Eli Lilly) have established their own generic company to sell and promote generic equivalents.

　Most chemists already know the amount of each ingredient in their competitors' shampoos. Since the cost of chemicals in shampoos is very low, it would be foolish to cut corners and add filler. With that said, allow us to add a qualifier. You have certainly seen those two-gallon bottles of shampoo that sell for $2.99. These "el cheapo" varieties do contain thickening agents (fillers) and are notoriously ineffective. For the price, what can you expect?

Q. Aren't shampoos just like liquid dish soap?

A. No. Shampoos *are* made from liquid detergents such as ammonium lauryl sulfonate, but they are much safer for hair than liquid dish soap. Triethanolamine is a base used in the preparation of mild detergents used in bars soaps, liquid soaps, and shampoos. Shampoos contain a great many other ingredients, much more than soaps. Some of the more common ingredients are: lauramide DEA (helps with lathering), lecithin (for shine), hydrolyzed animal protein (for repairing split ends), gylcol stearate (detangles and adds luster), methylparaben (a preservative), methylisothiozoline (an antibacterial), Canadian balsam (lacquer), and citric acid from citrus fruits to lower the pH. When shampoos are produced, they are very basic and the pH must be lowered to that of human skin and hair. Many brands produce an oily, a regular, a dry, and a salon shampoo. They use the same general formula with the addition of a few basic chemicals or by increasing the amount of one chemical already present.

Q. There are a few things about what you just said that aren't too clear: Why do shampoos need preservatives in them, and why would a manufacturer include lacquers or stiffening agents in shampoo?

A. The preservatives, usually tetra or disodium EDTA or methylparaben, sequester (tie up) trace amounts of metals. Metals are usually introduced during the manufacturing process. Trace metals catalyze (speed up) the breakdown of fats and oils on the hair and scalp. Another preservative is BHT (butylhydroxytoluene), which blocks reaction with oxygen. Because of the presence of BHT, shampoos can turn bad (spoil) with time. Lacquer or stiffening agents are added to repair "split ends."

Q. How do dandruff shampoos differ from regular hair-cleaning products?

A. Dandruff is a natural physiological process in which epidermal cells (top skin layers) move to the surface, die, and fall off as flakes. It is only when the flakes become large and more numerous that dandruff causes a visible problem. Antiflaking agents are usually shampoos or lotions that contain one or more of the following: coal tar, zinc pyrithizone, salicylic acid, selenium, or sulfur. One manufacturer produces a blue-colored antidandruff shampoo containing selenium sulfide. The label claims that it "Contains the ingredient most prescribed by physicians." While the product packaging correctly states that the shampoo "contains" this ingredient, it is misleading because this nonprescription shampoo has so little selenium sulfide, by law, that if it had more it would have to be a prescribed medication. Don't be misled. It's one thing to "have" the chemical as part of the product, but quite another to have enough to be really effective. *All other selenium sulfide shampoos, unless they have been prescribed by a doctor, have the same amount of this compound and work equally well.*

Q. Exactly how do these antidandruff shampoos work?

A. Please let us caution you: *No antidandruff shampoo on the market today has been shown to control dandruff completely.* However, they can relieve itching and decrease flaking to some extent. Dandruff is not a disease but rather a nuisance. The amount of time it takes for these dead cells to move from the dermis to the hair is about twenty-eight days for the average person. For those who suffer from dandruff the migration rate is ten to twelve days.

It is difficult to discern exactly how all these products work. Selenium sulfide and zinc pyrithione retard cell migration. No one has a clue how coal tar works, but it has worked for centuries! Antiseptics kill microbes on the skin but no proof exists that they decrease flaking. Sulfur and salicylic acid work by simply breaking the flakes into very small pieces.

Don't ignore the possibility that you may have seborrheic dermatitis, which is a disease. It is characterized by flake formation on other hairy parts of the body (eyebrows, etc.), redness to affected skin, and greasy yellow-brown flakes. Should you have any of these conditions, see a physician.

Q. What is pH balanced shampoo? Why should a consumer care about pH balance in hair preparations?

A. All shampoos have a very high pH (basic) when first produced at the factory. Since human hair and skin are slightly acid, lauric, citric, or some other weak acid is added to bring the pH down into its normal range (pH = 5–8). Nearly all shampoos are "pH neutralized" by manufacturers to prevent their base components from irritating skin and eyes. Neutralization is the process by which a strong acid (hydrochloric acid) is made to react with a basic substance (sodium carbonate) to form a solution very close to neutral (pH = 7) or by which a strong base (soap) is made to react with an acid (citric) to produce a solution close to neutral. If your shampoo irritates you, it's not because of the pH level, but rather some ingredient(s) the manufacturer has added.

Q. Is it generally the case that shampoos contain these antiflaking agents, or must a special shampoo be purchased?

A. Antiflaking agents are only found in antidandruff shampoos or lotions.

Q. **I see commercials that compare the relative effectiveness of the more well-known dandruff shampoos like Head and Shoulders® with those claiming to be more powerful products like Denorex®, Tegrin®, or Selsun Blue®. Are they really all that different? I always thought that the latter three products were recommended for more serious scalp conditions such as eczema, seborrhea (seborrheic dermatitis), and psoriasis. If this is correct, how do they work?**

A. First let us look at the active ingredients on each label. Head and Shoulders®—zinc pyrithione; Selsun Blue®—1 percent solution of selenium (a toxic metal) sulfide; Denorex®—coal tar and menthol; Tegrin®—coal tar; Pert Plus® dandruff shampoo—zinc pyrithione; Ionyl® dandruff shampoo—salicylic acid (2 percent); and X.SEB® dandruff shampoo—4 percent salicylic acid.

As of this writing, the Food and Drug Administration (FDA) has only formally approved zinc pyrithione and coal tar as effective and safe in our efforts to control dandruff. Note that the FDA does not approve of the others as "effective" but it does consider them safe, so they can be marketed over the counter.

Now to the function of each ingredient: the mechanism of how coal tar works is unknown but it really does a great job in controlling symptoms of dandruff, mild cases of seborrheic dandruff, and psoriasis. It slows the reproduction of excess flakes, narrows the capillary blood vessels, kills bacteria, stops itching, and has an astringent effect on the scalp. Could you ask for more? Yes, it smells bad! Menthol is a mild antiseptic and is of no value for dandruff. Salicylic acid is a skin-peeling drug (a keratolytic) that loosens dandruff cells so they may be easily removed. Zinc pyrithione is a cytostatic agent and slows the growth of dandruff cells. While we could not find sulfur shampoos at any drugstore, be advised that sulfur removes scale and is FDA approved for this purpose. It is interesting to note that Ionyl® shampoo, which lists 2 percent salicylic acid, claims to be effective against not only dandruff but seborrheic dermatitis and psoriasis. A competitive product, X.SEB®, lists 4 percent salicylic acid as the active ingredient but only claims it can control plain dandruff. We hope you are wondering what is going on here. The active ingredient in Scalpicin® lotion is hydrocortisone, which is a mild antiseptic that cannot control dandruff. "Hydrocortisone preparations relieve inflammation, so they may have some role in alleviating the redness and itchiness of seborrheic dermatitus. They are of no use against ordinary dandruff."*

The only product to make the FDA claim of effectiveness is Head and Shoulders®. In order to use the FDA seal in their marketing, the manufacturers of this shampoo had to prove to one of the FDA's medical advisory panels that their product, a 2 percent suspension of zinc pyrithione, is safe when used as directed and that it can effectively control the redness and itching associated with dandruff and seborrheic dermatitis. The FDA seal does not mean that the product can prevent dandruff or seborrheic dermatitis. Many other products on the market can work as effectively as Head and Shoulders®. However, for some reason, these manufacturers have chosen not to advertise the fact that their shampoo is as effective as Head and Shoulders®. If we had to purchase a dandruff shampoo other than Head and Shoulders®, we would feel safe in purchasing a product that had a 4 percent zinc pyrithione or a shampoo that contained a different set of ingredients that were approved by the FDA.

Claims by advertisers do not have to prove that a shampoo is effective. However, the claims must not be misleading. For this reason, we have relied on findings published in the *Federal Register* or scientific evaluations by experts.

Q. I notice that many shampoos contain ammonium lauryl sulfate. But I also notice that my toothpaste contains this substance, too. Am I shampooing my teeth?

A. Well, most toothpastes contain surfactants (detergent), and ammonium lauryl sulfate is a very popular one. It is so popular partly because it is soluble at room temperature.

---

*The Essential Guide to Nonprescription Drugs, edited by D. Zimmerman, Harper and Row, New York, 1988.

Q. So often the manufacturers of shampoos spend hardly any time talking about how well their products clean hair; instead they talk about how their respective products lead to healthier, more manageable, stronger, thicker hair. And now more than ever we hear them talking about vitamin-rich emollients, protein-rich formulas, and the like. How are we to wade through all of this and make a choice that is right for our hair and its needs?

A. Vitamins and added protein have nothing to do with cleansing ability or the condition of the hair after shampooing. The same is true for floral essence, honey, and the multitude of "stuff" that is added to help market a shampoo. Try plain unadulterated "baby shampoo." It is safe for babies, so it won't hurt your hair, and it is very effective. This is as close as you'll get to "pure" shampoo.

Q. So what's *not* in baby shampoo that *is* in all the others?

A. "Baby shampoos" do not contain any of the following, which *can* be found in regular shampoos: herbal or other sorts of essence, strong detergents such as sodium lauryl sulfate, Canada balsam, thickening agents such as pulverized cellulose, animal protein, irritating salts that can be astringent, and the multitude of other ingredients that are added to "hair conditioning shampoos." It is the absence of these and other compounds that makes baby shampoo very popular with people who must wash their hair frequently (for example, athletes).

Q. Then why isn't everyone rushing to buy baby shampoo rather than all the other glitzy products on the market?

A. The formulas of baby shampoos are quite simple due to the restrictions on producing a product that is not irritating to tender babies. But this simplicity makes for dull advertisements; baby shampoo cannot repair split ends, condition hair, add luster, or impart a special essence to hair. In a word, plain pure shampoo is hard to market.

Q. You have discussed the fact that some shampoos have conditioning qualities in their ingredients, but what exactly do hair conditioners do?

A. The pH of your skin and hair should be between 5 and 8, but shampoos are very basic (with a pH greater than 8). Hair conditioners contain weak acids such as lauric or citric acid to return the pH to levels closer to natural skin and hair. They also contain proteins from soluble animal keritans. These are obtained from animal hoofs and hides and help to repair split ends.

Hair Coloring

Q. What does hair coloring involve?

A. Did you know that hair only has two pigments—brown-black and/or red? To these pigments one can add permanent and temporary dyes. The latter, which only act on the surface of the hair, and the "permanent" kind that acts all the way to the root shafts. Temporary dyes can be easily washed out, while permanent dyes cannot.

Q. Does the use of hair coloring, hydrogen peroxide, or lighteners change the pH of the hair?

A. They do alter the natural pH of hair, but that is minimal compared to the damage these harsh chemicals can do to the hair shafts. Because their use incorporates some rather harsh chemicals that damage the hair, it may be necessary to use conditioners for a while. Regular, plain shampoos and simple conditioners will work fine.

Hair Curling

Q. How do hair curling preparations work?

A. Hair links are held together with what is called a disulfide bond or attachment. *Di* means two, and *sulfide* is a form of sulfur. Actually, it's quite simple. One link of hair is "stuck" to another link of hair on numerous spots with the attraction of one sulfur atom for another (-S-S-). The same process occurs in skin and is responsible for the toughness of skin and hair. Suppose those disulfide bonds are broken with something like thiogylcolic acid. This removes the attraction of one hair strand for another and the disulfide bond (-S-S-) now becomes free.

The free hair can be easily stretched, molded, or set into any desired form. At this point, compounds such as hydrogen peroxide are used to reform those disulfide bonds and create the shape desired. Chemists call this process oxidation, while most of us just call it "setting."

Q. **Is the same disulfide in "setting gel"? This often clear gel is placed on a clump of hair strands before they are rolled up in a roller.**

A. No disulfides are used in "setting gels." Such gels control the shape of the hair in rollers by using a plasticizer such as PVP. After the solvent evaporates, the PVP is still rigid.

Hair Sprays

Q. **What about hair sprays? Are they safe? How do they work?**

A. Hair sprays work by depositing a layer of resin which is dissolved in a volatile (easily evaporated) solvent. After the solvent evaporates, a layer of plastic is left on the hair. If you have ever seen people out on a windy day yet their hair doesn't move, then you know their hair spray works. These hair sprays (most of which come in nonaerosol formulas or pump applicators) are plasticizers, and the chemical reaction involved here is polymerization. As we explained earlier, polymerization is the reaction of many small molecules (monomers), which condense to form extremely long molecules (polymers). Epoxy resin cement hardens by a polymerization reaction. Hair sprays, too, contain a resin dissolved in a volatile solvent that forms a plastic on the hair. The most common plasticizer in hair sprays is polyvinylpyrroldone (PVP). Try this experiment: If you apply a thick layer of hair spray to a glass surface and then let it dry, you can actually pull it off in a large thin sheet.

Q. **Since the whole business of chloroflourocarbons and the depletion of the Earth's ozone layer was raised we really don't hear that much about hair sprays. Now the talk is about pump sprays and the like. Besides the propellent, is there any difference in the basic products?**

A. Chlorofluorocarbons have been banned in North America for over seven years. Aerosol sprays now use carbon dioxide as the propellent. The chemicals used in pump sprays are basically the same as the aerosol spray for the same product. Some people believe the pump sprays apply the product more accurately. The product being propelled remains the same in any case.

Mouses, Gels, and Creams

Q. **Many people today use mouses and gels to sculpt their hair to get a contemporary look. What is in these products that makes them so useful?**

A. The same plasticizer, PVP, that is used in hair sprays.

Q. **Won't this plasticizer dry out a person's hair and make it brittle? Are there any serious risks to using these products?**

A. The prolonged use of hair gels or hair sprays containing plasticizers can damage hair by dehydrating (removing moisture from) the hair shafts. This will cause a change in the natural pH and resulting resiliency of the hair. Hair is a complex mixture of proteins which are easily "denatured" or broken up into smaller fragments by heat or strong chemicals. Another hazard from the use of these hair gels or sprays is the extreme flammability of either the solvent or the dry resin on the hair. As chemical educators, we have seen women's hair catch on fire, from merely getting a dangling hair too close to a laboratory burner.

Q. **We are told that just a small amount of a product like VO5® will bring new life, body, and shine to damaged hair. How?**

A. Don't ignore Brilcream® and Suave® grooming lotions, among others. They all have the same basic ingredients: mineral oil (with several emulsifying agents so the mineral oil can be suspended in water), lanolin, stearic acid (penetrating agent), zinc pyrithione (antidandruff agent), and several ingredients present in minute quantities. These lotions and gels do an excellent job of restoring moisture and natural oils to your hair. They are very inexpensive to use because they are so concentrated.

Q. A number of these creams or hair preparations also have "special formulas" designed for color-treated hair. Is there really any difference in the basic makeup of the product?

A. These "special preparations" for color-treated, or heavily bleached hair contain much higher concentrations of lanolin and mineral oil (or some other thick oil) than regular preparations for the hair. Oils are mixed with an emulsifying agent which allows heavy oils to saturate water and thereby aids in the passage of the oil into the skin or hair.

Depilatories

Q. What is a depilatory?

A. It is a substance used to remove body hair chemically. It is a more concentrated solution of the substances used to break the sulfide bonds in hair permanents, i.e., calcium thioglycolate. The high concentration breaks nearly 100 percent of the disulfide bonds—this fragments the hair. These fragments are easily washed off. While it seems the hair is dissolving, it is really just broken into very tiny pieces.

TOOTHPASTES

Q. What types of chemicals are in toothpastes?

A. Toothpastes need abrasives to grind off stains, fluoride to help prevent cavaties, a surfactant to wash away debris, and an artificial sweetener to enhance taste.

Q. Exactly what are those ingredients on the label?

A. First read the labels of several brand-name fluoride/tartar-control toothpastes, and a store brand as well. The formulas are nearly identical. Sodium fluoride in water; hydrated silica (abrasive); sorbitol (moisturing agent); tetrapotassium pyrophosphate (prevents the conversion of plaque to damaging tartar); sodium saccharin (artificial sweetener); titanium dioxide (white color); carbomer (thickening agent); F, D, and C blue #1 (approved dyes).

Q. Why are baking soda toothpastes so popular now?

A. Dentists have always recommended baking soda for daily brushing because, as a weak base, baking soda controls the acid colonies in the gum lining which serve to convert plaque into tartar. It is also a very mild abrasive. Plain baking soda powder may well be preferable to baking soda paste because the former is just as effective and much less expensive. Baking soda powder pastes are popular now because of the manufacturers' good marketing.

Q. What's in those whitening toothpastes?

A. Some are simply "standard" toothpastes with a very strong abrasive such as aluminum oxide, which actually grinds off the discolorants on the teeth (and the enamel as well). Others contain compounds that release hydrogen peroxide in the mouth. It's much less expensive to rinse with a 3 percent solution of hydrogen peroxide, which can be purchased at any supermarket.

Q. I am curious: what is the basic composition of a toothpaste?

A.

THE COMPOSITION OF A TYPICAL TOOTHPASTE

Substance	% by weight	Function
Water	37	Solvent
Glycerol	32	Holds water in
Dibasic sodium phosphate	27*	Abrasive*
Sodium lauryl sulfate	2	Surfactant
Sorbitol or Carmageen	1	Thickening agent
Fluorides, pyrophosphate, other additives	1	Enamel hardeners, antitartar agents, sweeteners, preservatives, flavors, antiplaque agents

*Other abrasives include calcium carbonate, calcium pyrophosphate, hydrated aluminum oxide, magnesium carbonate, talc, tricalcium phosphate.

Q. What is tooth enamel made of, and how does fluoride toughen it?

A. Enamel is primarily composed of the mineral hydroxyapatite. When fluoride is introduced, the enamel is converted into fluoroapatite, a substance much tougher and resistant to attack from acids and therefore prevents cavities (tooth decay).

Q. What is tooth decay? What causes it?

A. Healthy teeth are covered by a protective enamel which is very tough due to the presence of a mineral containing both calcium and phosphate—hydroxyapatite. When a thin coating of polysaccharide, from food, comes in contact with bacteria on the teeth, an acid is formed that reacts with the calcium and phosphate in the enamel to cause it to break down. Microorganisms can move through this damaged barrier to carry the infection into the interior of teeth. This condition is called *dental caries* or more commonly referred to as *cavities* or *tooth decay*. While teeth do have a natural process by which the lost calcium and phosphate can be replaced by calcium and phosphate in saliva, the plaque must be removed daily by grinding it off with the abrasives found in toothpaste or tooth powder. The material used for grinding must be abrasive enough to remove plaque, but not so abrasive that it damages tooth enamel. Surfactants, such as sodium lauryl sulfate, are useful because they help to remove the ground-off material.

Q. What is plaque?

A. It is a thin layer of a polysaccharide (sugars, starches, and gylcogen) that sticks to the surface of the teeth and provides a breeding ground for bacteria.

Q. What is tartar?

A. When plaque reacts with the acid colonies below the gum line, a very hard substance called *tartar* is formed. Tartar clings so tightly to the enamel that it must be removed by a dentist or dental hygienist with a special pick.

Q. Does it matter if tooth-cleaning products are pastes, gels, powders, or creams?

A. There are really no chemical differences in which the various forms of tooth-cleaning products are packaged, as long as you brush according to your dentist's recommendations. We checked the labels on two brands that sold a toothpaste and a tooth-brushing powder. The ingredients were exactly the same except that the paste had water and a thickening agent.

Q. What about the products today that are striped? For years, Pepsodent® used to have red stripes as it came out of the tube. Today, we have products like Aquafresh®, and others, which have what appear to be three separate toothpastes in the same tube. Do these colors represent separate cleaning agents?

A. This question caused us to cut open several tubes of this brand and analyze the constituents in each color. They were exactly the same! Perhaps a great marketing ploy for kids and adults. However, there is a new dental cleansing agent on the market now which is applied two layers thick to the toothbrush. It is not a gimmick. The product comes in a cannister with two chambers. One chamber consists of regular toothpaste while the other chamber has hydrogen peroxide dissolved in a gel. With one stroke of the plunger, you get both. This product is very expensive and you may wish to discuss this further with your dentist.

Q. How do denture cleaners differ from toothpastes?

A. Since they are applied to the artificial denture material, either by soaking or brushing, they are considerably stronger oxidizing (bleaching) agents and the pastes are much more abrasive.

Q. What difference is there between denture-cleaning pastes, powders, and soaks?

A. Pastes and powders work pretty much the same way. They contain an abrasive, a mild bleach, and a surfactant. Soaks usually release hydrogen peroxide slowly into a surfactant solution.

Q. How do denture adhesives work? Why doesn't the mouth's fluids (e.g., saliva) attack the adhesive and make people's dentures fall out?

A. These adhesives are soft and malleable but they are also insoluble, having been made from polymers that are activated by the heat of the mouth. Not being soluble, these adhesives are in no way affected by the hot or cold beverages we drink, or by saliva.

Q. I always see the commercials showing how to *apply* the denture adhesive but never how to *remove* it. If the creams and powders aren't affected by liquid, how are they removed in preparation for a new application the next morning?

A. They are removed by simple mechanical methods such as brushing, scraping, or with some water.

MOUTHWASHES, BREATH MINTS, AND SPRAYS

Q. Why do people use a mouthwash?

A. Mouthwashes are used to freshen the breath and to kill microbes. Mouthwashes also remove protein debris that would react with bacteria to produce the condition called *halitosis* (chronic bad breath). When they are formulated with antibacterial agents and detergents, mouthwashes can remove other debris. Hydrogen peroxide (3 percent) has the added advantage that it can whiten the teeth if used regularly. The addition of fluoride to mouthwashes seems to be effective in delivering topical fluoride protection for children. It is less effective for adults, since their teeth have stopped growing. Some mouthwashes contain sodium carbamate, which changes to hydrogen peroxide in the mouth and is an unnecessary cost. One of the most popular mouthwashes and throat gargles is Listerine®. The American Dental Association has recommended the original, brown Listerine® solution only, as an effective mouthwash to prevent plaque. No other claims for the effectiveness of Listerine® are made. The other forms of Listerine® don't qualify. Generic forms of "brown" Listerine® are just as effective as the brand name since they have the same ingredients in the same concentration.

Q. These days much is made of mouthwashes with plaque-fighting capabilities. What extra ingredients are added for this purpose?

A. Tetrasodium pyrophosphate is used in some mouthwashes to control the conversion of plaque into tartar. These should be labeled as *antitartar* mouthwashes, rather than *antiplaque* products. The mouthwashes that are really antiplaque usually contain a strong surfactant and a strong antibacterial agent, such as cetylpyridium chloride. There is a mouthwash still on the market that used to claim that its product, when used before brushing, could remove more tartar from the teeth than plain brushing alone. About a year ago, the FDA ordered the manufacturer to stop making such claims.

Q. What's the difference between mouthwashes and the gargling solutions people use when they have a sore throat? Are they separate products or not?

A. They are indeed the same products with the same ingredients. The purpose of a mouthwash is to remove debris on the teeth and leave a fresh taste. Most mouthwashes contain a detergent to remove the debris, a flavoring agent, and some sort of antiseptic. The latter are of questionable value in the mouth or throat. Many gargles also contain topical anesthetics, such as benezocaine or phenol and may give temporary pain relief. In fact, arguably the best gargle for a common sore throat is a warm salt (sodium chloride, or table salt) solution. Not only does it flush out bacterial decomposition products (phlegm), but warm salt water feels soothing to the throat and increases circulation of blood to the afflicted area. Three tablespoons of salt to one quart of hot water is inexpensive and probably better than anything you could purchase over the counter. Any advertisements claiming medical benefits for mouthwashes or gargles were banned in 1970 by the FDA, and the ingredients have not changed much since then. The product Listerine® was not affected by this ban since it was placed on the market in 1938 and came in under the "grandfather clause." However, it should be noted that the only mouthwash recommended for reduction of tartar formation by the American Dental Association is still the brown-colored (not the green) Listerine®.

Q. I see a lot of people using breath sprays before attending a meeting. How do they work?

A. These different brands of breath sprays all contain alcohol as their active ingredient. They also contain flavorings and moisturizers.

Q. Can you explain what's in a breath mint?

A. These products usually contain sweeteners, moisturizers, and some claim to have an ingredient that kills germs. The three most significant compounds, from brand to brand, are sorbitol, cuprous (copper) gluconate, and soluble chlorophyll. Sorbitol is a compound used in the synthesis of antifreeze, resins, and plasticizers. It is also used as a humectant (absorbs water) in printing; actually helps to ensure a smooth ink flow on ball point pen tips; serves as a humectant in peanut butter; and as a stabilizer in coconut oil, soft drinks, and wines. Nowhere does it say that sorbitol *kills germs.* Cuprous gluconate is the generic name for "Retsyn." We can find no antigermicidal action listed for this compound. Chlorophyll comes from the green pigment of plants. While it has been used as a colorant and antiknock agent in gasolines, its antibacterial action in the mouth is reduced because of its limited solubility in water.

Q. What is the most effective throat lozenge?

A. Actually no mouth or throat lozenge is much more effective than gargling with hot water or a 3 percent hydrogen peroxide solution. Some lozenges contain phenol, which is both an anesthetic and an antiseptic. Read the labels and select one that contains phenol.

ANTIPERSPIRANTS AND DEODORANTS

The chemistry of these products has not changed all that much since the early 1900s when Odo-Ro-No was introduced as the first antiperspirant, and perfumes served as deodorants. We Americans do seem to have an inordinate fear of body odor. Emphasizing this fear has resulted in billions of dollars for the stockholders of deodorant and antiperspirant manufacturers. The cost of manufacturing is often 3 to 15 percent of the total cost. The packaging of these products usually costs more than the ingredients they contain.

Q. What is the difference between antiperspirants and deodorants?

A. Antiperspirants constrict or tighten sweat glands and prevent normal perspiration. Bacteria need moisture to grow. When we perspire, the decomposition or breakdown of bacteria and skin material causes unpleasant odors. All of the antiperspirants sold in the United States contain one or more of the following: aluminum chlorohydrate, aluminum chloride, or zirconium chlorides. The solid stick forms and creams seem to work better than roll-ons, which are more effective than sprays.

Deodorants do not constrict the sweat glands. Instead, they contain antibacterial agents such as triclosan. The antibacterial action only lasts a few hours, so perfumes are added to mask or hide any odors. Many people prefer deodorants for several reasons: first, they object to having a natural body process interfered with; second, antiperspirants irritate their skin; and, third, regular use of antiperspirants can discolor clothing.

Q. What causes these foul odors? I wash regularly but still I get them.

A. Perspiration provides moisture for bacteria to flourish and grow. The endocrine glands secrete oils that decompose to form amines (which smell remarkably like rotting fish). Another product caused by perspiration is butyric acid, which is the same substance that gives rancid butter its unpleasant odor.

Q. Why is perspiration acidic, and salty to the taste—much like a tear drop?

A. Lactic acid is produced by the sweat gland, which accounts for the acidic quality. The salty taste comes from salt in our perspiration. A large percentage of these salts are simple sodium chloride, but calcium and potassium are also present in lower concentrations.

Q. Which is better, a deodorant or an antiperspirant?

A. It is a matter of personal choice. If you have delicate skin and find antiperspirants irritating, use deodorants. If you do not sweat profusely, then deodorants would also be a wise choice. Some people have to use antiperspirants due to their own special biochemical problems. We assume they have none of the problems we noted with respect to antiperspirants.

We would be less than candid if we didn't admit that our attitude toward antiperspirants isn't completely objective. Many men—and probably women, too—use Styptic Pencil®, a concentrated stick of aluminum chloride to seal off blood capillaries cut on the face (or legs) while shaving. While most would want facial (and leg) cuts to be sealed off, the thought of that compound under the arm can be a bit daunting.

Q. There are certain products on the market (especially for those who perspire at lot) which claim that, when used, the person can even skip a day without reapplying the product. Is this some kind of super antiperspirant?

A. We know the commercial to which you are referring. The big, husky guy on the silk sheeted bed says, "I used brand X antiperspirant yesterday and may not have to use it today." This stuff is not only loaded with aluminum chlorohydrate but aluminum chloride as well! Both compounds are excellent astringents and will close the sweat pores in underarms very effectively. However, since these products have such a high concentration of astringents, they may irritate sensitive skin. Are these products "super antiperspirants"? We don't think so. If one were to apply a conventional antiperspirant twice, the results would be the same.

Q. Some antiperspirant manufacturers claim that their products are made for a woman because women perspire more than men, or because their pH level is different than that of men. Should this information be factored into my selection process?

A. These antiperspirants use the mild compound zirconium aluminum glycine hydroxychloride, which is indeed quite gentle to the skin. The term "pH balanced" is meaningless in this context and has little to do with the action of antiperspirants on any skin type.

Q. Chemically speaking, what do manufacturers of antiperspirants/ deodorants mean when they claim that their products help their users stay dry and odor free longer? Do their products simply have more of the antiwetness agent?

A. They would like you to believe that. All antiperspirants can put only so much aluminum or zirconium salt(s) on the skin before irritation occurs. Deodorants have antibacterial agents but increasing the dose doesn't help, because they have a limited potency.

Q. **You have already talked about the basic components of soaps. What about deodorant soaps? Isn't soap always antibacterial?**

A. Soap is always antibacterial and the addition of the antibacterial agent triclosan should increase its antibacterial action. However, the combination doesn't seem to work any better than plain soap.

Q. **Why do the prices of deodorants and antiperspirants vary so much?**

A. Basically it's marketing. For example, there is a new antiperspirant and deodorant on the market from a popular men's perfume manufacturer. This deodorant is marketed for $2.19 for two ounces (or $1.10/ounce), but their antiperspirant sells for $3.00 for 2.5 ounces (or $1.60/ounce). The cost of the chemicals involved is actually higher for the deodorant than for the antiperspirant.

A FEW MISCELLANEOUS ITEMS

Colognes, Perfumes, and Shaving Lotions

Q. **What is "eau de toilet"?**

A. It is a French term for cologne. Colognes are perfumes that have been diluted by a factor of ten or more with alcohol or another solvent. Originally, colognes were made from citrus fruits.

Q. **Is there any real difference between colognes made for women and those made for men? If not, then why are their relative costs so different?**

A. The difference between colognes made for men and those made for women is subjective. Chemically, their differences are not very significant. Their relative costs are not any more than the perfumes from which they originated. Costs have little to do with their marketability. About 95 percent of the cost of cologne is tied to advertising. By now you shouldn't be surprised!

Q. What are perfumes made from? Are generic perfumes as good?

A. Perfumes are made from animal or plant extracts, a resin, and a solvent. There are three odors that come from this complex mixture, the *top note,* the *middle note,* and the *bottom note.* Sorry—"note" is perfumists' technology. The *top note* is the odor that comes off within a minute or so of application. It usually contains the small molecules in the mixture and is not generally indicative of the odor of the perfume, since it occurs with evaporation of the solvent. Larger molecules evaporate off from then until 5 or 6 hours have passed. This is the *middle note,* or the odor that you paid for. The *bottom note* lasts for another 12 hours and consists of the largest molecules in the mixture.

We know what you mean by generic perfumes. "If you love brand X, then you will love brand Y." With the use of modern chemical instrumentation, cosmetics chemists have been able to break down the complex mixture of brand-name perfumes into their chemical composition, and offer generic substitutes that are nearly the same. Think back a few years to the "musk odor" that was used in perfumes and now is found in deodorants and other cosmetics. This was originally obtained from the slaughter of arctic musk oxen. Cosmetics chemists have unraveled the mystery of musk ox odor secretions. The slaughter has long since stopped and it seems that these chemists were not only capitalists, but environmentalists as well.

Perfume *chemistry* really doesn't exist; it is far more a matter of trial and error. That's why new and very expensive perfumes come on the market each year and old ones disappear just about as quickly. Some have endured for decades, like Old Spice® for men and Heaven's Scent® for women. They produced exactly the odor that people wanted at their inception and didn't need an inordinate amount of hype to keep them popular over the years. Cosmetics advertising is a very expensive gamble.

Q. If there is no real difference between perfumes, colognes, and toilet water, why are their relative costs so different?

A. There is a difference in the concentration of compounds that are responsible for the odor of a particular product. Perfumes have the highest concentration while colognes have much less for a particular product. Toilet water is indeed cologne, and cologne is simply diluted perfume. The relative costs do not represent any major differences in the basic components present in each. It is simply what the market will bear for the parent perfume.

Q. **Why do certain colognes smell really good on some people but not as good on others? I've heard this has to due with body chemistry. Is this true?**

A. This is indeed true but much less common than most folks believe. By referring to "body chemistry" you mean skin condition and the nature of endocrine (skin gland) emissions. Perspiration for normal, healthy people should be pretty much the same. When an illness (however minor) or a biochemical-endocrine balance gets out of order, the composition of sweat and oil production becomes distorted for a period of time. This causes an unexpected reaction with a cologne or perfume but it usually "goes away."

Q. **Is aftershave lotion just another type of cologne? Or is it designed to serve some purpose that cologne is not?**

A. Aftershave lotions contain propylene glycol, menthol, and benzoic acid. These are all compounds designed to cool the skin, tighten pores, and heal irritation, unlike colognes, which just impart a fragrance.

Q. **Men who use electric razors often have preshave lotions recommended to them by manufacturers of the razors. What do these preshave lotions do and what are they made of?**

A. Preshave lotions are mostly lubricants (myrisyl propionate and casaua flour) that remain on the skin and facial hair after the solvent evaporates. These products are intended to make the skin easier for the electric razor to glide on, and they help make the facial hair stand up a bit so it can be cut more efficiently.

Lubricants

Q. **There is a lubricant on the market called KY Jelly®, which I believe is water-based. Why are such lubricants recommended for use with condoms? What's wrong with just using petroleum jelly, hand lotion, or any number of other items?**

A. KY Jelly®, being water-based, washes off easily with water. It is also used with rubber gloves when physicians perform internal (anal, vaginal) examinations. In addition, it is easily decomposed by heat. The use of KY Jelly® or a generic in lieu of petrolatum jelly with condoms is simple: petrolatum jelly weakens the latex condom and could cause breakage. Water-based jellies do not react with the structure of the condom.

Q. **Most everyone familiar with condoms (prophylactics) knows that they are made of latex rubber, but is that all?**

A. What did you expect, steel radials? Yes, they are all made from latex rubber. Unfortunately, some men or women are allergic to latex so alternate animal membranes can be used, but with caution: they may not protect from viruses as well as latex. The other ingredients commonly added to the surface are light mineral oil for lubrication and antisperm agents (spermicides) for the doubly concerned.

Q. **What is in petroleum jelly?**

A. It is more correctly spelled "petrolatum" jelly. Another common name for the same product is vasoliment (Vaseline® brand petrolatum jelly). It is a mixture of hydrocarbons that are obtained from the purification of crude oil. This yellowish mixture is further purified to obtain white petrolatum, which we use today. If you read the label from any brand of petrolatum jelly, it will read, "white petrolatum, USP." The letters USP mean that this product meets the standards of the United States Pharmacopeia, which is not a government agency, used as a standard for purity by the pharmaceutical industry. As you may know, petrolatum jelly seals off the skin from any surface damage due to irritation or mild abrasion.

Lip Products

Q. What is the difference between lipstick, lip gloss, and lip balm?

A. *Lipstick* contains castor oil, caprylic or capric triglycerides, and stearic acid, *plus* eighteen other components—and some labels also indicate that the product may contain twelve other compounds! Among the twelve other compounds is the color-forming agent. Again, we submit that cosmetics chemistry is not a science but rather an art. In fact, castor oil, while being a laxative, is also an insoluble lubricant and has many other uses.

   Lip balm is another matter, since its main purpose is to medicate and protect the lips. Your lips are probably the most delicate parts of your body. Lip balms contain moisturizers, healants, and protectants such as petrolatum jelly.

   Lip glosses add a shiny and moist texture to the lips. They usually contain lanolin, polybutene, mineral oil, kaolin (a clay), silica (sand), BHT (butylhydroxytoluene—a preservative), capric triglyceride and stearic acid (both can penetrate skin), *plus* fourteen other components, which *may* be present.

Eye and Nail Products

Q. What is the composition of eye shadow and eyebrow pencil?

A. This is a hard question since so much of cosmetics chemistry is tied up in patents. Eye shadow will normally contain talc and mica (rock fibers), polyethylene fluorethylene, magnesium stearate, and many "contain twenty other compounds." Eyebrow pencil has pretty much the same chemical composition as eye shadow, but with a bit more pigment added.

Q. What is in nail polish, and nail polish remover?

A. Nail polish is a mixture of pigment, nitrocellulose, and a lacquer dissolved in solvents such as acetone or ethyl acetate. When the acetone or the ethyl acetate evaporates, a hard and water-soluble coating is left on the nails. Nail polish removers are simply the same solvents, acetone or ethyl acetate, used to dissolve the coating. Nitrocellulose is used in nail polish as a flexible lacquer that can bend with the nail without cracking or flaking. Common pigments found in nail polish include: titanium dioxide; carbon black; ultramarine; organic dyes; and dyes of iron, chromium, and other metals.

Advertising claims that nail polish is "acetone free" simply mean that ethyl acetate is the solvent being used. Claims that acetone is more drying to the nails are simply not true.

Powder

Q. What exactly is body powder?

A. Commercial body powders contain talc and/or corn starch, zinc oxide, and perfume.

Q. Is there an inexpensive and simple formula to make body powder?

A. We recommend placing one part sodium bicarbonate with nine parts of cornstarch in a blender and slowly add a few drops of your favorite perfume. Purchase the sodium bicarbonate and cornstarch at your supermarket and you will save even more money. This formula will provide a very inexpensive, yet effective body powder.

Tissue

Q. What is toilet tissue made of? Sorry to keep asking this question again, but is there any real difference in the large number of toilet tissues on the market?

A. The best toilet tissues are made from purified wood pulp and skin softeners. The worst are just made from wood pulp—knots and all. One wipe and you should be able to tell the difference!

Q. Is there any difference between toilet tissue and facial tissue?

A. Toilet tissue is different from facial tissue in that the latter contains extra conditioners to make the product more smooth to the touch.

Q. **Much has been said about families refraining from using colored toilet tissue. Why? It seems odd that the same concern isn't raised about colored facial tissue, paper towels, and napkins. Why do you suppose that is?**

A. Colored paper products can contain trace amounts of metals to produce the color. Since toilet tissue is used in vastly greater quantities and on more sensitive parts of the body than facial tissue, paper towels, paper napkins, or the aggregate sum of all of these, it seems reasonable to concentrate it. Some people with very sensitive skin experience irritation from colored tissue products.

4

Inside the Medicine Cabinet

Reading labels is very important because there are some common compounds found in many preparations that most of us have in our medicine cabinets. Being informed can increase your purchasing power. You can save money by wading through the gimmicks offered in manufacturers' advertisements. Often the truth is simply that there are not many differences between competing brands. If a manufacturer wants to increase the sale of a particular brand of analgesic (pain reliever), then it has to come up with a marketing strategy. All analgesics sold are nearly the same. To increase sales of a particular one, the manufacturer can double the dose in each tablet (capsule, caplet, gelcap, or whatever) and change the instructions on the label. The consumer then needs to take one "extra-strength" tablet (capsule) instead of two regular-strength tablets (capsules). Now the product is touted as "new and improved," "extra strength," or whatever the manufacturer wishes to say in marketing a simple drug. Manufacturers know that they can stretch this a bit without breaking any laws.

MAINTAINING YOUR MEDICINE CABINET

Keep all of your prescription and over-the-counter medications in a cabinet well out of the reach of children. Set up a periodic cleaning schedule for your cabinet, checking all medicines or toiletries for discoloration or degradation (deterioration or break-up), and, if need be, discard them. Check the expiration dates on all medicines, prescriptions, and preparations. Don't save prescribed medications if you are no longer using them. Clutter can be dangerous! Medicines kept for an extended time should be protected from excessive summer heat, which speeds up their chemical deterioration. Be sure all caps are secured tightly. Many people find it helpful to prepare a chart and attach it to the inside of the cabinet door. The chart lists all contents of the medicine chest, the dates of purchase, what remains of each preparation, and when each medicine is expected to expire. If your pharmacist or physician changes any of your medications to generic drugs, place the brand name in parenthesis next to the generic name to reduce confusion.

TYPICAL ABBREVIATED CHART

Medicine/Item	Purchase Date	Status
Lopid (a)	12-3-94	8 Tablets
Penicillin Syrup (b)	12-19-94	1/3 pint*
Prozinan (minipress)	11-29-94	10 tabs (expiration date)
Antiseptic Cream	1-3-95	1/2 tube (expiration date)
Hyrdogen Peroxide	?	1 pint (expiration date: 11/95)
Bandages (6 inch)	?	2 pkg. of 8
Etc.		

*Must be refrigerated. (a) Al Smith, M.D. [phone number], (b) Sylvia Cotton, M.D. [phone number], Brownies Pharmacy [phone number], Poison Control Center [phone number], Ambulance [phone number], Emergency Room [phone number].

The Role of the Food and Drug Administration (FDA)

The Food and Drug Administration controls the sale of prescription, nonprescription, and other over-the-counter medications in the United States. It has the authority to ban the sale of unsafe drugs, cosmetics, health aids, and vitamins. The FDA can stop a manufacturer from making false claims for products or force it to provide instructions for their safe use. We have used the recommendations of the FDA's medical and scientific advisory panels to help us determine the safe and effective use of compounds that make up particular products. These recommendations are published monthly in the *Federal Register.*

Perhaps the greatest testimonial that can be made to the importance and potential impact of the FDA centers on the action it took about twenty years ago to prevent the mild tranquilizer thalidomide from being introduced into the United States. Thalidomide was being used extensively in Europe, and many pregnant women as well as elderly persons were prescribed the drug to relieve nausea or insomnia. One of the FDA's chemists realized the dangers of thalidomide and fought to prevent its introduction to the U.S. market.

The chemist fought the drug lobbies as well as many of her superiors before thalidomide was finally withdrawn. Due to the FDA's quick action, the United States was spared the more serious implications of thalidomide use. Unfortunately, many badly deformed babies were born in Europe: some had no limbs and others had "flippers" for arms. This tragedy was primarily concentrated in England and on the European Continent. The FDA may be slow, but it serves as the model for the rest of the world in the area of consumer protection.

In 1991 alone, the FDA challenged orange juice mislabeling, improved condom testing, took swift and unpopular action against the American Medical Association (AMA) monopoly, withdrew permission for the sale of many over-the-counter preparations and prescription pharmaceuticals, established a uniform nutritional labeling program for foodstuffs, and prescribed numerous additional actions that were to take place in the next few years.

If you have any questions concerning over-the-counter medications or you are just curious about them, write the FDA. Its staff will provide you with the information you need, or they will tell you where to look. Many libraries at major universities, or large public libraries, may also house FDA reports.

In this section, we will limit our discussion to nonprescription, over-the-counter preparations. Prescription pharmaceuticals are best left to your physician and/or pharmacist. A friendly reminder: purchase all of your prescriptions at *one* pharmacy; you can avoid the confusion and dangers of obtaining multiple prescriptions for the same medication(s) from different physicians. Get to know the pharmacists at the druggist of your choice. These trained professionals can be very helpful in detecting and preventing unexpected reactions; they know as much, if not more, about pharmacology than physicians.

Unless your doctor recommends otherwise, always insist on

generic drugs. This suggestion alone can save you hundreds of dollars each year. Generics are identical in chemical composition and biological response as the much more expensive brand-name pharmaceuticals. As long as you use generics, shopping for savings should be reserved for over-the-counter preparations. A friend used to tell us that a particular generic brand didn't work as well as a brand-name product. In fact, the two products were made by the *same company,* with the *exact same ingredients.* They were probably the exact same product but with *different labels!*

It is amazing to note that about five major corporations produce approximately 80 to 90 percent of all the over-the-counter preparations sold in the United States today. Many times the major producer is not listed on the package. For example, McNeil Consumer Products distributes the antidiarrhea compound Immodium® under its label, but Johnson and Johnson Company, which sells prescription Immodium® through the Janssen Company, owns McNeil!

Tremendous savings could be yours: purchase generic equivalents for brand name, over-the-counter preparations. You can save about 80 percent by purchasing generic ibuprofen as a store brand instead of the brand names Motrin®, Advil®, Nuprin®, etc. Be aware as well that there are only four aspirin manufacturers in the United States: Monsanto, Dow Chemical, Bayer-Sterling, and Norwich-Eaton. We listed them in decreasing order of sales. You will *not* find Monsanto or Dow on any aspirin container, but together they produce 80 percent of the aspirin sold in the United States. They sell bulk aspirin for most store brands of aspirin and to many of the brand-name companies for packing. The other two companies that produce aspirin here are Bayer-Sterling and Norwich-Eaton. The Bayer and Norwich companies produce aspirin only for their own labels. Purchasing generic aspirin (or any generic analgesic) can save you quite a bit of money and leave you with the assurance that generic aspirin is just as good as the brand name product. Generic aspirin, acetaminophen, naproxen sodium, or ibuprofen must undergo the same difficult bioassay and chemical tests as the brand-name product. A bioassay procedure is needed to determine capsule or tablet integrity (to ensure the product doesn't break up too easily) and to establish that the product is distributed evenly in the blood.

PAIN REMEDIES

Q. What is the difference between aspirin, acetaminophen, ibuprofen, and naproxen?

A. They all relieve pain and all are antipyretics (fever reducers). Aspirin can also reduce inflammation of the joints and help prevent colorectal cancer, blood clots, and in some cases even stroke. Some people think ibuprofen is more effective than aspirin for deep muscle pain, but the evidence is mostly anecdotal. Naproxen works in much the same way as ibuprofen, and stays in the blood stream about two hours longer than ibuprofen. Acetaminophen (also known as paracetamol in the United Kingdom) offers no relief for inflammation and is decidely inferior to aspirin as a pain reliever. However, it is less irritating to the stomach than aspirin and thus it is preferred by people with sensitive stomachs.

Naproxen sodium is a relatively new over-the-counter analgesic. The brand name is Aleve®. Naproxen sodium is sold in a "nonprescription strength" of 220 mg per tablet. Recommended dosage is one caplet every 10 to 12 hours. Despite a very strong and active promotion, it is not stronger or more effective than aspirin, acetaminophen, or ibuprofen. The advertising on the package, "Aleve® works on a variety of pains; headache, toothache, backache, muscular pain, pain of arthritis, menstrual cramps and aches and pain of the common cold," could just as well be used for the other over-the-counter analgesics. Aleve® will irritate the stomach about as much as aspirin.

Q. What is the generic name for aspirin?

A. It doesn't have one. It was a trade name in 1920. A German chemist's father had an upset stomach from taking salicylic acid for pain, so he prepared a more palatable derivative, acetylsalicylic acid, which he patented as "Aspirin." (Before the advent of aspirin, people obtained salicylic acid by sucking or chewing the bark of the white willow tree or extracts from it.) As a tablet, aspirin degrades (loses its effectiveness) if left in a hot environment. For example, if aspirin is left in the glove compartment of a car on a hot summer's day, it may spoil. One of the decomposition products of aspirin is acetic acid (vinegar). If when you check your aspirin it has a vinegar-like odor, you should discard it.

Q. How does aspirin work?

A. Aspirin works by reducing nerve impulses to the brain. An excess of some body secretions (known as prostaglandins) cause inflammation. Aspirin interferes with the action of the prostaglandins, which dilate (expand) the blood vessels in the brain, thus giving relief to the pain of headaches due to constricted vessels.

Q. Are there any natural analgesics?

A. The brain secretes substances called endorphins and enkephalins, which act to relieve pain. Of course, there is always the bark of the willow tree.

Q. Doesn't aspirin irritate the stomach?

A. Unless you have an ulcer, a gastrointestinal illness, or a sensitive stomach, aspirin will not irritate the stomach if taken with a full glass of water. Unfortunately, many people gulp them down without enough liquid.

Q. Then why do we hear that some people should not take aspirin because of the upset stomach it can bring about?

A. In our view, *not many* people do get upset stomachs after taking aspirin. The vast majority of people tolerate aspirin quite well when taken with sufficient liquid. Aspirin is an inexpensive and potent medication. It does so many more things than other analgesics, and in this lies the problem for manufacturers or distributors who market it. The profit margin on aspirin is quite low because of its widespread availability. Since it is difficult to impugn aspirin's effectiveness, the manufacturers of the more profitable ibuprofen and acetaminophen try to concern people about some unwarranted gastric irritation from aspirin. Actually, aspirin dissolves somewhat in the mucous lining of the stomach and causes an insignificant amount of bleeding to occur, about one drop of blood. All of the bleeding is due to the weight of the undissolved tablet on the lining. Drinking half to a full glass of liquid (water, milk, juice, tea, coffee, etc.) solves this problem. If you have ulcers or other gastric afflictions, or are elderly, contact your physician *before* taking aspirin.

Q. Not all that long ago, wasn't there considerable concern that some people—mostly children—can contract a condition known as "Reyes Syndrome"* from ingesting aspirin. Is this true?

A. Aspirin has been shown to cause Reyes Syndrome in a very small number of children. When this was discovered, it caused quite an uproar in the press. It is now known that this condition affects far fewer people than was originally estimated. As always, we urge you to consult your doctor if you have any concerns about giving aspirin or any medication to your child.

Q. Wouldn't Bufferin® or buffered aspirin be better than plain aspirin?

A. No. Buffered aspirin isn't really *buffered* at all. It is aspirin mixed with an inconsequential amount of antacid—not even enough antacid to cause the normal acidity of the stomach to change by 0.1 percent! Besides, the acidity of aspirin is about one thousand times weaker than the acids already present in the stomach.

There is little scientifically meaningful difference in the absorption rates of buffered (however that term is understood) and plain aspirin. Moreover, there are no data satisfactorily demonstrating that buffered aspirin provides faster pain relief, relieves more pain, relieves pain for a longer period of time, or is easier to tolerate than plain aspirin.

Q. What is enteric coated aspirin?

A. Enteric means "a medical preparation treated to pass through the stomach unaltered and absorbed in the intestines." Therefore, anything that is enteric coated dissolves in the intestine rather than in the stomach. Enteric coated aspirin is useful for anyone taking large doses of aspirin daily (people with arthritis, for ex-

---

*A condition that can occur during illnesses, such as influenza, which are accompanied by fever. The condition can include swelling of the brain, and coma.

ample). For those who seek occasional pain relief, enteric aspirin is not generally required. Enterics usually take thirty minutes to an hour longer to be absorbed. For this reason alone, most people prefer faster-acting pain relievers.

Q. You pointed out that aspirin can be taken orally or "enterically." Are there any other modes of application?

A. Enteric aspirin is absorbed in the intestine but it must be taken orally. There are some lotions containing aspirin which are rubbed on the skin. Unfortunately, because of its molecular structure, aspirin doesn't penetrate the skin readily. There are also aspirin rectal suppositories. They take forever to work and are really a messy way to handle a headache or other pains.

Q. I question the safety of aspirin. After all, don't nine out of ten (or is it four out of five?) hospitals use Tylenol®?

A. One reason nine out of ten (or four out of five) hospitals use Tylenol® (acetaminophen) is that they can purchase it below the manufacturer's cost. The manufacturer can afford to lose a bit of money in order to market its product. The Bayer Company is trying the same marketing strategy with its aspirin and has had some recent success.

There are some legitimate reasons for a physician to halt the use of aspirin when a patient enters the hospital. Aspirin is an anticoagulant; in other words, it thins the blood and prevents some clotting. For this reason it is prescribed to help prevent or lower the incidence of heart attack and stroke. However, because it thins the blood, aspirin should not be used by patients facing surgery, child birth, or any procedure that could result in the loss of blood. Nearly all the physicians we contacted said that they routinely order Tylenol® (acetaminophen) to relieve the mild pain of their patients who are in the hospital. After the patient is discharged, these doctors recommend any analgesic that was previously effective for the patient—including aspirin. The manufacturers of the more profitable aspirin substitutes—naproxen, ibuprofen, and acetaminophen—have convinced many Americans that aspirin is less safe and less effective than their products. We have become a nation of aspirinophobes.

In nearly all pain preparations that include two analgesics, aspirin has been removed by the manufacturers so that the combination can be described as "aspirin free." People are being led to believe that aspirin will result in heartburn, upset stomach, intestinal bleeding, or other complications. These are myths.* Only 4 percent of those taking aspirin encounter any gastric upset, and only 0.3 percent of these individuals encounter any bleeding at all. Acetylsalicylic acid (pure aspirin) is about one thousand times weaker than the acid in orange juice.

Q. The television commercials for Anacin® state that it has *two* ingredients for pain; that certainly must be better than just one, right?

A. Read the Anacin® label: it states that it contains "100 mg aspirin and 20 mg. caffeine." No one has ever considered caffeine to be an analgesic. It will stimulate you, however. Do you want to be stimulated while in pain? Remember, the FDA has outlawed the use of mixtures containing more than two analgesics in an over-the-counter preparation for pain.†

Q. Are aspirin powders or Alka Seltzer® tablets any better than plain aspirin?

A. The powders are not any "better," nor are they assimilated faster than plain aspirin. Alka Seltzer® has a lot of sodium (salt) and is no more effective than plain aspirin. Both are just different forms of the same basic pain reliever, for those who prefer to administer it in a more acceptable way. Aspirin powders are very popular in the Southern United States. The powder is poured into a glass of water, stirred, and swallowed. Unfortunately, aspirin does not dissolve in water, and the mixture is often gulped, with much of the aspirin lost at the bottom of the glass.

---

*See "The Ten Myths about Aspirin," R. J. Palma, Sr., and E. Guenesa, *Pan American Journal of Chemical Education,* vol 2 (1991): 243–51.

†See "Pain, Fever and Anti-Inflammatory Drugs Taken Internally," Report of the FDA's advisory review panel, and the *FDA Notice on Proposal to Withdraw Approval of Phenacetin,* 1980.

COMPARING POPULAR ANALGESICS
Cost Per Dose (CPD)*

Analgesic	Brand Name CPD	Generic CPD
Advil®	$0.45	$0.09
Bayer® aspirin	$0.18	$0.03
Bufferin®	$0.20	$0.08
Nuprin®	$0.33	$0.06
Datril®	$0.39	$0.09

---

*Data are averages collected from 36 stores in the Dallas/Ft. Worth area during 1993.

The generics used were ibuprofen for Advil® and Nuprin®, plain aspirin for Bayer® brand aspirin, and generic buffered aspirin for Bufferin®. You can develop a list like this for other products, such as Tylenol® and many more. Read the recommended dosage on a bottle of Tylenol® (the number of tables per dose), then divide the cost of the bottle by the number of tablets. This will give you the cost per tablet. Multiply the cost per tablet by the recommended dosage. This will give you the cost per dosage (CPD). Now repeat this process with generic acetaminophen. This will give you its generic CPD.

Q. What exactly does it mean for a preparation to be "topical," as in a topical analgesic or a topical anaesthetic?

A. Topical medications are *applied to* the skin and *absorbed through* the skin.

Q. How do topical analgesics, such as aspirin creams, work?

A. Aspirin does not go through the skin very readily. Manufacturers realize this and suspend the aspirin in oils (similar to cold creams). The oil has two functions. It must be able to dissolve into the fat or tissues directly below the skin, and it must also allow the medicine to be soluble in these tissues.

Q. Are there other topical analgesics besides aspirin creams?

A. Most of the topical analgesics sold don't even contain any aspirin. About 90 percent of the products sold today contain methyl salicylate and/or menthol. For example, Ben Gay® contains 15 percent methyl salicylate and 10 percent menthol. The product Icy Hot® contains 30 percent methyl salicylate and 14 percent menthol. The product Aspercreme® contains no aspirin (and its advertisements make this clear); the active ingredient is trolamine salicylate, which is a counterirritant like methyl salicylate. Menthol leaves an intense cool feeling on the skin, even though the area may feel warm to the touch.

Q. **How do these salicylates reduce deep muscle or joint pain?**

A. They irritate the skin slightly, thereby increasing blood flow to the injury.

Q. **What is a topical anesthetic?**

A. These are compounds that numb the skin, thereby reducing the itch or pain, and whose ingredient names usually end in "caine" or "cain." The most common topical over-the-counter anesthetics are benzocaine, novocaine, and bacitracin.

Q. **There are numerous products on the market that claim to bring soothing—sometimes penetrating—warmth to sore joints or to aching muscles. How is this feeling of comfort or warmth generated by creams, lotions, or ointments?**

A. Here again, the sensation of comfort and/or warmth that creams, lotions, or ointments produce is brought about by increasing circulation of blood in the afflicted area.

Q. **What are liniments?**

A. They are creams containing methyl salicylate, menthol, or similar compounds. They work by counterirritation, a mild pain from the liniment causes the pain impulses in the area to be "switched off."

Q. **A friend of mine uses a horse liniment for shoulder and joint pain. Is this safe?**

A. Dimethyl sulfoxide (DMSO) is a horse liniment and an industrial solvent that should never be used on humans. It dilates blood vessels and produces a warm sensation. It can be purchased over-the-counter in many pharmacies, but it cannot contain on its package any reference to use on humans. Although some athletes claim to use it daily, DMSO often leaves a garlic taste and smell to one's breath. The major drawback of DMSO is that it readily absorbs nearly any compound, causing that compound to be absorbed into the body. We have stopped using DMSO in our laboratories, and we urge you and your friend to consult a doctor.

Q. Why is camphor used so often in liniments and creams that warm the skin and muscles?

A. Camphor is a counterirritant used in medicine because it selectively stimulates cold sensors.

GENERIC DRUGS

Q. What are some of the top-selling generic drugs used in the United States?

A. A variety of drugs from antibiotics to sleeping aids are purchased in large quantities in the United States. The following is a short list of the most frequently purchased generic drugs:

SOME OF THE LARGEST SELLING GENERIC DRUGS

Generic Name	Proprietary Name	Use
Amoxycillin	Amoxil	Antibiotic
Hydrochlorothiazide with Amiloride	Maxzide	Potassium sparing diuretic
Furosemide	Lasix	Diuretic
Oxazepam	Serax	Tranquilizer
Paracetamol	Pannadol	Analgesic
Acetaminophen	Pannadol	Analgesic
Ibuprofen	Motrin	Analgesic
Allopurinol	Zyloprim	Gout treatment
Aluminum hydroxide with magnesium hydroxide	Mylanta or Maalox	Antacid

Generic Name	Proprietary Name	Use
Potassium chloride	Slow-K	Potassium replacement
Digoxin	Langxin	Cardiac failure treatment
Prazosin	Minipress	Treats high blood pressure
Diazepam	Valium	Tranquilizer
Doxepin	Sinequan	Antidepressant
Erythromycin	Sumycin	Antibiotic
Chlorothiazide	Diuril	Diuretic
Hydrochlorothiazide	Hydrodiuril	Diuretic
Amitriptyline	Elavil	Antidepressant
Temazepam	Serax	Sleeping aid
Propanoldol	Inderal	Beta blocker
Salbutamol	Ventolin	Anti-asthmatic

SOME WIDELY SOLD NONGENERIC DRUGS

Prescription	Use
Ventolin	Asthma
Minipress	High blood pressure
Tagamet	Ulcers
Zantac	Ulcers
Humulin	Diabetes
Zyloprim	Relieves gout
Inderal	Beta blocker
Bactrim	Sulpha drug
Clinoril	Anti-inflammation
Serax	Tranquilizer
Slow-K	Potassium replacement
Questran	Reduction of bile
Berroca	Multivitamin preparation

Some other common items that are in your medicine cabinet include: acne preparations, antiseptics and disinfectants, topical anesthetics, fungal infection treatments, corn removers, laxatives, diarrhea treatments, antacids, antiemetics, hemorrhoidal treatments, cold remedies, antihistamines, sedatives, stimulants, and vitamin-mineral supplements. Let's look at some of these.

ACNE PREPARATIONS

Q. So many advertisements are focused on young people who have acne and oily skin. There are a great many products claiming to be the best at removing the dirt and oil that bring on blemishes. There are creams, lotions, medicated pads, facial scrubs, and on and on. Can you help unravel this tangled mess?

A. The most common agent used in acne preparations is benzoyl peroxide. It functions by mildly irritating the skin tissue causing it to peel away. The benzoyl peroxide can then penetrate and kill the microorganisms that produce acne. Sulfur soap and salicylic acid are safe and work on a similar principle.

Q. What is an astringent?

A. Astringents are compounds capable of drawing the skin or other soft tissue together. They help to close the skin pores. In addition, astringents block noxious substances from entering the surface cells, and they prevent the passage of blood by shrinking red blood cells on the skin.

Q. I have often heard my parents say that they applied something called witch hazel to their skin to clear up acne. What is witch hazel, some old home remedy?

A. Witch hazel is a plant extract. It is an astringent (with the same basic properties noted above) and an aftershave solution. Since the product contains 14 percent alcohol, it is also used as an antiseptic. Since it has so many functions, it is still widely sold throughout the United States.

Q. There are also acne preparations, especially of the cream variety, that claim to work by "soaking up the excess oil" that helps to cause pimples. Do these preparations contain some other medication besides benzoyl peroxide?

A. No acne preparation works by "soaking up excess oil." The image of a "chemical sponge" is simplistic, and it doesn't exist. Some sulfur and salicylic acid creams used for acne claim to be absorbant but nothing like "soaking up excess oil."

Q. Couldn't I just keep acne from appearing by doing what Mom always suggested: drink lots of water, wash my face thoroughly twice a day, and don't eat many greasy or fatty foods?

A. There are many myths concerning the prevention and cure for acne. Here are some facts: Acne cannot be cured but it can be controlled. Diet does not make acne worse, or better for that matter. No medication is effective for *all* acne cases. Sexual activity—too little or too much—is not a factor in whether a person gets acne. Soap and water will not cure acne, but it does seem to limit the growth of bacteria. Nervous teenagers are no more likely to get acne than their calmer peers.

Q. I saw this fascinating commercial—it's been on for years—in which young people are asked to wash their faces and then apply a medicated acne pad. When the camera zoomed in really close, I could see all the "dirt and oil that plain washing doesn't reach." Is this for real or is there some gimmick to the commercial?

A. There's no gimmick here. A cotton pad soaked in alcohol or many other liquid compounds will work the same.

Q. What is in an exfoliant and how does it work?

A. Exfoliants are chemicals which are applied to the skin to remove surface skin cells. Like benzoyl peroxide or salicylic acid, exfoliants irritate the surface cells causing them to peel away.

HAIR REMOVERS

Q. Many people, especially women, have unwanted hair on their bodies. Years ago, people would pluck it out or shave it off; now they can use creams that seem to dissolve the hair. How does this happen?

A. These creams are called *depilatories,* which consist of calcium thioglycolate suspended in oil. There is a strong sulfur odor to the calcium thiogylocolate and to all thiogylocoate compounds. The prefix *thio* means that the compound has sulfur substituted for oxygen. When used on the surface of skin, depilatories *seem* to dissolve hair, but actually they break up the hair into small units that are easily washed off. The fact that depilatories can irritate the skin (some people are extremely sensitive to thiogylcolates) often limits their use.

DISINFECTANTS AND ANTISEPTICS

Q. Is there a difference between disinfectants and antiseptics?

A. Yes. Disinfectants kill all bacteria and some viruses and are not safe for use on the skin. Sodium hypochlorite, potassium permanganate, mercurous chloride, and some organic nitrogen compounds are examples of disinfectants. Antiseptics, on the other hand, are antimicrobial, nonirritating agents that prevent the spread of infections. Alcohols, hydrogen peroxide, Povo-Iodine, phenol, resorcinol, and plain soap are excellent antiseptics. Interestingly, pure alcohol is not as good an antiseptic as 70 to 80 percent solutions of alcohol. It has something to do with water exchange across the cell membranes (osmotic pressure). Usually the term *alcohol* means either ethyl or isopropyl alcohol.

Q. How does methyl alcohol differ from ethyl alcohol?

A. Methyl alcohol is called wood alcohol. It is present in wood smoke and wines. The toxicity (poisonous nature) of methyl alcohol is due to the formation of formic acid. Fifty milliliters (a small amount) is deadly if consumed. Ethyl alcohol is prepared by fermentation and is found in beer, wine, and distilled spirits (hard liquor). We'll have more to say about ethyl alcohol in chapter 6 on "The Bar."

Q. What is isopropyl alcohol?

A. Like methyl alcohol, it is also deadly if ingested. The only alcohol which is safe to swallow is ethyl alcohol. Isopropyl alcohol is used to give back massages, to disinfect, to remove moisture in gasoline tanks, and it has a number of uses as an industrial solvent. We caution you that *only 100 percent isopropyl alcohol* can be used in your gasoline tank to remove moisture. Most stores only carry 70 percent isopropyl alcohol. What is the other 30 percent? Water, so don't put it in your gas tank! We will have more to say on this subject in chapter 8 on "Your Car."

Q. If wines are obtained through fermentation, then how does methyl alcohol get in?

A. Methyl alcohol is correctly referred to as methanol. An older more descriptive name is "wood smoke." Methyl alcohol is obtained as a minor component of *any* distillation of fermented compounds. But we will have a lot more to say about wine and spirits in chapter 6.

Fighting Fungus

Q. When people think of fungal infections, probably the most common variety to come to mind is the itching and burning of atheletes' foot. What are some other kinds of fungal conditions that we might fall victim to? What types of products can help relieve such infections, and can you explain how these preparations work?

A. Athletes' foot is not the only form that fungal infections can take. There is also jock itch, vaginal infection, ringworm, molds, and yeast infections.

Antifungal agents work by destroying the microbes responsible. They kill these microbes by interferring with a portion of the microbe that is responsible for its growth or by destroying the protein section already present. The most common antifungal agents are: iodochlorohydroxoquin, miconazole, tolnaftate, and undecylenic acid.

Q. Women have been suffering from vaginal yeast infections for many years. What exactly is this condition and why is it so common among women? Can you explain how it is that only in recent years there have been over-the-counter remedies for this condition? How do these products work?

A. Vaginal yeast infections are characterized by a white, foul smelling discharge. The organism causing this infection thrives in warm, moist areas of the body. Although it is rare, yeast infections can occur elsewhere on women's bodies and can even occur in the groin area and on the feet of men. However, the warm, moist, and sunless vagina presents an ideal site for yeasts to live.

The most common over-the-counter medications for vaginal yeast infections are miconazole and clotrimazole. They work in the same manner described for antifungal agents. Hydrocortisone is also sold over-the-counter, but for itch relief only. Miconazole has been sold for vaginal infections for over ten years, but that is not to say that other medicines for vaginal infections have taken unreasonable amounts of time to move from prescription to over-the-counter status. Evidently, there are (and were) two schools of thought among physicians regarding self-treatment.

CORN AND CALLUS REMOVERS

Q. What exactly are corns? What medications can be used to remove them?

A. Corns are the result of overgrowth of the skin's outer layer due to pressure. This pressure on the skin is most often found on the feet, where the hard, dry skin growth of a corn forms, or on the hands, where it is referred to as a "callus." Probably the most effective remover of both corns and calluses is salicylic acid. It should come as no surprise, then, that wart removal products also contain salicylic acid.

Q. But didn't you just say that salicylic acid was effective in the treatment of acne? How is this possible?

A. Salicylic acid is a keratolytic (skin peeling agent); therefore, it can be used in the treatment of both acne and corns. In the case of corns, repeated applications of salicylic acid, in the form of drops or corn patches, will wear down the overgrowth of skin.

LAXATIVES AND ANTACIDS

Q. What are laxatives and how do they work?

A. Stimulants, stool softeners, and bulk formers are the three types of laxatives currently available on the market. The *stimulants* irritate or "jump start" the nerves to the bowel. They contain senna, bisacodyl, castor oil, and phenolphtalien and should be used with caution since they might cause very strong muscle contractions. *Softeners* usually contain dioctyl, sulfosuccinate, or poloxalkol, which draw water into the bowel to relieve constipation. *Bulk-forming* laxatives are usually psyllium, kaolin, or carboxymetacellulose, which absorb water into the large intestine and make the stool softer.

As with many over-the-counter products, continued use may lead to dependency. Persistent problems, such as chronic constipation, should be checked by your physician.

Q. **But what if my problem is diarrhea? What is in preparations to control this condition?**

A. Diarrhea results from an infection or irritation of the bowel. Some nervous conditions or excessive alcohol consumption can cause diarrhea. It is treated by electrolyte replacement, water retention, decreased peristalsis, and coating the bowel. *Electrolyte replacement* (introducing sodium, potassium, and bicarbonate to the bowel) can be achieved by drinking any of the popular sports drinks (e.g., Gatorade®). The bulk-forming agents described under laxatives are polysacharrides, except kaolin, a very hydrophilic (water absorbing) clay powder.

The spasms from diarrhea can be relieved by using tincture (an alcoholic solution) of opium, which is codeine and morphine (and therefore would need to be prescribed by a physician). Loperamide relieves spasms also. Bismuth salicilate is a thick liquid that can protect the bowel by coating *before toxic and infectious agents can act.*

Q. **What is in a good antacid?**

A. Antacids are compounds that can rather quickly neutralize stomach acid, reduce gas formation (if needed), and they taste fairly pleasant. Antacids pose no side effects. The more popular antacids are: aluminum hydroxide with some magnesium hydroxide added to prevent constipation from the aluminum hydroxide (Maalox®), calcium carbonate (Tums®), magnesium hydroxide (Milk of Magnesia®), hydroxymagnesium aluminate (Rolaids®), and sodium bicarbonate. In our scientific opinion, the ingredient in the pink-colored antacid, which is bismuth subgallate, cannot neutralize much excess acid in the stomach. Its purpose is to coat the stomach to protect it against further attack.

Q. What do manufacturers mean when they say that their antacid absorbs so many times its weight in "excess stomach acid"? Can liquids or those little tablets do that?

A. This statement is true but quite misleading. A person can take ten times the recommended dose for certain antacids and still not be able to neutralize (not absorb) much of the excess acid contained in the stomach. For other antacids, the recommended dose will effectively neutralize much of the excess stomach acid. It should be noted that antacids aren't designed to neutralize all stomach acid, just the amount of excess acid.

Q. Is there any difference between antacid tablets and the various liquid antacid preparations on the market?

A. In terms of neutralizing ability, there is no difference. However, some people have trouble chewing and swallowing tablets.

Q. Can antacids have side effects?

A. Yes! They can cause high levels of sodium in the blood as well as constipation. Constipation occurs with aluminum hydroxide preparations and is alleviated by adding small amounts of the laxative, magnesium hydroxide. Sodium has been removed from many antacids. Sodium bicarbonate remains the exception. It is sold in pills, powders, and effervescent tablets like Alka Seltzer®.

Q. What is simethicone, which seems to be a popular ingredient in antacid and gas-relieving products?

A. It is an antibloating agent added to some antacids to counteract the carbon dioxide gas produced from neutralizing stomach acid. It is also the primary ingredient in products sold specifically to relieve the pressure and pain of gas.

Q. Some commercials for products that ease upset stomach say that their preparations "coat" the stomach to reduce the upset feeling. How do these products work?

A. They absorb great quantities of watery-infectious waste material in the stomach and upper intestine, thus allowing the intestine to "dry out," protecting against further infection reaching the stomach lining. Some of these stomach coaters are: kaolin (purified clay), attapusite (natural aluminum magnesium silicate), bismuth salts, and activated charcoal.

Q. Is there any over-the-counter preparation that can control nausea and vomiting?

A. Antiemetics reduce normal nausea and vomiting by controlling the "gag reflex." The most popular brand of antiemetic is Emetrol®. It contains sugar and phosphates. You can save a lot of money by having your pharmacist sell you Coca-Cola® syrup or some other regular cola syrup. It is 78 percent less expensive, and since it contains both sugar and phosphates, it is just as effective as Emetrol. (Diet colas will not work since they lack sugar.)

HEMORRHOID PREPARATIONS

Q. What chemicals are in hemorrhoid products and how do they work?

A. Hemorrhoids and piles are varicose veins in the anal-rectal area. Their presence causes itching and pain. These varicose veins are actually a ballooning of the veins and can be either protruding (external) or internal. Simple hemorrhoids can be controlled with diet and commercial medicines. Petrolatum A and D jelly, either synthetic or from shark's liver, can protect the inflamed area. Glycerin, mineral oil, or lanolin can also serve as a protectant. Local anesthetics will numb the area by blocking pain-conducting nerve endings. Ephedrine or phenylephrine reduces swollen veins. Calamine ointment and/or zinc oxide are astringents that draw together and tighten the soft tissue, thereby giving a pleasant feeling of relief. These products can be found in any pharmacy or supermarket.

COLD MEDICATIONS

Q. What is the most useful cold remedy?

A. Probably the most sensible remedy is waiting seven days for your body to overcome the illness. Really, just about anything works for you *if you think it works*—even chicken soup! Standard treatments include: expectorants, cough suppressants, nasal decongestants, drying agents, and analgesics.

  Expectorants such as guaifenesin moisten the mucous secretions so they can be coughed up. *Cough suppressors* (antitussives) depress the cough center in the brain. Dextromethorphan is the only safe and effective cough suppressant sold over the counter.

  Nasal decongestants work by constricting the swollen veins in the nose and sinuses. Ephedrine, napthazoline, oxymetazoline, phenylephrine, or xylometazoline are standard nasal decongestants. *Drying agents* are called anticholinergics, which are just antihistamines such as bromophiramine and chloropheniramine maleate. Other drying agents are doxylamine succinate and beeswax.

  Many of the over-the-counter decongestants should not be used for more than a few days. These products tend to work for only a short time, after which the problem returns more severely. Ask your doctor or pharmacist for a product that does not lead to dependency.

Q. Are you saying that with all of the cold tablets, capsules, caplets, pills, powders, night-time cold remedies, and the like, that essentially there is very little chemical difference between them?

A. We never said that there are no chemical differences *between* expectorants, decongestants, or drying agents. However, we do mean to say that there is very little, if any, chemical difference between different brands of the *same type of cold medicines* (brand X decongestant is not any better than brand Y's decongestant). If there are differences, they focus on the amount of one or more ingredients in the remedy, not the basic ingredients themselves.

We also want you to recognize that the way a particular cold remedy is packaged has no bearing on its effectiveness. However, many people do find taking caplets to be easier than taking capsules, and some prefer syrups to caplets.

Q. When children and/or adults are suffering from a stuffy cold, one advertisement tells us to rub in Vicks® vapo-rub to ease the congestion so the person can breathe better. How can such a product relieve the symptoms?

A. Vicks® vapo-rub contains camphor, menthol, and eucalyptus oil as its active ingredients. However, we could not find any solid evidence that these compounds are decongestants, nasal decongestants, or drying agents.

Q. What is an antihistamine?

A. Antihistamines block the receptor sites that would cause the body to produce histamine (that watery nasal discharge). The specific shape of the antihistamine molecule fits exactly into the receptor sites. Bromophiramine and chloropheniramine (Chlortrimeton®) are very popular antihistamines available without a prescription. Diphenylhydramine (Benadryl®) is an antihistamine that causes drowsiness and is used in many popular over-the-counter sleeping aids (e.g., Sominex®). Other antihistamines used as sleeping aids are phenylamine, methapyrilene, and doxylamine succinate (Unisom®).

Q. Why would a sleeping medication use an antihistamine as an active ingredient? Is this the primary element that makes us drowsy when we take a sleeping pill?

A. Many antihistamines cause drowsiness as an unwanted side effect. They are used as the primary ingredient in over-the-counter sleeping pills because they are predictable and safe when taken as directed. Not all antihistamines cause drowsiness, and for this reason many people prefer them. The prefix "pseudo" indicates that the antihistamine has been changed slightly to avoid drowsiness: pseudoephedrine (Sudafed®) is an example.

Q. I am a label reader, and I noticed something a bit odd that you might be able to help explain. The twelve-hour capsules that I take for colds and allergies have 75 mg of phenylpropanolamine, which I take to be an antihistamine. But when I went to the drugstore to purchase an over-the-counter diet capsule, it, too, had that same 75 mg of phenylpropanolamine. Why is that?

A. Phenylpropanolamine is not an antihistamine. It is used as a decongestant in products such as: Alka-Seltzer Plus Cold Medicine®, Contac® cold medicine, Cheracol® cold medicine, A.R.M. Allergy Relief Medicine®, Coricidin Cold Tablets®, Dimetapp®, Naldecon®, Robitussin®, Triaminic®, and Tylenol® cold medicines. It is also found in many appetite suppressant tablets, such as Acutrim®. The mechanism by which phenylpropanolamine curbs the urge to eat is not clear at this time. In the dosage used for over-the-counter appetite suppression, it is safe but not universally accepted as effective.

SLEEP AIDS

Q. Are over-the-counter sleeping aids safe and useful?

A. They are safe if taken as directed. Those who use them may experience dry mouth, dizziness, and/or blurred vision as side effects. However, a glass of warm milk, or anything else that fills your stomach, will divert blood from your brain and cause drowsiness just as well.

STIMULANTS

Q. On the opposite end of the spectrum are those individuals who, rather than needing a good night's sleep, are unable to stay awake and alert. What stimulants are available without a prescription?

A. The only safe and accessible drug for stimulating the central nervous system is caffeine. A cup of coffee or tea has about 100 mg of caffeine. Many people don't realize that Camellia tea has quite a bit of caffeine, and some colas have more caffeine than coffee. Years ago, colas used to be prepared from the extract of the Kola plant. (Kola extract has a lot of caffeine and had been used to replace the small amount of cocaine originally in colas.) Popular stimulants in pill or capsule form have exactly the same amount of caffeine as a freshly brewed cup of stout coffee (100 mg). NoDoz® (Bristol Meyers) is an over-the-counter stimulant that contains 100 mg of caffeine and costs about $.35 per tablet. You can obtain the same amount of caffeine from a $.05 cup of home-brewed coffee.

VITAMIN AND MINERAL SUPPLEMENTS

Q. Are organic vitamin-mineral supplements better than synthetic ones?

A. Most organic vitamins and minerals are decidely inferior to synthetic ones and cost *much more.* Most natural vitamins are extracted from plants, processed, and then packaged. Natural vitamins are impure, unlike synthetic versions. In addition, preservatives are not included in the processing of natural vitamins so their potency is placed at risk over a shorter period of time.

Shark oil is not a better source of vitamins A and D. Vitamin C derived from rose hips is less stable than synthetic C. The same is true for minerals. Calcium from ore is just as good as calcium from oysters or egg shells. There is no *legal* or scientific definition for "organic" vitamins or minerals.

Q. What does USRDA mean?

A. It is the United States recommended daily allowance of vitamins and minerals that the average healthy adult needs to prevent deficiencies. The recommended amount is much higher for those who already have a deficiency.

Q. Is it possible to take too many vitamins and minerals?

A. You should avoid taking large doses of the fat-soluble vitamins A, D, and K. Also large amounts of iron, calcium, zinc, copper, fluoride, iodide, and potassium should be avoided since they are absorbed in the fat and take quite a bit of time to leach out. Water-soluble vitamins and minerals are excreted in the urine after the body has been saturated.

Q. Are there any differences in the type of vitamin-mineral supplements available?

A. Time-released supplements are the best because they supply your body with a constant blood level of supplements, even though there are some problems in absorption. Iron sulfate is not absorbed as completely as iron fumurate or iron gluconate. The absorption of iron is enhanced with vitamin C, though the reason for this is not well known at present.

Q. Can people save much money by purchasing generic supplements?

A. We conducted our own cost survey in the spring of 1992 and found that it is even wise to shop and compare generic supplements. The cost of equivalent generic supplements varied from $.42 per tablet to $.03 per tablet. This could amount to a savings of $140 annually.

Q. Do I need to take amino acid supplements?

A. Humans can synthesize twelve of the twenty amino acids needed. The other eight must be ingested. They are referred to as the *essential* amino acids. Just about any diet—it doesn't have to be a healthful diet—will supply all of the eight amino acids. Vegetarians usually mix a variety of foods to ensure they get all eight. Brazil nuts are a rich source of these eight amino acids.

Most people realize that certain vitamins and minerals are required to prevent diseases. For example, vitamin C is required to prevent scurvy (a vitamin deficiency disease characterized by bleeding gums, bleeding under the skin, and weakness). There are many types of diseases that are preventable with adequate levels of vitamins or minerals. Many doctors agree with the findings of the National Cancer Institute that about one-third of all cancers diagnosed in the United States are related to dietary deficiencies. Doctors recommend diets rich in fruits, vegetables, and fiber. Vegetables such as asparagus, cabbage, and mustard greens contain cancer-blocking indoles (formed from the decomposition of proteins and tryptophan).

The water-soluble B vitamins aid in preventing many skin diseases such as pellagra (rough skin due to niacin deficiency), dermatitis, and lesions as well as in the prevention of anemia. B vitamins can be found in seeds, pork, yeasts, legumes, liver, and grains.

Many underdeveloped countries that lack diets rich in fruits and vegetables suffer from vitamin A deficiency. This often leads to night blindness, or total blindness. Vitamin E, from plant oils, is required for healthy skin and strong blood hemoglobin.

TAMPONS AND PREGNANCY TESTS

Q. In recent years there has been concern raised about the use of tampons and the potential for a condition known as toxic shock syndrome. Is there something wrong with the tampons we buy?

A. Toxic shock syndrome is associated with irritation of the vagina due to improperly fitting tampons. Most women never experience toxic shock syndrome during their life. This malady can result in a very serious condition if transfered to the blood system. We doubt if there is any correlation between the brand of tampon used and the onset of toxic shock syndrome. To our knowledge, no such correlation has ever been reported.

Q. The latest addition to the items we store in the bathroom is the home pregnancy test. How do these tests work? Are they accurate?

A. When a woman becomes pregnant, she passes a specific hormone in her urine, which reacts with the chemicals in the kit. The resulting color indicates that the hormone is present in her urine. The test is very specific, since no other hormones or biochemicals in the urine can react to activate the color.

5

The Living Room

In this chapter we will discuss products that are found in and around the living room. Throughout the year, we spend a lot of time in the living room, with family, friends, or just by ourselves. Whether the room is formal or not, we try to protect our furniture and the flooring or carpeting with a variety of cleaning products. We will talk about polishes and waxes, carpets and carpet cleaners, air cleaners, and more.

WAXES AND POLISHES

Q. What are the basic components of furniture polish? How does furniture polish work?

A. Wood finishes are often covered with stains and varnishes then overcoated with a wax finish. Over time these types of finishes collect dust, tend to dull in surface luster, and appear to dry out. Periodically, these coatings need to be replaced to prolong the desired look of the finish.

Stains and varnishes are mixtures of synthetic or naturally occurring resins dissolved in a drying oil. The dyes alter the color or tone of the wood whereas the resins and drying oils provide a protective coating. Drying oils can evaporate and leave the resin behind, air can oxidize with the resin to form a coating, or both. Dyes added to varnishes are called *stains*. Mineral pigments added to varnishes make *enamels*.

Linseed and tung oils are the most common drying oils used for furniture. Gums and resins dry and produce a hard wood surface that repels water and enhances surface luster.

Over time the surface finish begins to wear off, collects dust, or both. Furniture polishes contain natural oils and scent that are absorbed by finished wood surfaces. The oil returns luster to the wood. The polishes tend to remove dust as well.

Q. How does furniture polish differ from furniture wax?

A. Waxes differ from oils in that they are normally solids or semi-solids at room temperature. Waxes are added to polishes and varnishes. Animal and vegetable waxes are similar to fats but are harder and less greasy. Waxes are fatty acids combined with high molecular-weight alcohols. Oils, on the other hand, use lower molecular-weight alcohols than waxes. Waxes, like polishes, air oxidize and form hard coatings on surfaces. Commercial wax coatings are mixtures of low molecular-weight waxes (soft waxes), high molecular-weight waxes (hard waxes), liquid waxes, and solvents.

Commercial liquid products are lower in high molecular-weight waxes and typically have solvents added. Solid waxes, such as carnuba wax, form hard, shiny coatings on surfaces.

Q. There are various dusting products that claim to pick up the dust without the need for polishing. How do they work? What do they contain?

A. Polishes by definition contain oils as well as gums or resins. Dusting products that are not designed to polish often contain just an oil that traps dust particles. Some products contain oils that soak into the wood finish and make it shine. This is what consumers call polish. We like to wipe the furniture gently, remove dust, and leave the surface shiny. Furniture oils are often less expensive in liquid form than in spray aerosols.

Most consumers tend to over apply sprays. A little goes a long way. Keep a polishing cloth around with a liquid furniture polish on it. You will be surprised at how little you really need to return the luster to wood and to polish at the same time. Natural oils like linseed and tung oils are more expensive than synthetic resins. Comparative shopping for liquid polishes will save you money.

Q. There are products on the market that claim to restore the beauty of wood finishes. How do they do this?

A. Waxes protect the surface of the wood from drying out and cracking. As waxes and oils are removed, the surface becomes dull. Beautifying products replace the lost oils and replace part of the wax lost thus giving the surface a shine. Shine helps to restore the "beauty" to the product.

UPHOLSTERY AND RUG CLEANERS

Q. When buying various pieces of upholstered furniture, the store will suggest that customers have the fabrics protected with "fabric guard" to prevent stains. How do these stain guards work?

A. Stain guard chemicals used to leave the furniture feeling stiff. Hard waxes and coatings were added to the fabric to prevent absorption of spills. Stain guards work by repelling water absorption, and water repellents form stain-resistant coatings. Most food and pet staining materials are dissolved in water. With the invention of softer, water-repellent waxes and the development of Teflon®, stain guards have become widespread. (Teflon® [polytetrafluoroethylene] is chemically resistant and repels most liquids.)

Q. If I have such a stain or fabric guard on my upholstery, can I clean the furniture without ruining the stain guard effect?

A. Most food and pet stains should be quickly cleaned with a damp towel. Gently blotting wet stains so the towel can absorb the stain is better than rubbing the stain. Rubbing, or applying pressure can force the stain deeper into the fabric. Gently blotting a stain guard protected fabric should not hurt the coating. Strong cleansers may weaken the stain guard. Unfortunately, like waxes and polishes, stain guard protection will fade over time. The protective coating can be worn off quickly by abrasion, or slowly through aging.

Q. Some carpet stores also make the claim that various carpets have stain guard on them or that the carpets are stain resistant. Is this the same type of stain guard that is on the furniture?

A. Sometimes carpet stores do add the same types of stain guards as are used for upholstery. However, the plastics used for most synthetic carpets are developed to withstand heavy traffic. Many of these synthetic fibers are stain resistant themselves. If the carpet is made with Teflon® in the fiber or Teflon® fibers intertwined, it becomes more stain resistant. Again wax-based products are available for repeat applications. These types of products need to be replaced periodically due to wear.

Q. When I had my carpet installed, the house smelled for a while. What is in the carpet that causes such a smell?

A. In the manufacture of plastics as in some carpeting, plastic dashboards in cars (the new car smell), and other plastic items, oils are added to the plastic to keep it supple. These oils are absorbed into the plastic and slowly come out over time. The surface oils are the first to come out and this is what you smell. Over time the internal oils slowly leach out and the intensity of the smell decreases.

Q. I heard a news story some time ago in which the concern was raised that some people are actually allergic to their carpets. How can this be?

A. Most carpets are synthetic plastics, and very few people are allergic to plastic. However, everyday use of carpets by humans and pets leave hair and skin around. Mites, fungus, and molds love this protected environment with its constant food supply. People are often allergic to these pests rather than to the carpets. Periodic cleaning and vacuuming should take care of most of the problems. Remember, too, what we said about oils being added to plastics in carpets to make them supple. Some people could have an allergic reaction to these oils.

Q. There are various products advertised that claim to remove tough stains from carpets. What is in these products? How can they remove the stains?

A. Most stain-removal products contain concentrated soaps and detergents that dissolve fats and oils. If the stain hasn't dried, soap and a little blotting is often all that is needed. Inks soak deeper into the pile fibers of rugs: these stains tend to be a little trickier. Many of the dyes in inks are soluble in a mixture of alcohol and water or in paint thinner.* *Don't rub ink stains* as this will promote the spreading of the stain. Rust stains can be removed slowly by dissolving the rust in lemon juice (this will take some time). Commercial products have mixtures of these types of removers. Some even contain "enzymes" to remove grass stains. The best advice for removing any stain is to do it quickly. This will avoid disappointment after trying expensive products.

Q. **We hear about all types of carpet cleaning approaches. There's the stuff you spray on and work into the carpet, let it dry, and then vacuum up; and there are the cleaning machines that can be rented from most supermarkets. Of course, there is always the professional carpet cleaners. Is there any real difference between these methods?**

A. If you don't have time to clean the carpets yourself and don't mind spending the money, professional cleaners are the way to go. However, most of us have better things to do with our money.

Vacuum steam cleaners and foaming brushes provide the best results for cleaning carpets. These are available at modest rental cost from many supermarkets. The mechanical action of the brushes and the steam heat helps to loosen and remove dirt.

Mechanical foam cleaning machines are the next best. These are less expensive but don't provide steam. Carpets cleaned in this fashion take a lot longer to dry.

Foam cleaners are the easiest but are more expensive in the long run. Products that are only sprayed on and vacuumed off remove mostly surface dirt but not what is trapped in the carpet fibers. More frequent cleaning is required with this type of product, and at $3.00 or more a bottle to clean a small-sized room, these are expensive. They do dry very quickly and may help for light

---

*Both alcohol and paint thinner are highly flammable substances. Carefully read the directions for their use, and always work in a well-ventilated room.

stains after a party. Frequent vacuuming is still the best method to prolong intervals between shampooing.

Q. Is there an inexpensive product to eliminate pet and other odors from carpets?

A. Many owners of indoor pets such as cats and dogs realize that their pets may not always find their way outside or to the litter box. Accidents do occur. Manufacturers market several carpet powders that are to be sprinkled on and then vacuumed up later. Most of these dry powders contain almost 100 percent pure baking soda and a small amount of perfume! These products are expensive and the fragrances are not the most desirable. It seems that a box of relatively inexpensive baking soda mixed with a drop of your favorite perfume would be a lot cheaper than buying these commercial products. Baking soda mixed with fresh cat litter also helps to reduce pet odors.

Unfortunately urine on carpets is a little harder to take care of. The liquid soaks down into the carpet mats and padding and doesn't dry very quickly. After a while the carpet may start to mildew. Both of these problems can be helped with baking soda. The baking soda will dry out the carpet and padding as well as prevent mildew. For badly mildewed carpets the backing may need to be lifted and a layer of baking soda added.

Q. How is it that baking soda helps remove odors?

A. This material, sodium bicarbonate, is supplied as an inorganic powder with a high surface area (very fine particles). Odors are mixtures of volatile organic oils. The oils in the air are absorbed into the surface of the salt and are then stuck. The powder acts like an odor sponge. Many odors are what are called *esters* that react with bases. Over time the bicarbonate, a base, can destroy some of these odors.

AIR CLEANERS AND DEODORIZERS

Q. Speaking of freshening the room or the house, what do commercial air fresheners really do? There are so many: some are sprayed

into the air, others are solids that evaporate, while still others can be plugged into an electrical socket. Are there any differences between these products?

A. Many of the products are nothing more than perfumes that mask other odors in the air. Most sprays, powders, solids, and various of the ones that "plug in" release perfume into the air. Most people tend to think that a room that smells good is therefore clean. This is often far from the truth. Some of the sprays do help to remove odors from the air. They do this by trapping the compounds that create odors and make them fall out of the air. They are now on the carpet, the flooring, and on your furniture.

Some products contain ingredients that are considered disinfectants. These disinfectants are used to kill molds, mildews, bacteria, and some of the mites in the carpets. These products don't always have attractive smells.

Odors in the air are easily removed by airing the room out. What we don't realize is that lingering odors are coming out of the carpets, the draperies, and the furniture—slowly, over time. We not only need to air out the room but also to wipe down the room. Most odors can be kept in check by routine cleaning. Wiping down the furniture with an all-purpose generic cleaner, vacuuming the rugs, and airing the room out will get rid of most smells.

Q. What are electric air cleaners? Of what use are they?

A. There are several types of electric air cleaners on the market. Older types simply used fibrous filter materials. The filters trapped dust particles in the air as it was forced over them by a blower motor, much like the air filter in your furnace. Newer electric air cleaners also have a new type of efficient trapping system. Air is drawn across several electrically charged metal plates. Air and pollutants are electrically attracted and caught (much like an outdoor bug zapper). The charged pollutants are then trapped on charged plates. In order for the best filtration devices to work, large quantities of air must be drawn through the filtration system. For large smoke-filled areas this type of filtration system is ideal. In the home they might be a bit on the noisy side.

Another type of air cleaner uses a porous silicon plate that acts like a magnet for particles. A blower motor is employed to pass air over the silicon plate. Periodically these types of filters need to be removed and washed with water, unlike fiber-based filters that are thrown out when they get filled.

Q. I was watching one of the ever-popular infomercials: this one featured an ionizer for the air. The program said that it could take odors out of the air. Is this true and, if so, how does it work?

A. This type of product is simply one of the electric "bug zapper" types we have just described. They are all ionizers.

Q. Do electric air cleaners produce toxic ozone gas?

A. The Environmental Protection Agency (EPA) has tested many table-top air cleaners. These units have not been found to produce significant quantities of ozone, thus marketing ploys stating that a particular unit doesn't produce ozone are somewhat misleading. Dust on furniture is a nuisance but full-sized house electric air cleaners are very expensive. Unless you happen to be allergic to dust mites they may not be worth the added cost. Although these products remove smells, simple cleaning will often perform the same task adequately.

Q. What are filter-type air cleaners? Are they worth the money?

A. Air cleaners are purportedly useful in ridding the house of allergy-producing particles such as dust, ozone, spores, and pollen. Most air cleaners are useful in removing some air-born dust and pollen. Most of the time dust and pollen settle on carpets, walls, and floors. There isn't any clear evidence to suggest that air cleaners actually reduce or prevent allergic respiratory diseases.

Many particles, such as smoke and odors, may be partially removed by some air cleaners. Most odors, such as those from food and smoke from cooking, are too small to be removed completely by common filter-type air cleaners. It seems that the best way to remove most odors is simply to open a window.

Filter-type air cleaners work by drawing air through a series of plastic filters to trap large particles. Most of these filters should be removed periodically to be cleaned. Cleaning these filters consists of nothing more than running water over them. They will need to be replaced eventually, since the fibers will degrade over time. Some systems also contain activated charcoal (high surface area, heated carbon), but it's not very efficient. Some gases such carbon monoxide and ozone cannot be removed by these systems.

Q. If these air-filter systems are not very effective, then why do we have air filters on our forced-air furnaces?

A. Forced-air filters do remove some of the dust. Over time the dust would build up in the heating and cooling ducts and reduce the efficiency of the furnace and/or air conditioner. Maintaining a clean air filter is very important for keeping the air flow moving as well as trapping the dust.

PAINT

Q. My husband and I just moved into an older home and were about to begin the decorating process. The house is at least thirty-five years old. How can we determine if there is lead in the paint on the walls? If we do have it, how can we get rid of it safely?

A. Lead-based paints would be of concern if the paints were made prior to the 1940s. Lead-based paints for household use were removed from the market around that time. You should be safe. If your house would have been older, the paint becomes a concern, especially if small children are present. The lead pigments in the pain are a concern if they are eaten—and you know how small children love to put things in their mouths. Stomach acid dissolves some of the lead from the paint, resulting in acute lead poisoning, which may be fatal.

Local water testing labs, colleges, or universities should be able to analyze for lead at a small fee (usually under forty dollars), or check with your local paint dealer. Remove some paint with a scraper and take it to one of these facilities for analysis. Solvent-based paint removers work by softening the paint resin. This will soften the lead pigments and is for that reason not the preferred method. When scraping off lead-based paints always wear gloves, and place a small air filter over your nose for added protection. Remember to wash your hands and clothing after working with lead-based paints.

Q. When we went looking for paints for the interior walls, there were so many kinds: flat paint, high gloss, semi-gloss, water-based, and so on. What's the difference in their make up?

A. We talk about paints in more detail later on in chapter 9. Paints are mixtures of solvents, water or an organic, a hiding pigment (typically titantium dioxide), a colored pigment, and a synthetic resin that binds the pigments together when it dries. High resin content leaves the paint with a gloss finish. Sand or other gloss-reducing agents are added to give the surface a texture and to reduce glare. Flat or matte paints have more of these compounds than semi-gloss or high-gloss paints.

6

The Bar

Ethanol, ethyl alcohol, or grain spirits is the compound that has been used since antiquity as a socially acceptable beverage. Alcohol is the general term used nowadays for this ethyl alcohol or ethanol. Physiologically, alcohol acts as a depressant, like a general anesthetic. However, it also changes parts of the brain's cortex thereby reducing inhibitions. In this sense alcohol can act as a stimulant in some people.

Beer, wine, and other alcoholic beverages are sold in the United States without their contents being listed (the alcohol proof being the only exception). We do not wish to imply that these products are impure since they should have been inspected for safety by the Food and Drug Administration. Yet any competent chemist will tell you that it is not possible for the FDA or the United States Customs Department to test all or even the majority of alcoholic products imported by or produced in the United States. The point is, most of the products we eat or drink are fully tested and the ingredients are listed on the label. Alcoholic products are among the few which may or may not be tested. Wouldn't you like to know what compounds are present in a *pilsner* beer that are not present in, say, a *lager* beer or in an *ale*? What is the chemical composition of the fine *sherry* made in Spain? How does this compare with less expensive sherry made in the United States? What kind of grapes are used? If you thought all quality sherries were produced in Spain, you would be wrong. There was a time when all sherry had to be made in Spain, however Spain lost that legal battle years ago. Similarly, "London Dry Gin" can be made or produced anywhere with any ingredients the producer wants to use. If you thought gin had to be made from alcohol and juniper berriers, then think again. Gin, London dry or otherwise, can be distilled from barley malt, grain, grape wine, apples, or any other fruit. After fermentation, juniper berry extract can then be added.

We also thought that all brandies had to come from grapes grown in the Cognac region of France and that Scotch whiskey had to be produced in Scotland. You may think all of this is so much nitpicking, but it was only a short time ago when copper sulfate (a blue poisonous compound) was found in some beers produced in the United States. It was added to increase the foamy "head" of these beers without increasing the wholesale price. In the eighteenth and nineteenth centuries, brewing beer was still an art and not a science. A man named Cobbett denounced the practice of using any sort of carbohydrate available, such as maize grits, potato starch, or rice. In his article "Beer-Druggists," published in *Cottage Economy* in 1897, he also included a recipe for brewing beer and a recipe for *porter* (a heavy, dark beer).

The reader may feel that we are excessively concerned about labeling beer and wine. Yet consider this: If you purchase a bottle of beer, a can of hash, and a can of soup, the ingredients of the hash and soup are clearly listed on their labels, but the contents of the beer are not. Sure, there are some exceptions. Some white wines inform you that sodium sulfite or sulfur dioxide has been added to "stabilize" the color. Some *bock* beers list the fact that caramel is added to produce the dark color (bock beer is normally produced only in the spring).* The alcoholic content is also placed on all labels. This concern about labeling beer and wine is not a mere curiosity. Without proper labeling, the risk to public health increases. And even if your wine or beer proves to be harmless, you still must purchase a product of unknown composition. The potential risk is compounded now that there is a strong movement in the United States toward independent brewing of wine and beer. Small breweries produce small amounts of high-quality beers on a regional basis. While most of the wine produced in the United States still comes from California and New York, there is a growth in high-quality specialty wines from other states. In addition, many Americans have found that homemade

---

*Normally, the color of bock beer is the result of the specific ingredients used and the brewing process.

wines and beers are not only inexpensive, but very high in quality, and recipes are available. Americans can produce wine or beer at home without penalty, provided they do not sell what they make. Most specialized beers, ales, and wines are only produced at small regional breweries or vineyards.

Maybe you have no interest in brewing beer or making wine. Nevertheless, you still have the right to know the ingredients in the beverage you are drinking. This is the same right that protects you against those who wish to sell you ale that has been prepared with the poisonous copper sulfate added.

We hope to enlighten you here as much as possible in the limited space available to help you understand the mystery of alcohol.

SOME BASIC QUESTIONS

Q. What is this "alcohol" in our beer, wine, and hard liquors?

A. This type of alcohol is ethyl alcohol, grain alcohol, or ethanol. It is prepared by fermenting sugars or starches to obtain a solution containing no more than 14 percent alcohol. The fermentation process involves the reaction of microorganisms, such as yeasts, in the absence of air to produce a solution containing about 14 percent ethyl alcohol. Fermentation cannot yield a solution having an alcoholic content greater than about 14 percent, since too much alcohol destroys the microorganisms present and the reaction simply stops. The fermentation of grapes produces wines, malt (grain that has sprouted) produces ales and beers, and "hard cider" is produced from apple juice.

Q. You mentioned that ethyl alcohol is an alcohol we can safely consume. What kind of alcohol should we avoid?

A. We cannot think of any kind or type of alcohol that you can drink without risk. In addition to the intoxicating effects of ethanol, methyl alcohol, isopropyl alcohol, and all of the other alcohols you are likely to encounter in your home are all poisonous!

Q. What does the term "fermentation" mean?

A. Fermentation is the breakdown of starch (or other carbohydrates) with the aid of compounds that speed up the reaction. These compounds are called *enzymes*. If the enzyme diastase is mixed with grain, the starch in the grain will be converted into maltose. This solution of water and maltose is called the *wort*. If the wort is diluted and treated further, the maltose is converted into ethyl alcohol and water. This final alcoholic solution can be separated into a product that is 95 percent alcohol and 5 percent water.

Q. **If the fermentation reaction can produce no more than 14 percent alcohol, how are 90 proof whiskeys made? By the way, what does the term "proof" mean?**

A. To increase the alcoholic concentration above 14 percent, the wine, whiskey, or other spirits must be *distilled*. Distillation is a process in which the alcoholic solution is heated high enough so the alcohol boils off at a temperature of 78 degrees Celsius.* The water in the solution boils at a much higher temperature (100 degrees Celsius) so the alcohol boils and is collected first. The term "proof," which was introduced in the sixteenth century, indicates how much alcohol is present. Two proof *is* one percent alcohol. So a 90 proof alcohol is exactly 45 percent alcohol. Alcohol was tested by pouring it on gunpowder. If the gunpowder exploded *after* the alcohol burned off, then the alcoholic solution was said to have a high alcohol content, for it had met the "proof."

Q. **If the alcohol present in wines, beers, and spirits is the same, why do many whiskeys have different colors and tastes? Why are all vodkas colorless?**

A. During the distillation process, the alcohol collected at 78 degrees Celsius is impure, as a small amount of water also distills over at this temperature. This small amount of water has the color, odor, and taste desired. Sometimes these compounds are referred to as "botanicals." The compounds are purposely left in to obtain the color, odor, and look desired in the final product. For example, the distillation of molasses or brown sugar in water yields *rum*. Vodkas are produced from grains, potatoes, or any other fer-

*See Appendix 2 for the Fahrenheit equivalents.

mented carbohydrate. The colors and tastes of the fermented sources are removed by passing the final product through charcoal, which strains all botanicals. The final product is the unaged liquor of neutral spirits and can be called vodka.

Q. How is it that this alcohol makes us "drunk"?

A. Alcohol acts like a mild depressant, slowing down both physical and mental activities. Large amounts of it can cause unconsciousness or even death. However, small amounts of alcohol seem to act as a stimulant by relieving inhibitions and relaxing tensions. Some studies have shown that moderate drinkers live longer than nondrinkers and are hospitalized for coronary disease 40 percent less than nondrinkers.

We don't wish to encourage alcohol consumption for anyone, especially since the transition from moderate to heavy alcohol consumption is unpredictable. While 40 percent of Americans drink alcohol responsibly, ten million Americans suffer from alcoholism, and many chronic alcoholics suffer from liver disease (cirrhosis). "Wet brain" is a term used to describe alcoholics who are unable to think clearly due to brain damage. It is *not* the use of alcohol that is a problem, but rather its misuse.

Q. Why is it that some people get drunk faster than others? In other words, why can some people drink a lot more than others and still not experience the same effects?

A. We're sure you know that increased weight, a person's sex, the amount of food consumed prior to drinking, medications in the system, the frequency of drinking, and the ability of the liver to detoxify alcohol are all contributing factors. Generally speaking, males and larger people can consume more alcohol before becoming intoxicated. When food is present in the stomach, alcohol will be metabolized more slowly. Persons who are being treated for hepatic (liver) disorders or who are taking medication should refrain from consuming alcohol unless approved by their physician. Even over-the-counter medications caution against combining their drugs with alcohol.

Q. Why do we get hangovers?

A. Alcohol consumption causes histamine to be released from the liver into the bloodstream, which dilates (expands) blood vessels in the brain. This can cause migraine headaches. Serotonin, a powerful vasoconstrictor found in the blood or tissues of mammals, can cause narrowing of the blood vessels in the brain. Serotonin levels are rapidly increased after the ingestion of sugars. Thus the old wives' tale that sugar can prevent a hangover might well be true. Serotonin levels drop precipitously during migraine headache attacks. Ingesting sugar helps to increase these serotonin levels. Acetaldehyde is a compound produced when the body metabolizes alcohol. Acetaldehyde is known to cause very bad headaches in humans and is responsible for many of the effects associated with hangovers.

Many alcoholic beverages also contain some by-products of the fermentation process which cause allergic reactions in certain people. For example, someone might become very sick from drinking scotch whiskey but have no problem drinking any other whiskey or spirits. Many people complain of headaches from drinking certain beers. Other people get a terrible headache from drinking certain spirits but not from any others.

Q. Could you explain what it is about alcohol that could make the body crave this drug?

A. It seems to us that most people have a misconception regarding the difference in the biochemistry of alcoholics and nonalcoholics. Normally, nonalcoholics do not crave alcohol any more than they would crave candy. Nonalcoholics can consume alcohol in moderate amounts without any cravings or major physiological changes. Their livers metabolize alcohol into simple waste products—carbon dioxide and water. The alcoholic metabolizes alcohol into some unusual compounds such as tetrahydroquinone. This compound is a synthetic narcotic much more potent than heroin. When it reaches the brain, it "sticks" to the nerve endings there like epoxy cement sticks paper together. Tetrahydroquinone is not easily removed from the brains of alcoholics.

This important breakthrough was noted by a pathologist who was analyzing the contents of the brains of derelicts. She noticed that every corpse had this substance in its brain. Tetrahydroquinone mimics the effect that alkaloids such as heroin and cocaine have on humans. No chemical has been effective in dislodging tetrahydroquinone from the brains of alcoholics. There was some earlier work that reported the use of a substance known as L-tryptophan in releasing tetrahydroquinone from the brain. Another study found that niacin, one of the more important B-vitamins, is synthesized in the human body from L-tryptophan.

Q. I've been told that the effects of alcohol can be counteracted with vitamin B_{12} shots. Is this true? If so, how does the B_{12} work?

A. Vitamin B_{12} is very effective in the treatment of pernicious anemia, which is the inability to produce a sufficient amount of red blood cells. It is also used for the treatment of serious nerve cell damage, which is common in alcoholics. Vitamin B_{12} is not absorbed readily by ingestion, so those who are deficient in this vitamin must take it either by injection or subdermal absorption in the tissues of the mouth.

BEER

Q. What is malting?

A. The fermentation of cereals, such as barley and malt for beers, is called malting. The more the cereals are roasted, the darker the beer becomes, as in the porter or stout varieties. Top fermentation is used to produce heavier English and other European beers, which are more acidic and stronger tasting. American beers are prepared by bottom fermentation and produce the light lagers. Pilsner is a light beer with a strong flavor of hops. If a beer is exposed to sunlight, a sulfur compound forms, which is often referred to as a "skunky" odor or taste.

Q. How is beer made?

A. Beer is made from barley and other grains. Before the brewing takes place, barley is malted in a process that involves *steeping, germination,* and *kilning*. Steeping is simply the process of soaking the barley in water. Germination is the degradation (breaking down) of the barley into starches, proteins, and enzymes. Kilning is the heating of the products of the germination step to achieve the desired color. High temperatures produce such darker beers as porters, stouts, and ales. Please note that we have not made a distinction between ale and beer in the table below. The alcohol contents shown are partly the result of the legal aspects of brewing beers and not the ability of the process to produce alcohol. Beers made in Europe are made from 100 percent malt. In the United States, beer need only be made from about 60 percent malt, with corn or rice added.

CHARACTERISTICS OF BEERS

Type	Alcohol Percentage by Volume*	Color
Ale	6	Light
Bock	variable	Dark**
Cream Ale	6	Light
Lager	4	Light
Light	3	Light
Malt Liquor	5	Medium-Light
Porter	6	Dark
Stout	7	Very Dark

*The alcohol as a percentage of the volume of the container.
**Many inexpensive bock beers achieve their color by the addition of caramel.

Q. What is mashing?

A. The malt is crushed and cooked to break down the starches before brewing.

Q. What is wort?

A. When cooked mash is filtered, the resulting liquid is then called wort.

Q. What are hops?

A. They are simply the blossoms of the hops plant. Hops contribute a bitter flavor that counteracts the natural sweetness of sugars. Hops also kill unwanted yeast that might give a bad flavor to beer.

Q. What is a lager?

A. This is a beer that has been stored for two to three months so certain flavors can develop.

Q. How are light beers made?

A. Usually enzymes are added to limit the fermentation process. This results in less alcohol being produced. Alternately, sugar can be added with the same effect. Many people think that light beers are regular beers that have been watered down. This is not generally true. The flavor of a light beer is much less enthusiastic than regular beers, which are considerably less robust than those produced in Europe.

WINE

Q. What are wines made from?

A. Wine is obtained by the fermentation of fruits, such as grapes, rather than grains. In the fermentation process wild yeast is sometimes on the skin of grapes and must be treated. Sulfur dioxide or sulfites are added to destroy the yeasts, the presence of which would turn ethyl alcohol into acetic acid (vinegar). Vinegar imparts a distinctive sour taste to wine.

Wines are classified by numerous methods. Classification by alcohol content is most common because many countries levy taxes on the alcoholic content of wines. An easy way of classifying them is to remember that table wines typically have less than 14 percent alcohol content by volume. Dessert wines have an alcohol content much greater than 14 percent. The fermentation process can only produce wines of about 14 percent. So wines with an alcoholic content of greater than 14 percent are fortified (spiked) with ethyl alcohol or brandy.

Q. What is brandy?

A. When wine is distilled a portion of it evaporates, cools, and is converted back to a liquid.

At about 80 degrees Celsius the liquid that distills is about 80 percent ethyl alcohol. Distillation is a process in which heat is supplied to a liquid having more than one compound present in an effort to separate (distill) those compounds. As the temperature is increased, the boiling point for each component is reached. Once the boiling point for each component is achieved, the liquid is converted to a gas that is then run through a cold coil and converted back to a liquid and then collected. This process yields a very pure liquid because few compounds have the same boiling point. The remaining 20 percent is water. The water portion contains the congeners (volatile components) of the particular wine distilled. Brandies can be up to 80 percent alcohol. This is about the same as vodka or whiskey.

Q. Exactly what are congeners?

A. They include oils, acids, esters, aldehydes, tannins, and other compounds that are not removed during the distillation process. They add to the distinctive taste of wine and other alcoholic beverages. These compounds are produced in very small quantities during the fermentation process. Since they are present in such small quantities, they are not harmful. The oils, acids, and esters present are similar to those present in coffee while the tannins are very much like those present in tea.

Q. What is the difference between light wines and sparkling wines?

A. Light wines are prepared by fermenting unripe grapes with a low sugar content. Sparkling wines, such as champagnes, can be made by corking the bottle while a little sugar is left. The active yeast in the bottle produces the carbon dioxide gas found in sparkling wines.

Q. Why do many beers and wines have chemical stabilizers added to them?

A. These compounds serve to maintain consistent appearance and taste, and they add to a longer shelf life.

Q. **What is it in the composition of a wine or champagne that allows it to be classified as "dry"?**

A. Wines which have a very low sugar content are called "dry wines."

Q. **What exactly does "aging" do for wines?**

A. This process removes some of the impurities in wine and also allows some wines to decrease their pH, and hence their acidity.

Q. **I noted sulfur dioxide listed on a bottle of wine. What is the need for sulfur dioxide in wine?**

A. It is a preservative used primarily in white wines to prevent the formation of a pale yellow impurity.

Q. **Don't some wine producers put nitrites (or is it nitrates?) in their wines? Why do they do this?**

A. Nitrates and/or nitrites are used in the preservation of foodstuffs. They were the original antioxidants and were able to preserve foods and meats by killing the bacteria responsible for many deaths: clostridum botulinum, or botulism. Unfortunately, these compounds also form very low levels of carcinogenic nitrosoamines. Nitrates have been replaced by safer compounds in the preservation of foods. No compounds have been found to preserve meats (especially pork products) better than nitrites. Therefore, their use is strictly limited by federal law.

Q. **What gives gin, whiskey, and other distilled spirits their distinctive tastes?**

A. Gin is simply distilled alcohol in which juniper berries have been added during the fermentation process. Traditional whiskey is fermented from barley, corn, rye, and other grains. Burbons are fermented from corn, while Tennessee whiskey is produced from "sour" mash. Rye whiskey is simply fermented from rye grain. Rum is fermented from molasses or brown sugar, and vodkas are just plain ethyl alcohol. Vodka can be fermented from potatoes or any sugar or carbohydrate.

The distillate (liquid coming over) is an 80/20 mixture of ethyl alcohol and water. The congener (the water portion distilling over with the ethyl alcohol) contains the rye, juniper berry, molasses, or other sources responsible for the distinct flavor and bouquet. These can be removed with activated carbon to yield 80 percent ethyl alcohol.

Q. Why is there quinine in my tonic water mixer? I thought quinine was a drug.

A. Quinine comes from the bark of the cinchona tree. In prescribed amounts, it was used to combat malaria. In small quantities it is present for flavor in tonic water and in the liqueur Dubonnet®.

7

The Kitchen

We will be concerned in this chapter with food preservatives; sweeteners; basic nutrition; flavor enhancers; spices; oils, fats, margarine, and meats; proper cooking methods, preparing foods to maintain their nutritional value, and cooking with alcohol; and the types of cleaners used in the kitchen.

Some people are allergic to a few chemicals used in food preservation. These compounds are in many foods found in restaurants: salads and wines, among others. Many salad bars have a sign informing patrons of the use of these compounds. Chinese restaurants, which are known for their heavy use of spices, especially monosodium glutamate, now have "salt free" or "sodium free" menus.

Often when we purchase prepackaged foods, we don't read the fine print on the labels. If we did, we would find that most of these items are mixtures, blends of natural products and chemicals that are hard to pronounce. What are these chemicals and what do they do? This is a very complex but important part of food chemistry, which we will try to answer in as simple a manner as possible.

FOOD SPOILAGE

Q. What causes food to spoil?

A. Most foods—meats, dairy products, fruits, and vegetables—"turn bad," decay, and deteriorate after a time. The presence of microscopic bacteria combined with oxygen in the air is the primary reason that our food degrades. Any process that inhibits the growth of microorganisms or stops oxygen from reacting with food serves the function of a preservative.

When food spoils, many products become not only visibly unappealing but noxious as well. Botulism (a type of acute food poisoning) is produced by the bacterium *clostridium botulinum,* an anaerobic bacteria that grows in the absence of oxygen. This bacteria is commonly found in foods that have low acid content: e.g., peas, corn, and beans. The toxins produced by these bacteria may be rendered harmless by heating (boiling) the vegetables for between thirty and forty-five minutes. However, it is a better idea not to chance it: just throw them out!

All of us have heard, read, or otherwise been warned that mayonnaise should not be left out at room temperature for very long. Its combination of oil and egg whites offers the perfect medium for germs to thrive. The microorganism *staphylococcus aureus* (staph) breeds in such low-acid foods as custard, salads, and sandwiches containing mayonnaise. Staph grows most readily at temperatures between 40 and 120 degrees Fahrenheit and produces a noxious waste product. Staph is different from the staphylococcal food poisoning from salmonella bacteria. Salmonella is itself poisonous, whereas staph and botulism produce dangerous toxins as waste.

Prior to the early nineteenth century, most foods were either eaten fresh or dried. Canning was then introduced to prolong the shelf life of foods. The early canning process simply used heat to kill bacteria. Typically, food was blanched (heated for a short time in boiling water) and then placed into sterilized glass containers. Blanching destroys some of the enzymes found in fruits and vegetables that degrade their surface appearance. (Blanching before freezing or canning is often recommended.)

When canning, metal caps are placed on the filled jars, which are then placed in boiling water. Since the jars are not tightly capped, the hot air can escape. Upon cooling, the hot air inside the containers escapes, creating a vacuum seal that prevents external bacteria and oxygen from entering the jars. It is important that air be excluded from the containers to prevent the glass jars from blowing up (air expands when heated).

Many fruits and some vegetables may be canned without

any problems. Unfortunately, some fruits, such as peaches, turn brown very quickly, and potatoes and beans were found to still be contaminated with toxin-producing bacteria. Because some bacteria were found to thrive in containers without air (*anerobic bacteria*), chemicals (preservatives) had to be added to the process to prevent the growth of such organisms. Chemical preservatives may be as simple as ordinary table salt; then again, complex organic and inorganic mixtures may be needed.

Q. How can oxygen in the air be bad for food?

A. Oxygen is a very reactive molecule. In foods it tends to react with many fatty substances to form peroxides, which break down and ultimately destroy these fats.

Antioxidants are added to foods to slow down the formation of peroxides. BHA (butylated hydroxyanisole), BHT (butylated hydroxytoluene), and propyl gallate are very common antioxidants. If you read the contents of packaged foods, you will see these and other preservatives listed.

Q. What chemicals are used for food preservation today?

A. Sulfites and the antioxidants butylhydroxytoluene (BHT) and butylanisole (BHA) are used in the United States. BHA also increases the shelf life of margarine and fats. The herbs sage, rosemary, and thyme are similar to BHA, which stabilizes fats against becoming rancid. Vitamin E is also an antioxidant. As a group, antioxidants work by preventing the oxygen in air from reacting with fats and other nutrients.

Q. Why is it that even though we place foods in sealed containers, and in many cases refrigerate them, they will spoil, often accompanied by mold?

A. Sealed containers help to preserve foods by excluding air for microbes to use. Refrigeration lowers the temperature and hence decreases the rate of decay. However, it is impossible to protect all foods from spoiling after a bit of time.

Q. We hear reports of food being contaminated. Is this just another way for food to spoil?

A. Yes. If food is contaminated with microbes, it will likely spoil quickly.

Q. It seems that different types of foods spoil in different ways. Why? For example: lettuce will turn reddish brown and then appear to break down and become watery, bread gets hard and stale with mold eventually forming, cooked foods will become smelly and have fungus-like growths on them.

A. The inside of a refrigerator has low temperature and humidity. These conditions aid in the removal of water from certain foods such as bread. Dark conditions catalyze (speed up) the reactions that cause foods such as bananas to become mushy and change color. Lettuce turns red-brown in color and becomes watery due to oxidation and the loss of water out of ruptured cells.

Q. If wine is created from fermented (spoiling grapes) and curing cheese has mold growing on it, then why are other types of foods not able to be eaten when they appear to spoil?

A. Fermenting grapes and curing cheese are not examples of foods that are spoiling. True, the processes of fermenting and curing involve microorganisms that change the food product through chemical reactions. However, the production of wine and cheese is not left to chance. The reactions are carefully controlled to obtain pure products. Spoiling of other foods may involve similar processes, but the conditions are uncontrolled and the microorganisms are left to the fate of the winds. The "spoiled product" of these uncontrolled reactions may contain botulism or merely decayed food that has lost both its nutritional and aesthetic appeal.

Q. Why do some foods appear to spoil faster than others even though they are in the same environment? A cucumber lasts longer than several stalks of celery in the salad crisper part of the refrigerator, but it doesn't last as long as carrots let's say.

A. We don't wish to oversimplify these phenomena, but the rate of spoiling of cucumbers, stalks of celery, and carrots in the refrigerator depends quite a bit on the hard cellular structure of these vegetables and the fact that the celery was probably cut. The rate of "spoiling" of these vegetables depends on the loss of water out of the rupture. Vegetables that have few if any bruises or blemishes will stay fresh longer because the potential areas for water to escape are fewer.

PRESERVING OUR FOOD

Q. How do antimicrobial preservatives work?

A. These preservatives typically work in one of three ways: They interfere with enzyme activity inside the microbes; they starve the bacteria; or they prevent or interfere with microbe reproduction. Preservatives that are not only safe to eat, but do not significantly alter the taste of foods and prevent the existence or reproduction of microbes are particularly useful for helping us maintain our food supply.

Q. What chemical preservatives are often found in foods?

A. The Food and Drug Administration (FDA) oversees the type, amount, and use of preservatives found in prepackaged or prepared foods. The most common preservatives that we are likely to encounter are sodium benzoate and sodium propionate. These preservatives interfere with the microorganisms themselves. And as we have just learned, sulfites and antioxidants (BHT and BHA) increase the shelf life of some foods.

Q. What are some common food preserving techniques?

A. The oldest method for food preservation is drying. Moisture is needed for the growth of microorganisms; when it is removed from such foods as meats and fruits, these items stay edible longer. The process is sometimes referred to as dry-curing. Salting and canning are also established methods of food preservation. Canning has already been discussed. Salting draws moisture from the food into the salt by absorption or a process called *osmosis*. In addition, salt kills many microorganisms. Brines (saltwater) can be injected into the food as well. Newer techniques include pasteurization, irradiation, freeze drying, and, of course, the chemical preservatives we have already mentioned. Freeze-drying is a technique in which the water content of a food item is removed by a process called *sublimation*, which changes the liquid to ice and then directly to water vapor. Because the liquid state of water is not present during the removal process, the procedure is quite rapid.

Q. We hear so much these days about the need to restrict our salt intake. But in looking at the contents of prepackaged foods, significant quantities of sodium are used in commercial food preparation. What are we to do? Can't manufacturers use other methods to preserve our prepared foods rather than loading up on salt?

A. We don't believe that the amount of salt found in most prepackaged foods is placed there for food preservation. The salt is added to improve the taste of the food. There is not enough salt in these prepackaged foods for effective food preservation. Salt or sodium chloride, is a very effective flavor enhancer in any concentration.

Decreased salt intake will not necessarily result in better health. "Sodium is a natural part of many foods. Dairy products, fish, many vegetables, bread, and almost all canned or prepared food products contain sodium. Many of these are good foods and you should eat them. . . . Unless you are trying to control high blood pressure, the reduction of saturated fat and calories in the diet are much more important for health," says M. Franz.* One of your authors has a relative who is on a sodium restricted diet due to a heart condition. Instead of avoiding table salt and using saltless food flavoring agents, the relative loads his food up with a lot of monosodium glutamate (MSG). He was under the impression that a "sodium restricted diet" simply meant that he couldn't use table salt anymore, and in his opinion MSG was certainly not salt.

Eat Well, Feel Well (New York, Pratt Pharmaceuticals, 1993).

Q. If people who are on salt-free diets or salt-reduced diets cannot consume table salt or MSG, how will they know what to avoid when shopping for food?

A. The term "salt" has been abused in our society. "Salt" normally means the compound sodium chloride or table salt. Sodium chloride is only about 40 percent sodium. If your physician decides that you should avoid "salt," it is meant that you should avoid *all compounds that are even partly composed of sodium.* This does make it extremely difficult for some people to shop for food since so much of prepackaged food contains sodium.

This does not mean that those who require a salt-restricted or a salt-reduced diet are forced to eat bland, tasteless food the rest of their lives. There are salt substitutes and "low sodium salts" available at the supermarket. Salt substitutes are prepared from salt-free herbs—Mrs. Dash® is an example. There are also "low sodium" and "no sodium" salts. Low sodium salt is made with a mixture of 20 percent sodium chloride and 80 percent potassium chloride. Since sodium (Na) and potassium (K) are adjacent to each other on the Periodic Table of the Elements (see Appendix 1), we should expect their chloride salts to taste somewhat similar. For this reason, "no sodium salt" is 100 percent potassium chloride, which is safe, but can taste bitter to some people. The sodium/potassium combination results in a product that is *lower* in sodium than table salt, but it is *far from being sodium free.*

Most of the other saltless salt substitutes such as Mrs. Dash®, Nature's Seasons Seasoning Blend® (by Morton Co.), and their generics, are mixtures of some of these various spices: black or white pepper, sugar, oil of onion, oil of garlic, parsley, lemon, celery seed, capers, dill, thyme, basil, chili peppers, paprika, and many others. The product distributed by the Morton Company (Nature's Seasons®) lists salt as the *first* ingredient. As we now know, this means table salt or sodium chloride is present in the largest amount relative to all other substances in this product. Some of the claims on the label are: "For a zestier, livelier, balanced, seasoned flavor shake on foods." So far, Morton's advertising is accurate and not misleading. But, we feel the following statement on this product's label is misleading: "When you can shake on Nature's Seasons Seasoning Blend®, why shake on salt and pepper?" The first two ingredients—those present in the highest amounts in this product—are salt and pepper! This is hardly the kind of substance which those on a restricted-sodium or sodium-free diet can safely shake on their food without concern.

Refrigeration

Q. We rely so much on refrigeration to help us keep our food fresh and flavorful. How does a refrigerator work?

A. Many microbes, such as bacteria, just don't survive well in the cold temperatures. Either the cold kills them outright or it slows down their ability to reproduce. Refrigerators contain a series of metal tubes connected to a gas compressor (the expensive part of a refrigerator). Scientists have found that some gases like freon (an organic compound containing fluorine) cool the surrounding area when they expand. The compressor (which is generally located outside of the area to be cooled) takes the freon gas and compresses it. The compressed gas is then expanded into the coils surrounding the area to be cooled. As the freon expands, it cools the area. Fans circulate the cold air. Home and car air conditioners work on this same principle.

Q. Is a freezer just a super refrigerator? In the case of both types of cooling systems, how is the temperature controlled?

A. Yes, freezers are very much like refrigerators. The temperature in either type of unit is controlled by a device called a *thermostat,* which responds to changes in temperature by sensing the temperature and then sending an electrical signal to the compressor. The magnitude of this electrical signal is proportional to the temperature. Most home refrigerators contain both a freezing section and a section for other foods, which must be cold but not frozen.

Q. Is it a good rule of thumb to say that the cooler the temperature the longer my food will be preserved?

A. This is not true. After the temperature of food is reduced to 32 degrees Fahrenheit, or zero degrees Celsius, the water contained in it is converted to ice. At say, 10 degrees Fahrenheit, the water in food is still present as ice and the energy content of ice at ten degrees is not much different than the energy content at 32 degrees. Food is preserved at low temperatures because the bacteria present that could spoil the food are inactive at these low temperatures. However, there is not much change in bacterial activity at temperatures below 32 degrees Fahrenheit.

Q. **While we're on the subject of cooling and freezing processes, what is freezer burn?**

A. Contrary to its name, the process has nothing whatever to do with *burning*. Inside the freezer any moisture (as humidity) is quickly frozen into ice. Hence the amount of water in the air is very low. When unwrapped or poorly wrapped food is placed inside a freezer, water is drawn out of the food into the surrounding air (through evaporation) leaving some foods dried out. This is fundamentally what is meant by freezer burn.

Q. **Why doesn't all food placed in a freezer experience freezer drying?**

A. The drying occurs when moisture is removed from food while freezing occurs. Much of this depends on the relative humidity in the freezer, the rate of freezing (it should be as fast as possible), and the moisture content of the food.

Q. **In recent years environmentalists and leading scientists have warned that continued use of certain refrigeration coolants, namely, chlorofluorocarbons, poses a grave threat to the Earth's atmosphere. How does this occur?**

A. Fluorocarbons are found in cooling units, such as refrigerators and freezers, and in aerosol cans. These compounds are lighter than air and quickly escape into the atmosphere. Fluorocarbons, and especially chlorofluorocarbons, react negatively with the Earth's ozone layer, that part of the atmosphere which blocks out much of the ultraviolet radiation (what are called UV rays) coming from the sun and helps to control the temperature on the planet's surface. As ozone is depleted from the atmosphere, more harmful UV rays reach Earth. Ultraviolet radiation is responsible for thousands of skin cancers diagnosed in the United States each year. If left unchecked, continued depletion of ozone would increase levels of ultraviolet radiation and gradually raise the surface temperature of our planet (resulting in what we now know as global warming).

Q. Why do some salad oils turn cloudy in the refrigerator?

A. Salad oils should be "winterized" (chilled and filtered) to remove fats that combine in cooler temperatures to make the oils thick and cloudy.

MOISTURE: WHAT KEEPS IT IN FOODS? WHAT REMOVES IT?

Q. What are anticaking agents?

A. The humidity (moisture) in the air makes many food products clump up. All of us have probably seen the contents of salt shakers or sugar bowls get hard, lumpy, and crusty over time. Because anticaking agents attract water, they draw the moisture to them, thus retaining the sugar's or salt's granular texture.

Q. I noticed a little packet in some rice that I purchased and even in cans of coffee. The packet was labeled "magnesium silicate— DO NOT EAT." Why do the manufacturers put these packets in food?

A. Magnesium silicate is an anticaking agent. It absorbs water more than just about any other compound. Therefore, it will prevent boxed foods (such as rice) or seasonings (such as table salt) from becoming moist and clumping up in their containers.

Q. Thus far we have learned about removing harmful moisture that, along with oxygen, can result in food spoiling. However, there are things like baked goods and fresh fruit that we don't want to dry out. But what can we do?

A. If foods are left out at room temperature, they dry out (become stale). The water contained in them is evaporating into the air. Many times we would like our foods to retain moisture and remain fresher longer. For most people, the use of airtight containers is the best protection against foods becoming stale. Some organic compounds—composed mostly of hydrogen, oxygen, and carbon—like mannitol and sorbitol contain many alcohol groups (called polyhydric alcohols); they attract water and keep foods moist. These compounds are called *softening agents.*

TRACE METALS

Q. **In this age of machinery and automation in which thousands of tons of canned food are packaged each week, should we be worried about trace metal contaminants? What exactly are these contaminants, and are they harmful?**

A. For the most part, the amount of trace metals found in canned foods presents no significant health risk. They are introduced during the processing and milling stages from the machinery used to process or package food. While they aren't dangerous, due to their presence in very low concentrations, many trace metals are absorbed by fats or fatty compounds in foods, and do react and degrade fats (oxidize them). Sequestrants (metal extractors) like citric acid (vitamin C) and EDTA (a metal scavenger) are added to foods to tie up the metals so that the antioxidants can protect fats against attack by oxygen.

PRESERVING TASTE AND TEXTURE

Q. **What is an acidulant?**

A. This is a weak organic acid (e.g., acetic acid) added to cheese, beverages, and dressings to give a mildly acidic taste that combats the aftertaste of poorly processed foods and juices. Lactic, citric, tartaric, and phosphoric acids are added to orange juice, jelly, candy, and other foods to increase their acidity.

Q. Are you saying that properly processed foods wouldn't need acidulants?

A. Properly processed foods would require much less acidulants, if any at all, depending on the food processed. Of course, one must be prepared to pay a significantly higher price for orange juice without acidulants. There is nothing harmful, bad tasting, or nutritionally questionable about the foods we normally consume that contain acidulants. In fact, most of the orange juice sold in the United States contains acidulants to improve its flavor, since most of our juice comes from various orange strains in Florida and Brazil. This mixture of orange juices plus acidulants provides us with an inexpensive juice, and with a fairly good taste *for the price*. We could avoid adding the acidulants if we were prepared to pay the price for fresh-squeezed orange juice. The commercial blends of orange juice aren't quite as acidic as those to which our palates are accustomed.

Q. In discussing ways to keep food fresh and appetizing, you mentioned that substances containing sodium are often used as preservatives. Through the years didn't we also make use of substances called nitrates and nitrites? Can you explain the difference between them and exactly what they are/were used for?

A. As was pointed out when we discussed wines, nitrates have been banned in the United States for quite a while. Originally they were used to preserve pork products such as ham and bacon, but evidence that they can cause carcinogenic compounds when heated forced the government to ban them in most foods and limit their use in others. The evidence at that time also indicated that nitrites were less likely to form carcinogenic compounds than nitrates. For this reason, nitrates have slowly been removed from our meats: no nitrates are permitted in food today. However, processed pork products, such as ham and bacon, are very susceptible to harboring trichinae. This is a nasty organism that enters the human body as microscopic worms in meat and meat products. When one eats infected meat, these parasites reproduce in the intestines; their larvae enter the bloodstream and travel to muscle tissue, where they grow. This causes pain; fever; muscle deterioration; and, in very few cases, even death. Heating meat to a very high temperature prior to consumption, is the accepted way of treating raw pork and pork products. Unfortunately, heating pork products that contain nitrates or nitrites is also conducive to the formation of carcinogens. Therefore, the federal government decided that the danger from trichinosis was much greater than any possible carcinogen formation; so, while nitrates were banned, nitrites were permitted in low concentration in pork products. Sometimes, compromise is the best solution for such problems.

Q. In comparing the various methods of preserving food, are some better than others? For example, is freezing better than canning or vacuum packing? The television infomercials about food drying machines would lead one to believe that this is the way to go. Is it?

A. In determining the "best" method of preserving food, one must consider the cost and time involved. Certainly, freeze-dried coffee, soups, and fruits are quite popular, but you might not be interested in the taste of freeze-dried steaks. Our feeling is that irradiated food is probably the most effective and least expensive food preservation process.

Q. What is irradiation and why is it so effective in preserving foods?

A. A safe level of gamma radiation is passed through foods to destroy molds, insects, yeasts, and bacteria. In many Third World countries (where radiation is not used) about 50 percent of stored foods is lost to insects and harmful organisms. Typically, this process increases the food's shelf life by a factor of ten in many cases and it is less expensive than all the other methods of preservation. There is no need to add chemicals, increase the temperature, or use special containers. Most people not brought up on a farm don't even recognize the slightly burnt taste of pasteurized milk but would be pleasantly surprised by the good taste of irradiated milk. Most of the industrial nations use irradiation as the primary preserving method but because of the abnormal fear of radiation, most Americans fear irradiated foods. Currently, only shrimp, wheat, fish, corn, potatoes, spices, grapefruit, and strawberries can be preserved by radiation, but that will change in the future when chemists finally educate the consumer to the safety of radiation in foods. If you relish the thought of eating plump, juicy fruit, not just in season, but all year through (and not from South America or Australia), you will enjoy irradiated foods grown in America at a far lower price.

FOODS

Vegetables

Q. Television advertisements for a leading tomato ketchup and a leading spaghetti sauce emphasize the fact that their products are thicker because they have "more tomatoes." Is that true?

A. The products appear thicker, but is the increased thickness due to more tomatoes or is it due to the addition of thickening agents such as agar-agar, guar bean flour, or many other compounds that swell up when liquid is added and are safe to consume? This is difficult for us to determine without reading the label. All manufacturers must list the contents of their products in descending order according to volume. Check the label. Your answer may be there. While you are at it, check for the thickening agents we just mentioned. Our "gut feeling" is that since added tomatoes usually would not significantly increase the viscosity (ability to pour) of these tomato products; it is more likely that a swelling agent has been added (or the amount of the agent already present has been increased). Certainly *more tomatoes* must be added, because they said so on television. However, it is not clear how many more tomatoes they used. It is also not clear what is being used as a frame of reference for thickness. Is it thicker than their regular brand, all other spaghetti sauces and ketchups, or is some other standard of "thickness" being used?

Q. Why are garlic and onions odorless until cut or crushed?

A. Crushing releases a sulfur molecule that evokes a pungent odor, which is a lachrymator (it causes tears). Onions, shallots, and garlic are widely used in cooking because they sensitize the taste buds and nose.

Q. Why are mushrooms used so much in Oriental cooking?

A. Mushrooms are used in most cooking because they are rich in protein, low in fat, and give a slightly meaty flavor to vegetable dishes.

Q. My mother used to tell me that it was better to eat vegetables with their skins on if possible (e.g., potatoes, carrots, cucumbers) rather than peeling them, since peeling was thought to remove the vitamins, which are just under the skin. Is there any truth to this?

A. Would your mother lie to you? Cooking vegetable skins and saving the left-over liquid for sauces was our mothers' way of ensuring that we got plenty of vitamins and minerals.

Q. I heard that eating vegetables raw is always better. Is this true?

A. Most of the time, yes. However, because carrots and spinach are very hard for humans to digest, we cannot extract all of the vitamins and minerals found in these vegetables. Cooking starts to break down the cell walls of the vegetables; minerals and vitamins are then more easily absorbed by the body.

Meat, Poultry, and Seafood

Q. What determines the color of meat?

A. The compound myoglobin is responsible for the color of meat. Pork has less myoglobin than beef. Poulty drumsticks are darker because they have more myoglobin than breast meat.

Q. Why do some cuts of beef appear white?

A. When a calf is fed milk and slaughtered at less than three months of age, the meat lacks much of its myoglobin and has a creamy-white color.

Q. Why does fresh meat that has been sitting in the butcher's case for just a short while appear brown on the outside and red inside when cut?

A. Some people believe that butchers treat their cuts of meat with a chemical spray to enhance its color. That is not usually true. While there are chemical compounds that can be used in a spray to achieve this color change in meat, their use is illegal.

   When the animal dies (is slaughtered), the heart stops pumping oxygen-rich blood to the muscle tissue (the part of the animal we eat). Without the oxygen, the myoglobin in meat cannot turn red. The interior muscles turn a purply color and then, over time, they turn brown. When the exterior of the meat is exposed to air as the butcher carves the various special cuts (steaks and the like), the red color of the oxygenated myoglobin is at the exterior (the fresh red color we see). Meat naturally reacts with oxygen to convert the red myoglobin to a dark brown, oxidized form. You can see this for yourself: the next time you cut your finger and wrap a paper towel around it to stop the bleeding, take a look at the towel just a little while after you've put it down and you'll see that the blood stain is already beginning to oxidize and turn brown.

Q. I have often heard that beef is less easy to digest in the stomach than, say, chicken or fish. Is this true? If so, why?

A. This is true because the connective tissue in beef is much tougher than that found in poultry or fish. It's not surprising, then, that some cooks will take a tenderizing mallet to certain cuts of beef before cooking them.

Q. So often we hear it said that fish is "brain food." What could be in fish that would benefit the brain?

A. This old wives' tale is due to the iodine in fish. Unfortunately, it is false. This obtuse theory is based on the fact that fish from the ocean have a much higher concentration of iodine than fresh-water fish. Years ago, some people suffered from *goiter* (a swelling of the thyroid due to an iodine deficiency in the diet). The use of iodized salt with a trace of sodium iodide, has helped to remove this disease as a medical problem. About fifty years ago, some people thought that there was a correlation between reduced intelligence and iodine deficiency. This fallacy has been removed from the literature.

Another theory is based on the presumed benefits of shark cartilage soup, which is also high in iodine. Shark cartilage is made from repeating monomers of polysulfate glucosamines. These long polymeric chains are reduced by hydrolysis (broken down into smaller pieces) when the soup is prepared. Many in the Orient claim that this soup has the ability to increase mental activity and to decrease impotency. Glucosamines play an important role in cerebral transmission, but there is no evidence that there is any such thing as polysulfate glucosamine deficiency or that increasing the amount of this chemical, or iodine, in the diet improves intelligence.

Q. Why do brownish-colored lobsters turn red when boiled? Is there some reason for cooking lobster alive?

A. Shrimp also turn red (or pink) after boiling. The reason for the color change is that heat liberates a yellow-red pigment in their shells. Actually, most lobsters appear blue-green (to us) before cooking.

The rationale for boiling lobsters alive is based on health considerations as well as the fact that lobsters start decaying very rapidly after death. They have a powerful enzyme in their digestive tract which starts decomposing their flesh quite rapidly after they die. Lobsters, like all shellfish, usually carry a higher concentration of pathenogenic microorganisms (such as viruses that carry hepatitis) than fish. Therefore, it is important that shellfish be as fresh as possible.

The death-spasms from lobsters being boiled alive is more than most people can stand. Fortunately, it is unnecessary: the spinal cord can be cut just before boiling.

Q. Every so often we'll hear on the news that each year a number of Japanese citizens die from eating blow fish. Why is this fish so dangerous?

A. The blowfish is also called the puffer fish, due to its antics after being attacked. (The Japanese call it Fugu.) As a defensive weapon, blowfish can give off the dangerous toxin *petravotoxin*. This toxin blocks transmission of impulses to the nerves by preventing sodium ions from entering neurons. About eighty Japanese die each year from respiratory failure after eating blowfish. This occurs even though cooks in Japan must have a special license to prepare the fish.

Dairy Products

Q. What is homogenized milk?

A. Nearly all milk now sold in the United States is homogenized. Milk contains lactic acid and forms an emulsion with water. Dispersed milk fat in water is considered to be an emulsion. If milk is not homogenized, the milk fat rises to the top in an insoluble layer. Homogenization is performed because the protein in the milk causes the fat globules to stick together. By forcing milk through small openings the fat droplets break down into smaller, drinkable units.

Q. What is pasteurized milk?

A. Virtually all milk sold today is pasteurized. The milk is heated to 160 degrees Fahrenheit for fifteen seconds. This kills all pathogenic bacteria and gives commercial milk a slightly cooked flavor versus the sweeter taste of raw (unpasteurized) milk.

Q. What is buttermilk?

A. It is the liquid left over from churning cream. Just about all the buttermilk sold is artificially soured skim milk and is not really buttermilk in the true sense. Soured milk contains all of the lactic acid from milk, which gives it a thick consistency and a sour taste. The yellow specks should be bits of butter carried over from the churning of cream, but commercial buttermilk has dyes added to it.

Q. My grandson drinks quite a bit of chocolate milk. I suppose that is a good way to entice him to drink milk.

A. This is not very nutritionally sound. The oxalic acid in the chocolate inhibits the body's ability to absorb all the calcium in the milk. The youngster will get all the other nutrients from milk, except most of the calcium. Try strawberry or some other flavor in his milk.

Q. Why do people in some countries drink goat's or sheep's milk?

A. Both goat's and sheep's milk are very rich in fats and have a stronger flavor than cow's milk. The taste for these less familiar milks is an acquired one. The main reason that sheep's and goat's milk are recommended is not for their nutritional benefits over cow's milk, but simple economics. Goats are able to survive in rocky, barren areas that cannot sustain cows. Sicily is an example of an area that is very poor and the land rather unproductive. The milk of sheep and goats is used to process dairy products. Probably the most well-known product is true provolone cheese. This cheese is a semihard variety with a sharp bite and a smoky flavor. Most provolone cheese found in the United States is made by combining cow's milk with a special strain of bacteria and then adding "artificial smoke." It is neither as rich nor as aromatic as real provolone cheese.

Q. What gives blue cheese its distinctive odor?

A. Blue cheese contains a very special volatile compound, an ester. You may recall that we have already spent some time discussing esters. Esters are formed when organic acids and organic alcohols react together. They are quite volatile: that is, they form gaseous molecules readily. The ester in blue cheese is responsible for its unique odor. Esters fit neatly into the sensory slots or cavities in the nose and transmit a unique signal via the neurons there to tell the brain what odor is present.

Q. Is butter naturally yellow in color, or do producers color it? If coloring is used, should I worry about food dyes?

A. The color of butter is variable depending on the time of year, the breed of cow, and the dairy herd's diet. Nearly all cows produce a deeper, yellow-colored butter in the spring, when the grass is very rich in yellow-orange carotene. To ensure a uniform color of butter, processors add the natural and safe yellow dyes, annato seed extract, or carotene. If you wish, you can purchase butter that has an off-white appearance with no color additives at all.

Q. Yogurt is all the rage these days. Why do the containers of yogurt say that they contain "active yogurt cultures"? What exactly is yogurt anyway?

A. Yogurt is made from whole or skim milk and special cultures. The milk must first be heated to destroy all traces of antibiotics. The first time one of your authors tried to make yogurt, he didn't believe there were antibiotics in commerical milk. They were present and the yogurt never formed. Antibiotics kill the "good" culture added to make yogurt. The culture—a lactobaccillus characteristic of cultures found in Bulgaria—is introduced to the milk at a temperature of 50 degrees Celsius.

Q. What are antibiotics doing in milk?

A. Milk cows are treated regularly with antibiotics to reduce infection and to increase milk production. Some antibiotics always reach the cow's milk.

Q. What makes sour cream sour?

A. The presence of lactic acid.

Q. When milk is left out of the refrigerator it gets warm, turns bad, and smells awful. But when it is poured into hot coffee or into a sauce on the stove that doesn't seem to happen. Why?

A. Fresh milk from the refrigerator rapidly comes in contact with bacteria in the air which act on the milk sugar *lactose* and excrete lactic acid, causing fatty globules to coalesce—and soon curdling takes place. This coagulation or curdling of the fat globules occurs because of another compound in milk that allows the globules to bond together forming a cream-like layer (curds).

   The curdling or spoiling of milk is not related to temperature alone, but depends on changes in pH concentration and other factors. Consider the result of adding a bit of milk to your morning coffee or tea: The most important factor in prevent curdling is the decrease in the concentration of fat globules from whole milk as it enters an acidic solution (in this case coffee or tea) that has about 80 to 90 percent less fat globules available for reaction. As you can see, even curdling milk is not a simple chemical process.

Q. **There are so many different kinds of cheese on the market. What is it about their respective compositions that makes milk transform into one cheese rather than another?**

A. The conversion of milk into various cheeses occurs because of the bacteria used to make each cheese, and other substances added for flavoring.

Q. **Why does cream get all stiff and fluffy when it is whipped?**

A. The air that is added during whipping causes tiny air pockets to form. These are supported by fat in the cream which gives it the appearance of firmness.

SPICES/FLAVORINGS

Q. **What is it about some foods that gives them a sharp or tart taste?**

A. The acid levels of foods is what produces that tangy taste sensation. Adipic acid, for example, is often added to foods and beers to acidify them and given them a sharp taste. The spirited taste of sauerkraut or a crunchy dill pickle is the result of the production of lactic acid by the anaerobic (without oxygen) fermentation of sugars in the cabbage or the cucumber.

Q. **What compounds give a bitter taste?**

A. A bitter taste is evoked by caffeine, nicotine, and related compounds that contain nitrogen.

Q. **What foods would contain nicotine?**

A. Vegetables: Nicotine is a natural insecticide.

Q. **What makes chili peppers, jalapenos, paprika, and other spices hot to the taste?**

A. The hotness is due to the substance known as capsaicin. If you don't think paprika is hot, try freshly ground paprika. There is actually an arbitrary hotness scale developed for capsaicin. Some chili peppers in northern Mexico and southern Chile are the hottest and therefore contain the most capsaicin. They are given a rating of ten, and all other hot spices are judged according to this reference. These spices stimulate the saliva glands and the colon.

Q. Is it the flesh of the chili pepper or jalapeno that contains the capsaicin, or is it the seeds inside?

A. The seeds have the greatest amount of capsaicin. If you are courageous, try eating (licking is safer) the flesh of a jalapeno pepper and then try a few seeds. If you reverse the order of tasting, you might never be able to taste the flesh of the pepper.

Q. What is the difference between black, white, and green pepper?

A. Black pepper is obtained by allowing unripe Piper Nigrum (black pepper berries) to ferment. White pepper (popular in Chinese food) is obtained by removing the outer skin and seeds of the ripe fruit and allowing it to dry. Green pepper (the mildest of the three) is picked immature (before it has completely developed) and then preserved, skin and all, by pickling. Green pepper is often cooked and served whole in braised poultry.

Q. What causes the odor of cloves?

A. A class of chemical compounds called ketones are responsible for the clove odor. These same ketone compounds give fruits, dairy products (e.g., blue cheese), butter, cottage cheese, and other foods their distinctive odors. Other ketones give odors to semi-dry hay, raspberries, and the oil of violets. Eugenol is the active part of cloves and is also used in dental pain remedies, such as Ambusol® and others. The oil of cloves is preferred by many because the active ingredient (eugenol) is absorbed more effectively than synthetic products such as benzocaine.

Q. What is the difference between nutmeg and mace?

A. Ground nutmeg is called mace.

Q. Everytime I eat a product containing cinnamon, I get gas. Is that normal?

A. Yes, cinnamon irritates the intestines and causes flatus (gas).

Q. Is aniseed oil a flavor enhancer?

A. No, but it does contribute to the flavor of the herbs we know as fennel and tarragon. While these herbs taste bitter to some Caucasians, many Africans and Asians cannot taste them.

Q. Where does the flavor of anise come from?

A. The compound anethole is responsible for the flavor of anise, fennel, and tarragon.

Q. What is vanillin?

A. Vanillin is the major component of oil of vanilla, which can be obtained naturally from the vanilla orchid. Since the supplies of this plant are inadequate, it is prepared synthetically from eugenol. It is so widely used because it can be detected by the nose in low concentrations. The chocolate we all love is a mixture of vanillin and extracts of the cacao bean.

Q. But didn't you just say that eugenol is the active part of cloves? How can it be the source of vanillin?

A. Eugenol is plentiful and can be treated chemically to convert it into vanillin. The chemically converted eugenol now becomes vanillin. There are several chemicals that can be used to oxidize eugenol into vanillin.

Q. I always thought vanilla came from a bean? Am I wrong?

A. We aren't sure if you are wrong or simply have a misconception of the word "bean." Oil of vanilla is extracted from the fermented seeds, pods (beans?) of the vanilla orchid plant, which is grown mostly in Mexico, Madagascar, and Tahiti. This may explain the high price and scarcity of natural vanilla.

Q. What exactly are flavor enhancers and how are they produced? Why do we need them? Aren't the natural flavorings or our artificial ones strong enough?

A. Flavor enhancers are compounds that heighten the flavor of another compound, even though the enhancing compound has no flavor of its own. A good example of a flavor-enhancing compound is monosodium glutamate. It has no taste of its own, except for being salty, yet it enhances the flavor of many foods, especially meats. Producers add monosodium glutamate to their meat products to bring out the flavor. For this reason flavor enhancers are not really flavorings. They do not give flavor to foods but rather enhance or intensify a flavor already present. Other common flavor enhancers would include salt, maltol, safrole, and inosinic acid.

Q. Are synthetic flavors safe?

A. It is not always economical to prepare foods with natural flavorings. Over the years scientists have spent a great deal of money trying to figure out exactly how to synthesize flavors. Natural flavors are usually a complex mixture of organic compounds. Many times natural flavors are comprised mainly of one or two substances. Organic chemists usually can synthesize these compounds. For example, menthol is the principal flavor found in peppermint leaves. It is much cheaper to synthesize menthol than to extract it from peppermint leaves. An excretion from the scent glands of musk deer has been widely heralded in perfumes; however, true musk is extremely expensive. Wintergreen berries contain the flavorant methyl salicylate. Although synthetic flavors can only approach true flavors, they reduce the cost of prepared foods and other products that contain them.

SUGARS AND STARCHES

Q. What causes certain foods to taste sweet?

A. All tastes are sensed on the tongue and in the nose. At the tip of the tongue we taste sweetness, whereas bitter tastes are sensed in the back of the tongue. The tastes of sour and salty are sensed on the sides of the tongue.

Q. Do we receive all of our perceptions of taste from the receptors in the tongue?

A. No. There are about eight thousand taste buds found in other parts of the mouth (lips, cheeks, etc.). The aroma and color of foods are more important than the sense evoked by taste buds. If you pinch your nose closed, most foods taste bland! Try this with an onion and you will be surprised. This is the reason that people with colds and stuffed up nasal passages complain that most foods have no taste.

Q. What is sugar?

A. There are many different kinds of sugars. Perhaps the most common variety is table sugar, which is obtained from sugar cane or sugar beets. The chemical name for this sugar is *sucrose*. *Fructose* is the sugar found in fruits and consequently found in bee honey. *Dextrose* is obtained from corn or grapes, while the sugar called *lactose* is present in cow's milk. Fructose is about 50 percent sweeter than sucrose and more soluble than either glucose (a sugar derived from carbohydrates) or sucrose. Fructose is more economical to use than sucrose (table sugar) because of the extra sweetness. Sucrose is about twice as sweet as dextrose and six times as sweet as lactose. Brown sugar is also sucrose but contains molasses, a by-product of the cane sugar refining process. Contrary to the beliefs of many, brown sugar is no more healthful than white sugar.

There are many other sweet compounds that are considered sugars and are very high in calories. Many sugars are listed on food labels under different names, or the source of the sugar compound may be used instead of the name of the sugar. Sorghum, molasses, and maple are some examples of using the source of the sugar and not the name of the sugar on labels. These three sources of sugars are complex mixtures of several different kinds of sugars as well as many more chemical compounds. Any phrase with the word *sugar* or *syrup* or the ending *-ose* is sugar by another name. If one of these are last on the food label, then you can usually consider the food to be almost sugar-free. However, any food containing two or more sugars or a sugar as one of the first three ingredients, should be considered high in sugar content. Some of the sugar compounds or sources of sugars which might be listed on food labels are: invert sugar, corn sugar, milk sugar, maple sugar, brown sugar, lactose, sucrose, dextrose, fructose, maltose, mannitol, glucose, galactose, "nutritive sweetener," dextrin, sorghum, honey, turbinato, xylitol, molasses, and sorbitol.*

Q. What are starches?

A. Starches are complex carbohydrates. Carbohydrates are composed only of three chemical elements: carbon, hydrogen, and oxygen. However, the possible arrangements of these elements in a compound are enormous. A useful way of organizing the multitude of carbohydrates is to classify them according to their reactivity. Monosaccharides are the simplist form, and cannot be broken down into smaller groups. (The name *saccharide* comes from the Latin *saccharum,* which means "sugar.") Oligosaccharides are more complex than monosaccharides, and polysaccharides are even more complex than oligosaccharides. Both oligosaccharides and polysaccharides can be broken down into smaller units in the body. Oligosaccharides can be converted easily into only about two to six sugar molecules while polysaccharides break down into many sugar compounds.

Q. How are starches digested?

A. Actually, starch in foods like pasta, bread, and potatoes must be broken down into a soluble form called *glucose,* which is then absorbed through the intestinal walls and transmitted via the bloodstream to the rest of the body. Glucose is then metabolized (broken down and absorbed by the body) through a series of rather complicated reactions, the waste product of which is the simple compound known as carbon dioxide. This process is actually the reverse of the process known as photosynthesis, whereby plants convert the energy of the sun into starches. Unlike plants, humans convert starches into energy and expel carbon dioxide.

---

*From M. J. Franz, "A How-To Handbook for People with Diabetes" (New York: Pratt Pharmaceuticals, 1993). Used by the authors with permission.

Q. There seems to be a lot more sugar in store-bought yogurt and jellies than in homemade jelly or plain yogurt. Why?

A. One reason is that common household sugar can act as a preservative. When combined with water it can form what are called hypertonic solutions. These solutions have a much higher (hyper) concentration of (in this case) sugar, than the fluids in cells. Water then flows from the cells of bacteria to the hypertonic sugar around it. It is a natural process in which water is moved around in order to achieve a more equitable dispersion of water and sugar. However, the cells of the bacteria lose water so rapidly that they shrivel up and die. Sugar destroys the harmful bacteria and, therefore, acts as a preservative. A more plausible reason for all the added sugar in yogurt and jelly is that the extra sweetness can hide the taste of many imperfections.

Q. What are artificial sweeteners?

A. They are nonnutritive compounds that evoke a sweet taste in the mouth. Sodium saccharin, a leading artifical sweetener, which is about four hundred times as sweet as sucrose, was discovered in 1890. Like many discoveries in science, it was the result of pure luck and a curious mind. Sodium cyclamate, another synthetic sweetener, is about as sweet as saccharin and was discovered in 1937, also by accident. Since saccharin has a slightly bitter aftertaste, glycine, the simplest amino acid, is added to counteract the bitterness. Aspartame (Nutrasweet®) is only one hundred times sweeter than sugar and, like all proteins, it cannot be used in cooking without breaking down. The shelf life of beverages artificially sweetened with aspartame is much less than other sweeteners, natural or otherwise. For this reason, colas and other sodas sweetened with aspartame must be removed from store shelves and destroyed periodically.

In 1988, a new artificial sweetener, potassium acesulfame (Sunnette®), was approved for sale.

Saccharin was found to form cancerous lesions in test mice at one time and was banned in the United States. Later studies showed that the amount of saccharin used in the earlier tests was too high for realistic tests, so saccharin was once again permitted for use in food and beverages. Sodium cyclamate was also banned in the United States in 1969 for use as an artificial sweetener and for the same reason—its potentially carcinogenic effects. Currently, it seems that the U.S. government is about to allow sodium or calcium cyclamate for use again. The ban on saccharin and cyclamates was triggered by the controversial Delanely Amendment. This law automatically bans any chemical food additive that causes cancer in mice. The law does not take into account any variables in the testing, such as the amount of food additive used in the study. For this and many other reasons, the independent scientific community has not accepted the validity of this law. Saccharin and cyclamates were never banned by most other governments and continue to be very popular abroad.*

Since aspartame has a high phenylalanine content, it is a problem for people who suffer from PKU (phenylketonuria): their bodies lack the enzyme needed to metabolize phenylalanine.

Q. Is the preservative quality of sugar the reason for cold cereal producers including so much of it in their products?

A. No. The reason that cold cereal is produced with so much processed sugar is due to the sweet taste to which we are accustomed. Dry cereal needs very little to preserve it.

Q. Can you explain why people who have been diagnosed with diabetes are restricted in their consumption of sugar? Does this just mean that they can't eat candy bars and other sweets?

A. Diabetics produce very little insulin from the pancreas. The insulin hormone regulates the level of sugar in the blood. To control the glucose level in their blood diabetics must be tested and, if

---

*It is interesting to note the politics involved in these government decisions. After the ban on cyclamates, manufacturers returned to using saccharin since it was the only remaining artificial sweetener that was not banned by the FDA. In 1977, experiments which linked saccharin to bladder cancer in mice became public. These test results should have automatically triggered a ban, as was done with cyclamates. However, saccharin was the lone remaining artificial sweetener, so Congress, listening to the cries of its constituents, simply imposed a moratorium on the saccharin ban.

necessary, insulin must be injected or orally administered to stimulate the pancreas. Many diabetics can safely tolerate an occasional candy bar or sweet. Diabetics must restrict their consumption of all carbohydrates (which the body transforms into glucose before digesting it) and sugars. This means that pasta, breads, and other high-carbohydrate foods must be monitored as closely as sugar.

Q. On the opposite end of this question of sugar intake, why are some people actually encouraged to eat sugar? They seem not to feel very well if they don't eat enough of it. Can you explain this?

A. Hypoglycemics (people with low blood sugar) have difficulty maintaining a normal level of glucose in their blood. Their blood sugar levels frequently drop too low because of hyperactivity or release of excess insulin by the pancreas. This metabolic state is as dangerous to them as an excessive sugar level is to the diabetic. People suffering from this malady must take candy or sugar to raise their glucose level quickly, in much the same way diabetics must restrict their glucose level.

Q. So often we hear or read that foods such as jams are "fat free" and "cholesterol free," yet they are very sweet. Does this mean that they won't make us gain weight if we eat them?

A. Jams should never contain much, if any, fat or cholesterol. Jam is normally made from fruit, sugar, and other additives—none of which ever had fat or cholesterol. Manufacturers have learned long ago that the populace is very keen for these buzz words, even if the product could never have had these chemicals in the first place. However, fat-free and cholesterol-free jams *can* be fattening (high in calories) because there is *a lot of sugar* in them.

Q. Many products, such as various forms of chewing gum and candies, state on their labels that they are "sugar free," which means that they don't promote tooth decay. But how can something be sugar free and still be both sweet and a source of some calories?

A. These products are made with artificial sweeteners instead of sugar. They have *almost* no calories; any calories present must be in the other ingredients.

Q. Is it true that baking with honey, fruits, molasses, and the like is better than using regular sugar? If it's all "sugar," why should it make a difference?

A. There is no difference in the nutritional value of honey, corn syrup, white sugar, brown sugar, and other forms of sugar. The difference is wholly in the taste and the appearance of the food.

Q. My brother-in-law the nutrition fanatic refuses to eat table sugar because he says that it's been bleached to make it white and he doesn't want that stuff in his body, yet he eats brown sugar, honey, and molasses. Is he right about the bleaching?

A. Is brown sugar bleached to make it white? Yes, it is. Brown sugar is the crude extract from sugar cane, and it contains the by-product molasses. Molasses gives brown sugar its distinctive flavor and aroma. The nutritional value of brown sugar is about the same as purified white cane sugar or sugar from sugar beets. Brown and white sugars contain mostly "empty calories." In other words, the only nutritive value they possess is the energy (calories) they supply.

A calorie is the amount of energy needed to raise the temperature of one gram of water one degree Celsius. This is sometimes called a "small calorie." Dietetic calories, the ones we use to measure our energy input, are the equivalent of 1000 small calories. (They are actually kilocalories.)

Q. If we could just put pressure on our elected officials, government agencies, and the conglomerates that produce and/or manufacture the food we eat, we surely could have a "chemically free" food supply. Consumers should not have to eat or drink all these artificial additives.

A. We started this book by saying that our world is one filled with chemicals—well, our food is no exception. The food you consumer is a complex mixture of chemicals with odd-sounding names.

Even if we could remove every additive, preservative, flavor enhancer, color, and so on, our food would remain an extraordinarily complex arrangement of atoms and molecules. The table below contains a lengthy but partial analysis of a breakfast with no added chemicals. It may surprise you to learn that some of the compounds naturally found in these foods are toxic at the high levels that they are often found in (for example, methanol, butanol, hexylalcohol, and others). However, they are safe in the minuscule amounts in our food.

When you hear on the news or read in the paper that a particular chemical has been found in this or that food, you need to ask yourself if the amount at which it appears in the food item is significant. Is it present in potentially harmful amounts? Its mere presence in the food is not enough. Also, you need to find out if the toxic chemical can accumulate in the body over time (as lead can). If so, then the amount of the food you eat containing the chemical does legitimately become a consideration.

YOUR BREAKFAST AS SEEN BY A CHEMIST*

Chilled Melon

Starches	Succinic acid	Ascorbic acid
Sugars	Citric acid	Vitamin A
Cellulose	Anisyl proprionate	Riboflavin
Pectin	Amyl acetate	Thiamine
Malic acid		

Scrambled Eggs

Ovalbumin	Lipovitellin	Butyric acid
Conalbumin	Liviten	Acetic acid
Ovomucoid	Cholesterol	Sodium chloride
Mucin	Lecithin	Lutein
Amino acids	Lipids (fats)	Zeazanthine
Globulins	Fatty acids	Vitamin A

Sugar-Cured Ham

Actomyosn
Mycogen
Nucleoproteins
Pepids
Amino acids
Myoglobin
Lipids (fats)
Linoleic acid

Oleic acid
Lecithin
Cholesterol
Sucrose
Adenosine triphosphate
ATP
Glucose
Collagen

Elastin
Creatine
Pyroligneous acid
Sodium chloride
Sodium nitrate
Sodium nitrite
Sodium phosphate

Coffee

Caffeine
Essential oils
Methanol
Acetaldehyde
Methyl formate
Ethanol
Dimethyl sulfide
Proprionaldehyde

Acetone
Methyl acetate
Furan
Diacetal
Butanol
Methylfuran
Isoprene
Methyl butanol

Tea

Caffeine
Tannin
Essential oils
Butyl alcohol
Isoamyl alcohol
Phenol ethyl alcohol
Benzyl alcohol
Geraniol
Hexyl alcohol

Cinnamon Apple Chips

Pectin
Cellulose
Starches
Sucrose
Dextrin
Pentosans
Fructose
Malic acid

Citric acid
Succinic acid
Ascorbic acid
Cinnamyl aldehyde
Cinnamic alcohol
Ethanol
Propanol
Butanol

Hexanol
Acetaldehye
Acetone
Methyl formate
Ethyl acetate
Butyl acetate
Butyl propionate
Amyl acetate

Toast and Coffee Cake

Gluten	Calcium	Propionic acid
Amylose	Iron	Valeric acid
Starches	Thiamine	Caproic acid
Dextrin	Riboflavin	Acetone
Sucrose	Mono and Digylcerides	Diacetyl
Pentosans	Methyl ethyl ketone	Maltol
Hexosans	Niacin	Ethyl acetate
Triglycerides	Pantothenic acid	Ethyl lactate
Sodium chloride	Vitamin D	
Phosphate	Acetic acid	

---

*Used with permission of the Manufacturing Chemists Association, Washington, D.C.

The chemicals listed here are those normally found in pure foods. No found additives are listed and the chemical listing is not necessarily complete.

COOKING METHODS

Q. What does it mean to "blanch" food?

A. Blanching is the immersion of vegetables and/or fruit in boiling water for a minute or less. The point is not to cook the food, but rather to kill the microbes on its surface and prevent further spoilage. Frequently foods are blanched just prior to freezing.

Q. Why is steaming vegetables recommended instead of boiling?

A. When boiling foods, many of the essential vitamins and minerals required to maintain health are lost. These compounds may be destroyed by being in contact with heat for long periods of time. Also, we find that many vitamins and minerals are leached out (extracted) from vegetables in the added water required to boil them. Steaming reduces the number of vitamins and minerals leached out during the cooking process. Yes, raw vegetables are generally more healthy. But, if you don't like them raw, at least steam them.

Q. Why does steam take longer to cook foods than boiling water?

A. Steam is water that has been converted to its gaseous state. Although steam has more heat, it is a poorer heat conductor than boiling water and causes foods to take longer to cook.

Q. The color of most vegetables appears deeper and darker when they are cooked than when they are raw. Why?

A. The intensity of color in vegetables is determined by the pH and the concentration of dye in the food. Cooking can not only change the pH, but it will alter the concentration of dye. Notice that vegetables that have been cooked a long time appear washed out and faded.

Q. Does table salt (sodium chloride) raise the boiling point of water?

A. Nearly any substance (e.g., salt, sugar, baking soda) dissolved in water increases the boiling point of water. However, in most instances, when water is being boiled to receive vegetables and the like, it is unrealistic to expect much of a change in the temperature unless you are planning to put a large quantity of salt in the water. The addition of even small amounts of salt increases the "ionic strength" of water, which keeps pasta from sticking and vegetables from becoming mushy.

Q. Does cooking at high altitudes (say, in Denver, Colorado) cause any problems?

A. When the altitude is high, the atmospheric pressure is lower. This decrease in the force holding the gaseous water molecules in the liquid state allows water molecules to be easily converted to a gas (by boiling). Many prepared cooking mixes, such as cake mixes, have special directions for consumers who bake at high altitudes. Many times extra egg, water, and flour must be added to recipes to compensate for cooking at higher altitudes.

Q. What does it mean to "simmer" something?

A. The normal temperature at which water simmers is between 180 degrees and 210 degrees Fahrenheit. Water boils at 212 degrees

Fahrenheit. Simmering, then, is cooking at temperatures just below the boiling point.

Q. What is pressure cooking?

A. Before microwave cooking, people used pressure cookers to cook foods quickly at low temperatures. This method ensured that fewer vitamins were destroyed, and that the food was more tender. Basically, these cookers increase the pressure on the food inside, thus allowing water in the food to reach the boiling point at lower heat levels, which cooks the food faster.

Q. Is there a difference between baking, roasting, and what some people call broasting?

A. There is no difference between those three terms.

Q. Why do foods brown?

A. Most foods contain sugar or starch (poly sugars). When sugar is heated it starts to decompose and turns brown. Caramel, used as a flavoring and as a brown coloring agent, is prepared by heating sugar (hence the term *caramelize*).

Q. Unlike most other meats, ham doesn't turn brown when cooked. Why does that happen?

A. As we have learned, cured ham has nitrite added to it, which reacts with myoglobin to form a red compound that is stable at high temperatures. Many people don't believe that uncured, raw pork is actually grayish-white in color. Meat retailers add a food coloring to enhance the visual quality of uncooked pork. Cooking temperatures destroy the red food coloring used in pork, and the meat turns grayish-white anyway. Retailers have found that people prefer to buy pink pork versus gray pork.

Q. Why does moist heating at low temperature soften inexpensive cuts of meat?

A. The main substance in the connective tissues is a protein called collagen, which is converted (softened) to gelatin with moist heat, thus making the meat more tender.

Q. **What is meant by the term *braising*?**

A. Braising means to brown food in hot fat or oil, then simmer it in a covered pan with a small amount of water.

Q. **What is the "smoke point" and why is it important?**

A. The smoke point is the temperature at which a fat breaks down into visible smoke particles. The smoke point of oils do not remain constant during long cooking periods. As oil or fat is used, the smoke point decreases because the oils are continually being broken down as they are heated. Traditionally lard has been used in deep frying because it has a high smoke point. Oils have a smoke point considerably lower than lard. Oils typically smoke in a range of 420 to 530 degrees Fahrenheit (or 200 to 260 degrees Celsius). Many times peanut oil is recommended for wok or stir fry cooking because it has a very high smoke point and holds up well at high temperatures.

Q. **What gives barbecued meat its characteristic odor?**

A. The smell of barbecue and caramel is due to acrolein, a chemical that forms when protein decomposes with heat.

Q. **If heat is the only factor in this process, then why don't we get that barbecue smell when deep frying or pan frying? Heat is involved in both of these methods.**

A. Yes, you are quite correct. The odor from barbecuing meat is not just due to heat. We are accustomed to the odor of barbecue caused by the charring of sugars, spices, and other compounds in barbecue sauces and burning fat which drip on the coals.

Q. **Why is meat aged?**

A. When meat is stored for a few weeks, its enzymes undergo a change that is responsible for the softening of the connective tissue. This results in meat that is more tender.

Q. How do meat tenderizers work?

A. Tenderizers, such as papain (from unripe papaya), soften connective tissues in meat. Some slaughterhouses inject papain into an animal just prior to slaughtering it. Since papain enters the blood stream, it is carried to the muscles quickly.

Another type of meat tenderizer breaks down muscle fiber in the flesh of the meat. These tenderizers are typically enzymes (like papain) obtained from fungi or bacteria.

Q. I know that a lot of people marinate various cuts of meat, poultry, even fish. Does this process help to tenderize these foods?

A. Marinating meats, poultry, or fish softens the connective tissue and reduces the required cooking time. The marinade contains acids such as lemon juice or wine. These acids attack the connective tissue and tenderize the meat.

Q. I have recipes that call for clarified butter. How can I obtain it?

A. Melt unsalted butter in a glass bowl in the oven at the lowest temperature setting for thirty minutes. Allow it to cool and lift out the solid fat disks. Flush the exterior of the disk with water and keep refrigerated. Since butter fat is not soluble in water, you will not lose any clarified butter by flushing it with water.

Q. Why does butter scorch when in the frying pan?

A. The protein in the butter (called casein) changes character when heated. Clarified butter, from which the protein has been removed, will not scorch.

Q. Why is olive oil so widely used in Mediterranean countries?

A. Olive oil is a very stable cooking oil. It needs no refining, preservatives, or refrigeration. Olive oil also has the added advantage of being monounsaturated. This has been shown to lower blood cholesterol levels. Olive oil also has a medium-high smoke point and a rich, full-bodied flavor.

Q. What does it mean for something to be monounsaturated?

A. The term *mono* means "one," and *unsaturated* stands for double bonds. A chemical bond is the force that holds atoms together in a molecule. When a molecule is held together with only one bond between all atoms, it is called a saturated compound. Lard and other fats are solids at room temperature because all the atoms in their molecules are held together by single bonds. If a molecule consists of atoms that have at least a double bond or a triple bond, the compound is called unsaturated. Molecules such as those in vegetable oil have many "unsaturated sites," and are referred to as polyunsaturated. Products such as olive or cannola oil are monounsaturated, which means they have *only one* double or triple bond in the molecule.

So, a monounsaturated compound has only one double bond in the whole molecule. Double bonds in a molecule indicate that it can react further (with hydrogen). Polyunsaturated compounds have many double bonds, while saturated compounds have none. Solid fats are saturated compounds; oils are polyunsaturated. Saturated fats, such as lard, have been shown to cause hardening of the arteries, while polyunsaturated oils do not, and mono-unsaturated fats may actually reduce the amount of blockage in the arteries.

Q. **If solid fats are unsaturated and liquid oils are either polyunsaturated or monounsaturated, how would you classify the thick margarines that can be poured? Also, what's the difference between oil and shortening? Many times, I see a particular brand of oil also sold as a solid shortening. Why?**

A. Thick, liquid margarines are prepared by mixing liquid oils such as soybean oil with solids such as hydrogenated cottonseed oil. Solid shortenings are made by partly hydrogenating (mixing hydrogen gas with) the oil, which attacks the unsaturation (number of double bonds), resulting in a solid, saturated fat.

Q. **What are leavening agents? How do they work?**

A. Baking powder is used as a leavening agent. It makes baked goods rise. The powder is a blend of calcium acid phosphate, sodium aluminum sulfate (or cream of tartar) mixed with sodium bicarbonate (baking soda). Water reacts with this mixture and produces tiny bubbles of carbon dioxide gas. These tiny bubbles of gas get trapped within the batter and make it rise. Heating also makes the the gas bubbles expand and subsequently makes the batter rise even higher.

Q. How does yeast work in batters?

A. Yeast is actually a fungus that is also used as a leavening agent. If the yeast cells come in contact with their food source—sugar or starch—they eat like little demons and generate carbon dioxide gas as a waste product. The carbon dioxide gas then leavens (expands) the batter. Yeast prefers to grow at temperatures between 110 and 115 degrees Fahrenheit. For this reason, many bread recipes let the dough rise in a warm atmosphere.

Q. Is there any problem with using leavening agents at high altitudes?

A. Yes. At higher altitudes leavening agents produce carbon dioxide gas that expands with greater force. Hence, a cake batter might rise too quickly and to a much greater volume.

Q. What is the difference in function between baking soda and baking powder? Sometimes I have accidentally mixed up the two in a recipe and the result is awful.

A. Baking soda is simply sodium bicarbonate, which reacts with acids in foods (or batters) to form carbon dioxide gas for leavening purposes. Baking powder is more complex. It contains baking soda and an added acid salt, which forms weak acids when placed in water. The reaction of acid salts and sodium bicarbonate produces carbon dioxide gas. Potassium hydrogen tartrate, calcium dihydrogen phosphate, and sodium pyrophosphate are the most commonly used acid salts for cooking.

Your baking problem centers on the nature of these two compounds. Baking soda requires acidity from either the yeast reaction or by using an acid salt (baking powder). If you use baking soda, you also need yeast. If you use baking powder, nothing else is needed. As you can see, it really does matter which of the two you use when baking. By the way, you can save money by blending your own baking powder. We recommend one part cream of tartar (a weak acid) plus one-half part baking soda. Add another one-half part of starch if you plan to store the mixture for very long.

Q. Why do some frying pans scorch food very quickly while other pans of the same type work fine?

A. After many uses, pots and pans develop spots on their cooking surface from burned-on foods. These spots do not conduct heat as well as a clean pot. When much of the bottom of a pan becomes coated with carbon, more heat is required to cook foods. The higher temperatures scorch food in places where there is no soot on the pan's surface.

　　Ideally, cooking pans should be made of fairly thick metals to distribute heat evenly.

Q. Why shouldn't aluminum pans be used when cooking tomato dishes?

A. Many foods stain aluminum cookware—potatoes, for example. Foods such as tomatoes, cabbage, onions, and fruits contain weak acids, which act as metal cleaners and remove stains. There is only one place for the stains to go, and that is in the foods you are cooking; this often changes the color and taste of the foods you prepare. Acidic foods also remove a small amount of aluminum. This, however, should not pose any health risks.

Q. How do microwave ovens work?

A. Microwaves are actually a form of light we can't see. This form of light causes water molecules to vibrate very quickly. As the water molecules vibrate, they give off heat. This heat cooks our food. Water is an especially good molecule for microwave cooking since it absorbs microwave rays very efficiently. This is why dry foods don't heat very quickly in a microwave oven.

Q. How can a microwave cook food so fast? When microwaves were first introduced, people were afraid that food cooked in them would not be safe to eat—why? Is there any basis for these fears? Others considered microwaves safe but thought that the taste or texture of the food cooked in them would be different. Is it?

A. Some people thought that microwaves could transfer harmful energy to food. Part of this misconception lies in the public's awareness of the danger microwaves pose to heart monitors. The tales of physical damage being caused to people in the American Embassy in Moscow (during the days of the former Soviet Union) by microwave sleuthing didn't help our knowledge of microwaves. These reasons, as well as others, led to the misconception that microwave-cooked foods would be dangerous to eat. Microwaves just agitate the water molecules in the food and this causes the food to heat up fast. This type of cooking does not change the basic composition or nutrient content of food.

Microwave cooking *can* alter the texture of some foods. For example, breads heated in this way become mushy. A sound knowledge of what can and cannot be cooked effectively in a microwave oven should reduce the likelihood of messy surprises. Read your manufacturer's instruction book carefully.

NUTRITION

Q. What is cholesterol?

A. Cholesterol is produced in the liver, and its name comes from the Greek for "bile solid." Cholesterol can accumulate on the cardiovascular artery walls causing arteriosclerosis (clogging of the arteries). In a recent study published in the *New England Journal of Medicine,* it was found that 1000 mg of vitamin C and 200 units of vitamin E taken daily reduced the plaque (cholesterol build-up) on the artery walls by 40 percent—sort of a "cholesterol flush."

Q. Where do we get fats in our diets?

A. Dietary fats come primarily from butter, cream, margarine, vegetable oils and shortenings, meat products, seeds, and nuts. The American diet contains too much fat. In fact, 40 percent of our calories come from fats, and 13 percent of that is from saturated fats.

Q. What are some of the most common types of fat in our diet? What are some of the sources of these fats?

A. Fats are technically fatty acids. Many liquid fats are called oils. Fatty acids are found in a variety of foods.

FATTY ACID	SOURCE
Arachidonic acid	Liver
Butyric acid	Butter
Caproic acid	Butter
Caprylic acid	Coconut oil
Capric acid	Coconut oil
Lauric acid	Palm kernel oil
Linoleic acid	Soybean oil, fish oil
Myristic acid	Nutmeg
Oleic acid	Olive oil
Palmitic acid	Palm oil
Stearic acid	Beef tallow

Q. I read that fish oils can significantly reduce blood cholesterol levels. Is this true?

A. Fish oils are very high in polyunsaturated fats. However, the effect of fish oils on blood cholesterol levels has not been well documented. However, the effect fish oil has on the function of blood platelets is less than the result of taking one aspirin tablet.

Q. Can fish oils reduce the occurrence of heart disease?

A. There is some evidence from a few Norwegian studies indicating that diets rich in fish oils may reduce heart disease. The studies included people who also had diets rich in total fat and cholesterol. It is possible that the polyunsaturated fatty acids in their diet were a factor. Another study indicated that diets supplemented with fish oil lead to lower cholesterol and triglyceride blood serum levels. Triglycerides are lipids (soluble fat in blood). Ninety-five percent of lipids in the American diet are triglycerides.

Q. What is the source of cottonseed oil?

A. Obviously, it is found in cottonseed but it is also found in soybeans, corn, and rapeseed oil. The chemical name for cottonseed oil is linoleic acid, which also can be found in linseed oil produced from flaxseed. Linseed oil is a drying oil.

Q. What is an iodine number?

A. Perhaps you have seen this term in some health books or nutrition magazines. The iodine number is directly related to the amount of unsaturation in foods. As the degree of unsaturation (double bonds) increases, the higher the iodine number becomes. Foods containing high iodine numbers have a lot of unsaturated oils and fats. The iodine number is an index of nutrition: the higher the number, the more nutritious the food. Most products do not record this number so it is wise to keep a list.

OIL OR FAT	AVERAGE IODINE NUMBER
Coconut oil	9
Butter	35
Beef tallow	40
Palm oil	52
Lard	60
Olive oil	80
Peanut oil	90
Cottonseed oil	112
Corn oil	120
Fish oils	140
Soybean oil	140
Safflower oil	140
Sunflower oil	140
Linseed oil	200

Source: *Journal of Dietary Science* (Brisbane, Australia)

Q. What is protein?

A. Protein is made of many smaller units called *amino acids*. Eight of these amino acids are considered *essential amino acids*. Our bodies do not create them so they must come directly from the food we eat.

Q. How can I be sure I am getting all of these essential amino acids?

A. Most protein from animal sources contains all of the essential amino acids our bodies need. Meat, milk, fish, eggs, and cheese supply all eight of the essential amino acids: phenylalanine, leucine, isoleucine, methionine, threonine, tryptophan, and lysine.

Q. What is the difference between fiber and roughage in our diets?

A. The fiber, bulk, or roughage in our foods are all primarily cellulose. Cellulose is a carbohydrate that we cannot digest, because we lack specific enzymes, unlike cows, goats, sheep, and other animals that have them. Unfortunately, termites can also digest cellulose.

   Some of the foods rich in fiber include fruits, vegetables, bran, and nuts. Dietary fiber has been shown to decrease our risk of contracting colon cancer. One possible reason might lie in its mechanical effect on the large intestine. As water passes through the intestine it is absorbed by fiber and provides considerable bulk. The rapid movement of this bulk may aid in the swift elimination of carcinogenic agents.

   It is important to distinguish between soluble and insoluble fiber. Soluble fibers, such as oat bran, psyllium, or microcrystalline cellulose (like that found in the product Citracell®) do little to reduce cancer of the colon. However, there has been quite a bit of evidence that seems to show that soluble fiber helps to prevent heart attacks. Insoluble fiber does little for heart disorders but does reduce the incidence of colon cancer. One way of remembering the distinction is to keep in mind that insoluble fiber is the dietary equivalent of twigs, sticks, or straw. As they move through the digestive tract, they scrape the lining of the colon free of any dangerous materials.

Q. I can't always eat a balanced diet and I don't eat vegetables. Is this harmful?

A. Most of the time we should be able to obtain all of the required vitamins and minerals from the foods we eat. But diets lacking in certain foods, such as vegetables, may lead to several problems including anemia, night blindness, blood loss, and scurvy. The recommended daily allowance of vitamins and minerals, published by the National Academy of Sciences and the National Research Council, lists the daily allowances according to age, sex, and energy requirements. Being pregnant also rates a special daily allowance.

VITAMIN AND MINERAL DAILY REQUIREMENTS

Vitamin	Source	Amount	Disease Prevented
A	Eggs, butter, greens	5000 IU*	Night blindness
B_1	Grains, milk, pork	1.5 mg	Beriberi
B_2	Eggs, liver, grains	1.7 mg	Clotting failure
B_6	Yeast, bran, grains	2.0 mg	Mouth sores
B_{12}	Meat, clams, oysters	6 ug†	Pernicious anemia
Biotin	Beef, peanuts, liver	0.3 mg	Skin disorders
C	Citrus, greens	60 mg	Scurvy
D	Milk, eggs	400 IU	Rickets
E	Yeast, meats, eggs	30 IU	Anemia
Folic acid	Liver, grains	0.4 mg	Diarrhea
K	Cauliflower, greens	7 mg	Hemorrhages
Niacin (B_3)	Meats, grains, greens	20 mg	Pellagra
Pantothenic acid	Same as B_3	10 mg	Dermatitis

*International Unit   †micrograms

Mineral	Source	Amount	Condition Prevented
Calcium	Milk, dairy products	1.0 mg	Bone dissolution
Copper	Shellfish, grains	2.0 mg	Decreased metabolism of cells
Iodine	Seafood, eggs	150 ug	Goiter
Iron	Meats, eggs, raisins	18 mg	Fatigue, dizziness
Magnesium	Green foods	400 mg	Damage to nerves, circulation
Phosphorus	Various sources	1.4 mg	Incomplete calcium intake
Zinc	Shellfish, meat	2.0 mg	Decreased cell growth

†micrograms

Q. Can nutrients be lost by cooking or canning?

A. Cooking causes foods to lose their nutritional value because heat breaks down nutrients. Even canned foods lose their nutrients after standing for long periods. Below is a list of nutrients and the extent to which they are lost when food is cooked.

LOSS OF NUTRIENTS FROM COOKING

Nutrient	Percent Loss
Vitamin A	40
Vitamin C	90
Vitamin D	40
Vitamin K	5

Canned foods can lose as much as 20 to 30 percent of their vitamin C content after being on the shelf for twelve months.

Q. I have heard that peach pits are poisonous. Is this true?

A. Apricot and peach pits contain a trace of cyanide, but not enough to even make you ill. Fruit jams that have pits (for example, quince), have a trace amount of cyanide but are *not* dangerous.

Q. Why do some people have trouble digesting milk?

A. Most people of northern European ancestry can consume milk and milk products because they have the enzyme *lactase,* which breaks down the *lactose* in milk. Many people of African or Asian descent don't have this enzyme. They can tolerate cheese or yogurt because the lactose is broken down during fermentation, but a glass of milk, or a dish of ice cream may be difficult to digest. Of the world's populations whose members are more susceptible to the problem, northern Europeans suffer much more than other groups.*

Q. What causes the color in foods?

---

*P. Atkins, *Molecules* (New York: W. H. Freeman, 1987), p. 100.

A. There are many natural colors in foods. Beef fat is yellow from the betacarotene in grass. Safflower petals supply the color rouge. Carrots are orange from carotene, but originally carrots were colorless. Hybrids finally gave us a carrot rich in carotene. Persimmons, the yellow of butter, and the color of oranges are also due to the presence of carotene. Carotene is added to margarine to give it the color of butter. The pink color of cooked lobster and shrimp, as we learned earlier, is due to the formation of a type of compound called a ketone.

Q. Are artificial food colorings safe?

A. The Food and Drug Administration (FDA) enforces the use of artificial colors and the introduction of new ones. Currently, it accepts only about thirty food colors. Half of them are natural extracts and the other half are synthetic.

Q. What does GRAS mean?

A. The acronym GRAS stands for a list of food additives that the FDA considers to be "Generally Regarded as Safe." This list was first published in 1960 and has been amended several times since. Cyclamates were removed from the list, as was Red Dye #2. The list includes flavorings, stabilizers, flavor enhancers, preservatives, antioxidants, moisturizing agents, surface active agents, acids, alkalines (bases), and buffers, as well as colors. There are over 2,500 chemicals currently on this list. It has shrunk somewhat during the years and very few new compounds have been added. It costs over one million dollars to even test a new compound for inclusion on this list. The entire list can be obtained from the FDA. *It is important to note that compounds on this list are safe only if used in the amounts and in the foods specified.*

Q. Is fasting healthy?

A. In the early stages of fasting, the body's supply of protein is rapidly depleted. After a while the rate of protein metabolism slows down and the brain instructs the body to start burning up fat as its energy source. Eventually, fat reserves are exhausted and the body turns to the residual proteins for energy. The result is dramatic. The emaciated appearance that results indicates nearly complete depletion of muscle proteins. Contrary to some popular beliefs among fad dieters, *fasting is not healthy.* In fact the reverse is true. The rapid breakdown of fat and protein produces ketones, ammonia, urea, and other poisonous wastes.

Q. Since most underdeveloped countries are suffering from a shortage of meat protein, what are the most efficient ways of supplying it?

A. If the weight of edible protein is divided by the weight of the total protein required to produce it and then multiplied by 100, we can calculate the efficiency of protein production. Eggs and milk are about 23 percent efficient. Turkey (poultry in general) is about 18 percent efficient. Pork ranks fourth with 12 percent and beef ranks last at 4 percent. Of course, these ratings from the President's Science Advisory Committee (1976) do not take into account the cost of the animal feed. When accounting for feed cost, it turns out that poulty production is most efficient.

Q. How do vegetarians survive without meat proteins?

A. The vegetarian's food consumption provides protein from a variety of sources other than animal tissue. Plants such as vegetables have a great deal of protein. Usually a good protein balance is obtained by mixing a cereal grain with a legume (peas, beans, peanuts, etc.). Some of these combinations are listed below. (It must be noted that extreme or radical vegetarianism can be quite dangerous. Usually vitamin B_{12}, calcium, iron, riboflavin, and vitamin D are absent. The addition of dairy products to a vegetarian diet can provide excellent nutrition while still avoiding red meat.)

SOURCES OF CEREALS AND LEGUMES

Geographical Area	Food
Mexico	Corn and beans
Japan	Rice and tofu
England	Beans on toast
United States/Canada	Corn, beans, nuts, bread
Africa	Rice and beans

CLEANING UP

Q. What sorts of chemicals are in dish washing powders for automatic dishwashers?

A. They generally consist of a very strong detergent, an alkaline compound to increase the pH, sodium silicate to prevent damage to the dishwasher, a surfactant to prevent "spotting," and some fragrance. Generic dishwasher powders are usually made by the brand name companies and distributed by independent supermarkets under their store brand. They are identical to the high-priced and heavily advertised brand name products.

Q. I saw a commercial on television in which a few drops of a particular brand of dish soap completely removed all the grease from the surface of some water. What makes this brand name dish soap so special?

A. Just about any brand of dish soap can emulsify grease and fat. In fact, all soaps and detergents break up grease into soluble droplets that are easily rinsed off with hot water. There is nothing special about this brand or any other brand of dish washing liquid. It just costs more.

Q. How do oven cleaners work?

A. Most aerosol oven cleaners contain lye (sodium hydroxide). Yes, this is the same component we found in many liquid drain cleaners. Lye turns fat and burned-in sugars into soap so that they can be easily wiped off.

Some of the newer oven cleaners contain organic salts that attack grease (fats) and sugars. These are less dangerous than lye-based cleaners. Common sense should still apply. Any cleaner that takes off burned-on food will likely pose a hazard to the mucous linings of your mouth, throat, and lungs if you are exposed to it for a period of time. Be careful. Use appropriate protection and ventilate the kitchen.

8

Your Car

In this chapter we will briefly discuss the chemistry of antifreeze, batteries, gasoline, defrosters, de-icers, oils and oil additives, maintenance, radiator cleaners, and more. There is a great deal of money to be saved when purchasing products for your automobile. Wise shoppers pride themselves on being informed. Marketing ploys abound when ignorance or laziness gains a foothold.

In order to keep your automobile in the best condition, proper lubricants, fuels, cooling solutions, and protective compounds must be used.

GASOLINE

Q. I know that I spend a lot of money purchasing gas for my car. What exactly is gasoline?

A. Gasolines were initially obtained from the distillation of petroleum. Today, other techniques are used to obtain gasoline, such as *cracking*. We will talk about this shortly.

Gasoline contains colorless organic compounds that usually are between six and ten carbons atoms in length. These compounds distill below about 300 degrees Fahrenheit. About 30 percent of petroleum crude can be converted to gasoline. In a high-temperature heat-cracking process, higher-boiling organic compounds are broken down into lighter hydrocarbons, or gasoline. Unfortunately these high-temperature cracked gasolines may contain unsaturated organic compounds. These unsaturated compounds, which usually help as anti-knock additives, may polymerize (harden) to form high-temperature resins inside your engine. Stabilizers are therefore added to the gasoline to reduce polymerization.

The Clean Air Act of 1970 requires that all motor vehicles built after 1975 use unleaded gasoline. Tetraethyl lead is a poisonous additive to gasoline that was used to increased its octane number and thereby reduce engine knock. Gasolines containing lead were dyed for further identification by the consumer. Other less toxic alternatives are currently available such as some magnesium-containing compounds to raise the octane number of gasoline. To reduce emissions and the improper combustion of gasoline, alcohol is often added. In Colorado, alcohol is added every winter for several months.

Octane is an organic molecule containing eight carbon atoms. The octane number of gasoline is nothing more than a measure of the gasoline's ability to be detonated in a car's engine. The higher the number, the better (cleaner) its capacity to burn in the engine. (We'll have more to say about octane in an upcoming question.)

Q. Is there a best brand of gasoline?

A. In many small regions only one refinery produces all the gasoline sold by major and independent retailers. Most independent gasoline stations purchase their fuel from a major brand-name refinery. In some areas each major gasoline retailer adds a different additive "package" to the gasoline purchased from the same refinery. Frustrated? If you have a newer automobile, try a gasoline that follows BMW testing and try to use the same gas station all the time. If your automobile is three or four years old, then any gasoline that doesn't result in knocking and pinging will do fine! Using discount retailers can save you as much as $300 annually.

Q. What do you mean by a gasoline following BMW testing?

A. What we are talking about here is a very simple test that most automobile companies perform. BMW testing involves running their car engines on the gasoline supplied by the major gasoline refiners. The products are evaluated for performance and results are reported in their product literature. Most of us do the same thing. We've come to rely on a certain brand of gasoline from a local retailer that appears to perform to our expectations.

Q. Which gasoline additives should I use?

A. Most gasolines have an additive "package" blended into them. These "packages" contain detergents, anti-icing agents, antirust agents, trace metal scavengers, and deposit modifiers (to prevent knocking or pre-ignition). If you perform normal, routine maintenance on your vehicle, you shouldn't need any gasoline additives. However, there are a few occasions when you might wish to consider their use.

When the relative humidity is very high, you would be wise to consider de-icers (ethyl alcohol or glycol). Sometimes they are called "gasoline driers." Save a lot of money by purchasing *denatured* ethyl alcohol at a hardware store, but be careful not to use alcohol with water in it. A fellow we know tried to use rubbing alcohol (70 percent isopropyl alcohol and 30 percent water) in his gasoline and cursed us for weeks. We tried to explain to him that he had not even read the label, which clearly stated "30 percent water."

Other additives that you may consider for use are carburetor or fuel injector cleaners. Check the manual for your make and model to see if you need either of them. Most automobiles don't require them and their purchase would be a waste of money. The estimated annual savings by not using any fuel additives is about $780! If you are stubborn and insist on putting an additive in your gasoline, pass up the automotive section of your store for the hardware section. Buy a gallon of mineral spirts or toluene; these are the same compounds found in the high-priced additives. You can save about $102 annually. Use the same amount of these as you would if you bought the higher-priced de-icers.

Q. You've mentioned that the brand of gasoline isn't all that important. But which grade of gasoline is best?

A. Unless your car's maintenance manual specifies premium or midgrade, we'd recommend purchasing regular unleaded gasoline. If your engine pings or knocks, you probably need a tune-up or a mechanical adjustment. Before you take your car to the mechanic, try another brand (not another grade) of gasoline. If the pinging and knocking persist, then see a mechanic. Certainly a higher octane-rated gasoline will stop the knock and ping, but you can seriously damage your engine in doing so and waste a lot of money in the process.

Q. How could gassing up with an octane that is higher than the car needs hurt the engine?

A. High temperature cracked gasolines are often used for their higher octane numbers. These gasoline mixtures contain unsaturated organic compounds called *olefins*. These olefins can polymerize under the high temperatures in your engine during combustion. The resins tend to gum up the engine. Use the octane number recommended by your car's manufacturer.

OCTANE RATINGS OF SEVERAL HYDROCARBONS

Hydrocarbons	Octane Number
N-Heptane	0
N-Hexane	25
N-Pentane	62
Octane -4	73
Cyclohexane	83
N-Butane	94
Propane	97
Isooctane	100
Benzene*	106
Methanol (methyl alcohol)**	127
Ethanol (ethyl alcohol)**	128
T-Butylalcohol**	113
Xylene	117
Ethyl t-butylether**	118
Toluene	120

*Banned, carcinogen
**Common octane boosters currently used to replace lead and improve the octane rating of gasoline blends.

Q. What does "octane rating" mean?

A. The octane number of gasoline is an indicator of its relative ability to resist engine knocking or pinging. A compound called iso-octane has been given an arbitrary octane rating of 100 because it doesn't knock much (see the list on page 190). On the other hand, n-heptane, which knocks a great deal, is assigned a value of 0. Methyl and ethyl alcohol have very high octane ratings, well over 120. The Brazilians use ethyl alcohol as a fuel in automobiles because they grow an abundance of sugar cane from which ethyl alcohol can be produced. The carburetors of their vehicles have to be modified in order to function at such high octane levels. Because imported oil is very expensive in Brazil, ethyl alcohol is a viable alternative.

Q. In the automotive section of stores I sometimes see additives that are called octane boosters. What do they add to the gas to pep it up?

A. Commercial octane boosters are some of the chemicals found in the hydrocarbon-octane rating list we have just presented. Octane boosters are added to increase the efficiency of detonation of gasoline in the car's engine. The boosters mentioned in the list are mostly saturated hydrocarbons except for toluene, benzene, and xylene. These three organic compounds may contribute to engine residue if they are not completely burned.

Q. What is dry gas and how does it get the water out of my gasoline tank?

A. Most of us know that oil and water don't mix. However, alcohol is soluble in both gasoline and water. Most dry gases contain alcohols like methanol, which is soluble in gasoline; as it burns up with the gasoline you use, it carries along with it a small amount of water. The alcohol takes the water with it as the gasoline combusts to power the engine.

Q. I have heard or read about gasolines having detergents that clean the engine. Really? How do they do that?

A. Detergents are gasoline additives that help remove the build-up of resins formed from the polymerization of olefins, and they remove some organics left by the incomplete combustion of gasoline. Most of the additives are proprietary to the major oil companies. Also, certain fractions of petroleum distillates are better at removing engine build-up and are added by gasoline manufacturers.

OIL

Q. What makes a good motor oil?

A. Without using any brand names, we can help you understand which oils are superior. Motor oil is a complex mixture of hydrocarbons obtained by distilling crude oil. The nature of the mixture of hydrocarbons obtained depends on the source of the crude oil and the distillation procedure. To our knowledge, the only completely synthetic motor oil produced today is made by Mobil Corporation. It is quite expensive, but since the mixture of hydrocarbons is specifically designed for optimum use as a lubricant in engines, it is recommended by many manufacturers.

A chemist friend of ours works at the largest automotive oil additive company in the world. He uses and recommends motor oils that are produced by companies that sell nothing else but motor oil. Since their profit comes from the sale of motor oil, they can't afford to sell anything but the best oil possible. Accordingly, these companies also use their most expensive oil additive package. Companies that also sell tires, batteries, gasoline, and other products can afford to offer a less expensive and inferior motor oil. Our recommendation is simple: if a company sells anything besides motor oil, chances are you might be purchasing an inferior oil.

For years Mobil's synthetic oil (Mobil 1®) was in a class by itself. But as of early 1994, most major oil companies have begun producing synthetic oils. These oils are specially blended fractions of petroleum distillates that are designed for lubrication, heat stability, and to reduce engine wear.

Q. Which oil additives do you recommend?

A. We advise against adding any oil additives beyond those already in the oil. Actually, oil additives may destroy the "package" of additives already present in the motor oil. If your automobile burns or drips oil, then consider a viscosity thickener or perhaps a higher single grade viscosity oil (30 to 50W).

Q. What is a viscosity thickener?

A. Regular motor oil is rated on a test scale developed by the Society of Automotive Engineers (SAE). Viscosity is the resistance to flow. High viscosity is desirable at high temperatures so that a car's piston values will be well lubricated and wear on the engine is reduced. At low temperatures, viscous oils tend not to flow. They become thick like molasses. Low viscosity oils allow for maximum valve protection in cold climates. A thickener increases the viscosity of regular motor oil at high temperatures. A 20W SAE oil flows one-half as fast as a 40W SAE oil. The addition of a viscosity thickener to 20W oil will produce a 20-40W or multi-grade oil. The thickener starts increasing the viscosity of the 20W oil at high temperatures by uncoiling into a series of long molecular strands or chains.

Q. Why are some motor oils clear and others colored?

A. Some oils also have an odor while others don't. The origin of the crude oil is responsible for the color differences and the presence of sulfur (sour crude) causes the odor. The color and odor have nothing to do with the quality of the motor oil.

Once you have decided which brand of oil is best for you, stick with it and don't change brands until you change all of the oil in the crankcase.

Q. What do the letters SG, SF, CC, and CD mean on the oil I purchase?

A. SG and SF are American Petroleum Institute (API) engine service classifications for motor oil. SG was implemented in 1989 and SF in 1980. If your automobile was manufactured prior to 1989, SF oil will work fine. CC oils are hard to find and utterly useless.

CD refers to turbo-charged engines. CD-2 is an oil that is used under severe conditions. CE was introduced in 1983. CF-4 is a heavy duty diesel oil introduced in 1990.

Q. Is there anything to these commercials for oils that are so durable and long-lasting that they can be drained from the crankcase and the engine can still run without damage?

A. Some oil packages are better at lubricating at higher internal engine temperatures. This means that higher temperatures are required to degrade the oils. When you drain the oil from the crankcase a small amount does remain to lubricate the engine. All products will eventually degrade and the engine will freeze as the temperature rises. Some silicone oils are usually more stable at higher temperatures than petroleum distillates, but the silicone varieties are very expensive. These oils are made for higher engine temperatures, but often they do not lubricate as well. Routine oil level checks and oil replacement reduces the need for this type of expensive oil.

ANTIFREEZE AND DE-ICERS

Q. What are antifreeze/coolant solutions made of?

A. Commercial antifreeze solutions are prepared from ethylene and/or propylene glycol, corrosion inhibitors, metal scavengers, detergents, rust inhibitors, a substance to control leaks, and an antifoaming agent. The glycols depress the freezing point of water and increase its boiling point. Since nearly all commercial antifreeze sold in the United States is basically the same, we recommend that you purchase the least expensive permanent brand of antifreeze and save about $6 to $10 annually.

Q. For those in northern climates where the temperatures shift from very cold winters to very hot summer days, can the same antifreeze/coolant solution be used all year? Won't it deteriorate after several months, thereby needing flushed out and replenished to meet each new winter and summer?

A. Antifreeze can and should be used in both climatic extremes. Although cold temperatures don't degrade antifreeze, high temperatures may. However, the antifreeze/water mixture would boil prior to deteriorating. Winter or summer, the antifreeze keeps on working. Periodic replacement is a requirement to maintain fluid lost by leaks and evaporation.

Q. How is it that the same material that cools the radiator in summer can keep it from freezing in the winter?

A. When propylene glycol, a common antifreeze, is added to water it lowers the freezing point of the water as well as increases the water's boiling point. Most substances dissolved in water have this same effect. Antifreeze keeps water from freezing at 32 degrees Fahrenheit and from boiling at 212 degrees. The water coolant mixture is circulated from the radiator to the engine by the water pump. Heat is transferred from the engine to the coolant liquid prior to returning to the radiator. The radiator relies on the outside temperature to cool the liquid. Hence, the antifreeze is required to prevent water from freezing in cold climates as well as to prevent the water in the radiator from boiling in warmer climates.

Q. Is ingesting antifreeze dangerous?

A. Caution should be used when disposing of or adding antifreeze. *Ingesting (consuming) even very small quantities of ethylene glycol is dangerous and may lead to drowsiness, coma, respiratory failure, and even death.* The propylene glycol antifreeze is relatively harmless, though we do not recommend that anyone drink it or consume it in any other forms. Small animals should not be allowed to come in contact with ethylene glycol. Be particularly careful since ethylene glycol has a sweet taste that animals like. *And always keep antifreeze and other automotive products out of the reach of children.*

Q. What are some of the substances used to control small leaks in the radiator?

A. Radiator products that claim to seal small leaks use metal and plastic particles or asbestos fibers and plastic particles. When the radiator is hot the coolant liquid expands and the pressure on the inside of the radiator increases. As the pressure increases, liquid carrying the small particles is forced out of any holes that exist. These products rely on the particles getting trapped in the holes. The metal particles or fibers become jammed in the larger holes and the polystyrene spheres fuse when heated to form a solid plug.

Q. Do I need to add radiator cleaner annually?

A. Radiator cleaners are only needed for radiators that become plugged up with mineral scale: iron, calcium, magnesium carbonates, or oxides. If you change your radiator solution every other year, this situation should not arise. In areas of the United States where the water is extremely hard (very high in minerals), clogged radiators may occur no matter what you do. Usually a weak acid, such as oxalic acid, is used to dissolve the mineral scale, followed by a neutralizer such as sodium carbonate. These are only needed for radiators that are really in bad condition: in fact, you probably should consult a radiator shop. Some radiator cleaners are made from sodium phosphates—the same ingredients found in some household cleaners—and don't need to be neutralized, but either type must be flushed out with water following its use. We suggest draining the radiator every other year and then flushing it out with a solution containing one-quarter cup of a detergent high in sodium phosphate for each gallon of water used.

Q. During the winter I see de-icing fluids advertised for windshield washer wells. How do they work?

A. They are similar to commercial antifreeze and also melt ice and frost on glass. You can prepare a windshield washer solution yourself by mixing one part of commerical permanent antifreeze to nine parts of a fifty-fifty mixture of alcohol and water. The antifreeze prevents the solution from evaporating too quickly. This amounts to an annual savings of at least $10.

Q. If the misture contains alcohol, won't some people think it will explode or catch on fire being so near a hot engine?

A. If the mixture is combined in the proportions we specified, there shouldn't be any concern about it being flammable—it's 49 percent water.

Q. **I have also seen sprays that claim to de-ice the windshield if it's all crusted with a layer of ice. Do these products really work? If so, how? Is it the same material as in the windshield de-icer fluid we just talked about but in more concentrated form?**

A. These types of de-icers are often inexpensive alcohols masquerading as expensive products in concentrated form. The speed at which commercial de-icers or homemade products work depends on how thick the ice is. Unfortunately, when the ice is too thick even a de-icer will take quite a while to work. At that point a handy ice scraper is the next best product to remove the ice. Never use hot water to melt the ice on your windshield. Glass expands when heated and contracts when cooled. If this is done too quickly, the windshield may crack.

OTHER FLUIDS

Q. **When my car gets a maintenance check, sometimes I'm told that it's low on hydraulic brake fluid. What is this stuff?**

A. This fluid is made of high-performance polyglycols that dissipate heat and have very high viscosity. It is specially designed to transfer hydraulic force from the pedal through the master cylinder and to the brake pads, which press on the rotors to stop the car. The term DOT on the label means that the product meets the United States Department of Transportation standards.

Q. **Sometimes I'm told that my car is a little low on automatic transmission fluid. What's this pink fluid made of and what does it do?**

A. It consists of antioxidants, dispersions, antifoam agents, friction modifiers, viscosity agents, and seal conditioners. Automatic transmission fluid transfers heat while lubricating gears, bearings, and seals. Its main function is to transmit power by hydraulics. Type F (Ford) and Dextron are the two major types. Dextron can be used in any automobile with an automatic transmission, except a Ford Motor Company product. The recommended automatic transmission drain intervals differ among manufacturers, so check your owner's manual. Since all automatic transmission fluids must meet DOT standards, you might as well purchase the least expensive brand and save money.

Q. The cold weather windshield de-icer and the radiator antifreeze contain some very powerful chemicals. And now we've added motor oil, break fluid, and transmission fluid. I'm getting very worried about the affect that all of these chemicals could have on the environment. I'm releasing antifreeze into the environment every time I wash my windshield, and with all the millions of cars on the road, we must be leaking a lot of damaging chemicals every day. I know of several people who maintain their own cars. Where do all those fluids go? Should we be worried?

A. Most of the polyglycols used in antifreeze products are degraded into harmless components by the sun and by naturally occurring bacteria. Cars emit far more toxic waste from incomplete combustion of gas as a result of improperly tuned engines than would ever be emitted by most automobile fluids, except for engine oil. Engine oil does not degrade very quickly and should be properly disposed of. We will discuss this further in chapter 9.

BATTERIES

Q. My neighbor recommends using carbonated soft drinks to clean corroded battery terminals. Is he kidding?

A. Corroded battery terminals are best cleaned by scraping them with a metal wire brush. However, carbonated soft drinks do contain phosphoric acid which dissolves the metal oxides (corrosives) that build up around the connectors. The soft drink solution should only be considered when a metal scourer isn't available. Excess carbonated beverage should always be washed off. Be careful not to short the terminals with any water—*your battery could explode.*

Q. I don't mean to distract you from your discussion of batteries, but since we're on the subject of carbonated soft drinks and their uses, could you clear up another question? This same neighbor has an older car with chrome bumpers and trim. He tells me that the same soft drink can be used to clean those surfaces. Is he pulling my leg?

A. Dilute acids (phosphoric acid in the case of your neighbor's soft drink) are often very good at removing surface oxides on metals and the dirt that they trap. Vinegar as well as lemon juice contain acids and may also be effectively used. This step is usually followed by rinsing the surface with water to prevent further oxidation (corrosion) of the metals.

Q. I know that the battery provides the electrical charge for my car, but what does this have to do with chemicals?

A. The 12 volt automobile battery consists of six cells wired in a series—that is, one after another. Each cell has two electrodes that conduct the electricity. These batteries are recharged by the alternator when your car is running. The weight of automobile and truck batteries results from the presence of lead plates and corrosive sulfuric acid. Simply stated, batteries are devices that convert chemical energy (energy found within all chemicals) into electrical energy. As a battery is discharged, lead is converted (oxidized) to form lead sulfate. Sulfuric acid is used to produce the sulfate.

Sulfuric acid is used up as car batteries are discharged. Therefore, measuring the density (specific gravity) of the acid contained in the battery will determine the state of charge. *Remember, sulfuric acid is a strong acid. Be careful when handling batteries.*

Water is used up as batteries are charged and discharged. Distilled water should be used to replace any water lost. Tap water works almost as well in a pinch.

Q. If batteries "use up" sulfuric acid, then do we have to replace the acid? If we only replace the water (distilled or otherwise), where does the sulfuric acid come from that reacts with the lead?

A. The sulfuric acid used in most car batteries is very concentrated, so much so that it will burn if it makes contact with your skin. The level of sulfuric acid found in conventional batteries is usually sufficient throughout the life time of your battery. When the water level drops in the battery, replacing the water is all that is necessary. In the United States we can't buy such concentrated sulfuric acid over the counter, but service station mechanics have sulfuric acid that they can add to the failing cells in your battery. Testing the specific gravity (density) will help the mechanic determine the faulty cell(s). The specific gravity will be too low in a faulty cell.

Q. Aren't there batteries now that don't require water?

A. "Waterless" batteries are typically of two types. One type consists of a gel that can conduct electricity. The other type is a sealed unit that prevents water loss by evaporation. These batteries reduce operator maintenance but the respective shelf life of each is not significantly extended.

Q. Why does my car fail or hesitate to start on extremely cold days?

A. If your battery is in reasonably good shape and your car is mechanically sound, the problem with cold weather is not your battery. Cold temperatures turn your motor oil into a thick syrup. (The cold raises the viscosity of your engine's oil.) This in turn makes your battery work harder to supply enough energy to turn the motor over. In this environment, a battery with higher cranking amps might be useful.

    In colder climates, people who can't keep their cars in a garage have various methods to help get their vehicles started. One interesting device is somewhat like an electric blanket. It consists of a magnetized pad that can be placed on the bottom of your oil pan. It is then plugged into an outlet. Warming the car's oil decreases its viscosity, thereby reducing the energy required to start the car on cold days. *Remember, this type of pad must be removed after the car is started.*

Q. What is meant by cranking amps?

A. The key to purchasing a car battery is in the term *cranking amps*. While the term *volt,* as in a "12-volt battery," is a measure of the amount of charge a battery can supply, the word *amp* (from *ampere*) is a measure of flowing charge. Simply put, an amp describes the amount of charge flowing per second through the electrical circuit. Most car manufacturers will tell you what cranking amps are required for your vehicle. More energy (higher cranking amps) are usually required for larger vehicles and for vehicles that operate in colder weather.

Q. Are other types of batteries similar to car batteries?

A. In part, all batteries store chemical energy. Another common battery is the *dry cell* battery. As the name implies, there is little or no moisture contained in it. This type of battery consists of zinc, graphite, ammonium chloride, zinc chloride, and magnesium dioxide. Dry cell batteries are inexpensive but they cannot be properly recharged, and they do not last very long.

Alkaline batteries are very similar to the dry cell type in that they contain many of the same chemicals. However, potassium hydroxide, a strong, caustic alkaline is one of the main components (hence the name). These batteries have a significantly longer life than conventional dry cell batteries, but are much more expensive. Again, these batteries cannot be recharged. They are often used in equipment that requires power for long periods.

Some of the earliest batteries contained mercury. The *mercury* battery is very similar to the alkaline battery. The cell reactions are identical. However, mercury is toxic, and disposing of them in the trash can is environmentally unsound. Disposable batteries for household use no longer contain mercury. Consumer disposal of batteries resulted in many landfills being contaminated with mercury. All compounds of mercury are poisonous. For example, mercury chloride is water soluble and used in rat poisons and insecticides.

Lithium batteries are becoming increasingly popular. They are very lightweight and have high energy output. They are made of the very reactive metal lithium and an exotic compound called sulfuryl chloride. Lithium batteries revolutionized the introduction of pacemakers. Scientists worked for many years to develop a battery that would have a long shelf life, a high cranking power, and be small enough to implant into the harsh environment of the human body. Scientists tried everything from nuclear batteries to improved types of mercury models but with little success— at least until they happened on to lithium.

Nickel–Cadmium batteries (Nicads) are another very popular battery. They, too, are lightweight and give a constant voltage for long periods of time. These are very popular in cordless devices such as watches, video camcorders, and portable radios. They can be recharged, but they have what is called "memory." After they are discharged to a particular level they can't be recharged fully. As time passes and multiple recharges are performed the batteries tend to last for shorter and shorter durations. Generally, it is recommended that the batteries be completely discharged before recharging occurs: this prolongs their life.

CHARACTERISTICS OF SOME BATTERIES

Type	Operating Voltage*	Misc.
Dry Cell	0.9–1.4	a, f
Nickel–Cadmium	1.1–1.3	b, c, d, e, f
Lead (automobile)	1.29–2.05	b, c
Mercury	1.30	a, b, c, d, e, f
Alkaline	0.9–1.2	a, b, e, f
Lithium	3.4	a, b, d, e

a = not rechargeable
b = long operating life
c = unsafe for the environment
d = expensive
e = lightweight
f = safe to operate

---

*voltage per cell in battery

Q. Is it true that Epsom salts (magnesium sulfate) can revitalize an old car battery?

A. There is no real evidence that this is true. Most of the evidence is anecdotal and dangerous. What may help to resuscitate a battery with a shorted cell is to empty out the electrolyte, flush the battery with water, and replace with fresh acid. This is dangerous and not suggested for nonprofessionals.

How to Care for Your Car Battery

1. Periodically check the fluid level in the battery if it is an unsealed one. Replace water lost with distilled water if possible. Tap water is usable if distilled is not available. (Tap water contains too many dissolved minerals and might reduce the efficiency of your battery.)

2. Keep the terminals tightly clamped onto the connector posts.

3. Check the alternator belt frequently. A loose belt might shorten the life of your battery.

4. Never allow the battery to completely discharge. Besides not being able to start your car, it may destroy the battery. A trickle charger is very inexpensive and often a wise purchase. These chargers restore the battery's chemical energy by using household electricity (electric energy).

5. Be sure that metal objects, such as tools, are not placed across the two battery terminals. Not only do you run the risk of ruining your battery, it could explode. Hydrogen gas is produced during the use of a car battery. It is very flammable. Placing metal tools across the terminals could cause a spark that would ignite the hydrogen gas.

6. Do not smoke around car batteries. Again, hydrogen gas is formed during their use. Smoking might put you in the next county.

7. Clean and tighten battery terminals regularly. Clean your terminals with a wire brush and wash corrosive deposits off with a tablespoon of baking soda and a little water. Greasing the terminals with a little petroleum jelly will prevent corrosion.

PROTECTING YOUR CAR'S FINISH

Q. Speaking of corrosion, I live in a colder climate and during the winter I see cars on the road with this brown stuff brushed on their chrome bumpers. Is this some product to prevent the pitting of chrome from road salt?

A. Salt and sand are applied to roads during colder months to melt snow and ice and to provide traction for automobiles. Road salt corrodes the metals used in auto manufacturing. To reduce corrosion a coating may be applied to protect chrome bumpers from contact with salt. The coating is generally a very viscous oil that prevents contact of salt with the metal. With few if any cars being produced with chrome trim, the need for such protective materials—for chrome at least—is significantly reduced.

Q. Why does road salt melt ice and snow? And why does it corrode automotive paint finishes?

A. The freezing point of water lowers as impurities are added. When salt is added as a de-icer the salt crystals start dissolving into the ice. Salt is very soluble even in cold water. As the salt is added the freezing point of the water lowers and more of the ice melts. In extremely cold climates salt is no longer of use since it is unable to melt the very cold ice. So much salt would have to be added that it would prove to be too costly and impractical to apply.

   Automobile paint finishes provide a barrier to the salt and thereby prevent corrosion. But small nicks and dents can expose the underlying metal, and air oxidation of the iron in the steel creates rust (iron oxide). Rust in contact with your car's metal actually creates a very simple battery in the presence of salt. Rusting continues underneath the paint and spreads along the car's surface.

Q. Very often on the TV there will be advertisements for car-care products. Waxes are a big item. Is there really any difference between the various kinds of wax on the market?

A. Car-care products are heavily advertised on TV. To answer your question directly—no, there are few important differences between brands of car wax products. For companies to survive, advertisers lure you to their product with gimmicks. In reality, car waxes are very similar.

Waxes add a protective coat to the painted surfaces of automobiles to add luster, provide a barrier against corrosion by salt and rusting by air and water where the paint has been damaged. Waxes are degraded by exposure to sunlight (UV radiation) and more frequent applications may be needed in warmer climates. We have used many of the available products over the years without noticing many differences. The liquid waxes are applied very easily but there is a lot of waste. We tend to overapply and get more of the wax on the polishing rag than on the car. Paste waxes require a little more work to apply and don't appear to provide any added visual benefit, although a thicker coating may be applied.

Q. Is there any difference between a car wax and a car polish?

A. Polishes should restore the luster to a good wax finish. Polishes accomplish this by removing dirt trapped in the top layer of wax as well as restoring smoothness to the finish. A high-gloss finish is very smooth. Over time your automobile's wax finish becomes rough and dull as it is exposed to dirt and debris, rain, sunlight, and heat. Car polishes don't provide any added protective benefit beyond that of a good car wax.

Q. During one of those infomercials, I saw a car finish product that was claimed to be so strong and durable that lighter fluid could be poured on the hood and lit yet all the while the finish remained untouched. What kind of product can do that?

A. Most products can withstand high temperatures for a short period of time. A hot car engine or the sun causes enough heat on the hood of a car to fry an egg. Most waxes are designed to withstand such heat. What the advertisers don't tell you is that the fire you see is on the surface of the lighter fluid and not in direct contact with your automobile's finish. As the lighter fluid between the flames and the car evaporates and quickly burns, the flames go out. Lighter fluid boils at a much lower temperature than water. As long as there is fluid between the fire and the car the likelihood of damage to the car's finish is minimal. *We caution you not to duplicate this stunt on the surface of your car, or on any other surface for that matter.*

Q. Sometimes in the summer my car will get specks of tar on it from the road. What can I use to remove it?

A. Commercial tar removal products are expensive. Check the ingredients label on a brand name product and you will find that the same type of chemicals are also found in oil-based paint thinners. These products will remove some of the wax finish as well and leave the surface appearing dull. The wax finish should be replaced to prevent corrosion. *Caution: Paint thinner is highly flammable. Dispose of all applicator materials properly. Also, paint thinner will dry out your skin. Use gloves when applying it to the surface of your car.*

Q. I took my car into the shop to have some bodywork done and was told that there are all sorts of paint types that are used on cars: enamel, acrylic, lacquer. It all looks red to me. On what basis would I choose from among them?

A. We will be discussing these types when "paints" are focused upon in the next chapter.

Q. What is in the body filler materials that auto body repair people use? I've heard it called "plastic" or Black Magic.

A. There are various body repair materials available to the consumer. These products contain plastic epoxy resins, fillers for strength, and pigments. The plastic epoxy resin-type of filler is designed for strength, durability, adhesion to the body of the car, and ability to be sanded smooth. Professional auto body shops use high-speed sanders to smooth out the filled surface. Several passes with the sander are usually required as well as sandpapers with various degrees of coarseness. Once painted it is very difficult to tell where the repair has occurred. Although these materials are very good at patching dents, dings, and rust spots, they are not as flexible as the thin metals used for car doors. The filled epoxies tend to crack instead of bend.

PROTECTING YOUR CAR'S INTERIOR

Q. Are the upholstery cleaners for car interiors the same as those for living room furniture?

A. Yes. Cloth interiors should be treated as you would cloth-covered furniture. Oils added to plastic and leather are gradually removed by heat. It is recommended that during cleaning you restore these oils. Furniture polishes will help maintain the luster of leather and plastic. The product known as Armor All® puts oils back into leather and plastics and slows the aging process.

Q. What about products for cleaning the carpets of auto interiors? Will household carpet cleaners work just as well?

A. Household carpet cleaners are fine for removing dirt and debris trapped in the fibers of the carpet. Even for the most careful car owner tar and grease will eventually build up. Household cleaners are not designed to remove tar and may not be strong enough for grease. Solvents such as some paint thinners containing toluene may help remove some of the grease and tar. *Remember, safety must come first. Solvent-based paint thinners are very flammable. Be very careful.* Yearly carpet degreasing will help to keep your carpets presentable. Always check for color fastness of the carpet by testing degreasers and tar removers on a small hidden spot of your car's carpet.

Q. I see all sorts of products for cleaning vinyl upholstery and interiors (dashboards, consoles, and the like). Are they all basically the same?

A. Yes. Most all-purpose household cleaners will work to remove dirt and dust. However, heat and sunlight also remove oils (called plasticizers) from plastics and leather. Some of the commercial automobile cleaners replace the plasticizers, thereby keeping the plastic supple and preventing cracking. By replacing the oils in plastics and leather their shine is restored. A light coating of mineral oil rubbed on with a cotton cloth will help replace the faded shine of plastic components in your car. Don't use too much, a little goes a long way. You don't want the plastic to feel greasy.

9

In and Around the Garage

Traditionally the garage has been the storage place for many types of chemicals, especially since it is where numerous chemical products are used. Here we find house paints (interior and exterior), paint removers, adhesives, metals, cement and concrete, thinners, cleaners, and the like. The garage is also where we may first encounter the need to dispose of household chemicals.

PAINTS AND PAINT REMOVERS

Paints are comprised of three basic components: (1) a polymeric binder (what is called the vehicle) that reacts with air to form larger particles; (2) pigment, which supplies the desired color and gives the paint the ability to hide a previous color; and (3) a volatile solvent that evaporates. The solvents are usually petroleum distillates, or hydrocarbons. In oil-based paints, linseed oil is generally employed as the binder. The pigment can be titanium dioxide (white pigment with good covering power), carbon (black), chrome orange (lead chromate, which is actually yellow to orange as seen on many school buses), brown or red iron oxides, or organic dyes of various colors. Years ago, white lead was used as a pigment in oil-based paints, but has been banned for household use because it is extremely toxic. Acute lead poisoning of children, from the ingestion of paint chips, is the primary cause for lead-based paint being pulled from the market.

Water-based paints use a synthetic polymer with rubbery properties as the binder. They are called *latex* paints. The synthetic polymers in latex paints are formed into an emulsion with water. An emulsion is typically tiny droplets of water surrounded by an oil (or vice versa), like the protein and oil emulsion found in mayonnaise.

Early latex paints were made from styrene and butadiene polymers and water. Soap was added to keep the emulsion stable (so it didn't separate). After the water solvent evaporates, the styrene/butadiene polymer reacts with air and forms an insoluble coating that traps the pigment.

Acrylic or *acrylic latex* paints are about one-third more expensive but are washable and much more resistant to damage from sunlight. *Teflon®* paints are very popular because of their great stability in heat. In the production of Teflon® paint, fluorine is substituted for the hydrogen atoms found on the organic structure of the polymer. Some metals covered with this type of paint carry a twenty-year guarantee against corrosion.

Q. What is lacquer?

A. Most lacquers are made from synthetic polymers. Lacquer is simply a vehicle and plastic without dyes or pigments. Originally, lacquer was produced from the excretion of an organic wax-like material produced from Lac bugs. The color depended on how well the lacquer was separated from the Lac bugs and the environment in which the Lac bugs had been raised. Natural lacquer ranges from yellow to deep orange-red in color. Synthetic lacquers are now the most common form of lacquer. These man-made lacquers are usually made from nitrocellulose or cellulose acetate. Solvents for lacquers are typically alcohol, benzene, and toluene.

Q. But lacquer paints contain color. How could they not have dye or pigments?

A. The term "paint" simply refers to a protective coating containing pigments. Synthetic lacquers are colorless to off-yellow in appearance. When organic dyes are added, stains are produced. The dyes are soluble in the lacquer and a clear coating is produced. Pigments are insoluble in the lacquer and are therefore used for their ability to hide or cover other colored surfaces. When pigments are added to lacquer we have a lacquer paint.

Q. I thought that pigments and dyes are the same thing?

A. Although both are used to color or add tint to surfaces, pigments are insoluble in the vehicle used. Dyes, on the other hand, dissolve in the vehicle. Pigments are used to mask or hide a surface while dyes are used to color a surface.

Q. What is the difference between alkyd and latex paints?

A. Latex paints are heavy, viscous polymers suspended in water. They are named after the natural juices of rubber and dandelion plants. As the water solvent evaporates, they leave the polymer coating on the surface. Alkyd paints "cure" (polymerize) after the solvent evaporates.

Q. What paints are good for outdoor use?

A. Paints to be used outdoors must withstand the harsh environmental changes not usually found inside. Paints that don't chalk are preferred for outdoor use. Oil-based and water-based acrylic paints form a hard coating impervious to water and air. Outdoor coatings usually contain compounds that are resistant to ultraviolet light (from the sun), which tends to degrade polymers. Better grades of paints typically have a higher percentage of titanium dioxide or pigment. Pigments are insoluble, inorganic compounds: usually the higher percentage of pigment the better the hiding power of the paint. Aluminum oxide is another commonly used white pigment. Although this pigment is durable, its hiding power is not as good as titanium dioxide.

Q. What about paints for indoor use?

A. Most washable paints are appropriate for indoor use. Whether you choose sheen, matte, or gloss is just a matter of personal taste. A high-gloss finish reflects light, whereas matte finishes contain chemicals that diffuse light to make the surface appear dull. Most paint brands will work fairly well. It seems that the biggest difference between paints is the amount of pigment used. The more pigment used in the paint formulation the better the hiding power.

Q. What is waterproof paint?

A. Nearly all washable paint is waterproof. The polymeric binders repel water and protect surfaces. Perhaps you are thinking of marine paint. These hard, polymeric coatings resist salt water, wind shear, severe impact, biological attack, and many other conditions.

Q. What is a primer?

A. Primers are colorless to white in color and are used to increase the adhesion of paint to surfaces. Undercoats (paint-like products put on before the desired paint color is applied in order to mask the surface and allow the paint to adhere better) are colored primers. Primers can add corrosion resistance to metal surfaces if they contain metals such as manganese phosphate or zinc phosphate. Primers are especially useful for surfaces that may be dented. Primer is a paint or a lacquer intended as a first coat on a surface.

    Paints do not stick well to all the surfaces we want to paint. A primer coat can be applied that sticks well to the surface to be painted, as a middle coat. This type of primer anchors the paint to the surface. Primers contain materials that adhere well to the surface *and* to paints.

Q. Why do paints stick to surfaces?

A. Most paints are carbon-based polymers being applied to surfaces such as wood, which are also carbon based. Polymers are attracted to surfaces like wood.

    Metals are a different story. Plastic doesn't like to stick to metals. Most iron-based metals, such as steel, and aluminum-based metals have very thin layers of oxygen on their surfaces as an oxide coating (rust, if you will). This thin oxide layer reacts with certain unsaturated molecules found in some paints. When this happens, the paint won't adhere to the surface. In order to apply paints to metals, a primer is generally used that chemically reacts or interacts with the surface oxides on metals. The primer contains compounds with two parts, one part reacts with the metal and the other part binds to the paint.

Q. What is lucite paint?

A. It is a polymer of methyl methacrylate and it is transparent. Lucite can be further polymerized with a surfactant and is the base for acrylic paints. These paints don't absorb ultraviolet light and therefore don't degrade and lose their color.

Q. What is whitewash?

A. The whitewash that most people think of is a very simple paint product made from milk, egg whites, and calcium carbonate. The proteins found in milk and egg whites serve as the binding element and calcium chloride serves as the pigment. It is a rather poor paint that chalks easily. The first paint formulation patented in the United States was a type of whitewash.

Q. How do paint removers work?

A. Remember that paints typically contain a plastic (either a natural resin or a synthetic polymer) and pigment. Since paint polymers are generally organic, it seems natural to use organic solvents to help remove paints. Mixtures of simple organic solvents such as methanol, turpentine, and petroleum distillates are found in most paint removers. These solvents swell the polymers used in the paint formulas (it makes them curdle up on the painted surface) so they can be scraped off. Paint resins undergo a several-stage process of joining the resins together, which makes them fairly insoluble. Therefore, most dried paints can only be swollen with solvents. Paint is much easier to apply than to remove. *Most paint-removing solvents are flammable and toxic. Several of them produce the narcotic effect of drowsiness and should only be used in well-ventilated areas. Read the cautions and warnings on the product labels and follow their instructions for maximum safety.*

Other types of paint-removing processes are quite complicated and should only be performed by qualified technicians. One process involves heating the paint with a blow torch. Such a method is sometimes used for plastics, which do not always hold up well in the presence of heat. A second method, used to remove paint from metal surfaces, involves sand blasting, which is nothing more than a high-powdered technique of chipping away at the paint.

Q. What is a polyurethane furniture finish?

A. Polyurethane is a way to form a very hard, transparent coating on furniture. It is formed by the polymerization of urethane, a very reactive compound that, when under proper conditions, will react with itself to form long chains of polyurethane plastic. It is used in medical supplies; in clothing (Spandex®); and, when mixed with air, it can form hard foams. Polyurethane coating is easily washed and provides a very water-resistant and stain-resistant surface.

Q. What is the difference between varnish and shellac?

A. Shellac was originally a polymer obtained from an excretion made by Lac bugs (see our discussion of Lacquer). Today, shellac is made from nitrocellulose. Hence, varnish and shellac are the same. Some true shellac may still be purchased. It is not any better than most varnishes; however, it may be useful in restoring antiques with a natural finish.

Q. How can I clean my paint brushes?

A. If you are using a water-based paint, try hot, soapy water first and then a solution of sodium phosphate (Spic 'n' Span® or something similar). Oil-based paints must be cleaned with mineral spirits or toluene. Alcohol simply doesn't work! Save money by purchasing the mineral spirits in generic form. Ask for mineral spirits and not some name brand.

Q. What is thinner?

A. Paint thinners are usually volatile (easily vaporized) solvents such as hydrocarbons that are added to facilitate the application of oil-based acrylic and enamel paints. Remember our earlier warnings about how flammable thinner is and that it can damage your skin (see p. 206).

PLASTIC

Plastics are made from small molecules called monomers, which are used to produce extremely large molecules (sometimes referred to as macromolecules). The very large molecules are also called polymers. Plastic is a very pliable substance that can be molded into many shapes and can assume many forms: packaging, wrapping, bottles, containers, textiles, plumbing and building supplies, paints, furniture, flooring, adhesives, glues, medical supplies, pens, razors, toothbrushes, hair sprays, trash bags, and a host of other items. Two billion dollars is spent annually in the United States on plastics; this is but three percent of the total value of all goods and services.

With our tremendous use of plastic, how do we dispose of it? Seven percent of the total weight of municipal waste is plastic. Eighty percent of the plastic ends up in land fills. So what can be done to dispose of plastics? Incineration is very expensive and produces hazardous wastes which are toxic or irritating. Recycling would be a logical choice but only 1 percent of all plastic is currently recycled. Some people think that biodegradable (decomposable) plastics are the answer. Frankly, we know without any question that biodegradable plastics are useless. If exposed to oxygen they do degrade but in landfills they are so covered with debris that oxygen is virtually absent. Biodegradable plastics are a marketing ploy by petrochemical companies. So at this point you may think using paper bags will help the environment. Trees *are* a renewable resource but plastic compacts to 0.1 percent of its original size.

The advantages of plastic versus paper packing (or vice versa) still stir debate among environmentalists and the general public. Plastic is not nearly as biodegradable as paper. In fact, it is possible that plastic containers may last as long as 468 years in water. However, today's landfills consist mostly of unreacted paper products (36 percent) while plastic only accounts for 7 percent. A major problem now is the inability of paper to degrade as quickly as possible in landfills. The biodegradation (rotting) of paper requires oxygen, water, and some sunlight or heat. This combination of conditions seldom occurs in most landfills. (In fact, completely intact books and paper containers from eighty years ago are still found in landfills.) Intelligent landfill management, especially pumping in water and air, are the exception now. We believe the scarcity of landfill sites in the future will demand efficient utilization of all landfills and an increase in use and concern for the safety of alternate methods, such as methane gas recovery, burning and recovery of chemicals, at least a sixfold increase in the recycling of materials (similar to Japan's effort today), and other available techniques that are not now used due to the closed "mindset" of government and industry. In the interim, we believe the extreme ease and efficiency in compaction of plastics (99.9 percent) should dictate their use in place of paper for the near future.

Q. Are there any natural polymers?

A. Christopher Columbus found Native Americans playing with a natural polymer, a light cream or amber vegetable gum. Later the Europeans called it rubber. Raw rubber comes from the rubber tree and has been used for years in the manufacture of chewing gum. Some other examples of natural polymers include: DNA, silk, silicates, asbestos, gutta-percha (used in golfballs), erasers, and Buna rubber (water hoses).

Q. What is vulcanized rubber?

A. It was produced accidentally by Charles Goodyear in 1839. He dropped a mixture of crude rubber and sulfur on a stove. The new product was stronger and more resistant than raw rubber and was eventually used in tires. The word "vulcanize" was derived from Vulcan, the Roman god of fire. If vulcanization is carried too far, ebonite or vulcanite is formed, both of which are extremely hard and chemically resistant.

Q. What is vinyl plastic?

A. Conceptually, the word "vinyl" conjures up the thought of a cheap, tough, flexible, yet smooth and shiny substitute for leather. Actually, chemists refer to vinyl as a *thermoplastic,* a material that changes its structure when heated. Polyvinyl chloride (PVC), vinyl acetate, acrylonitrile, vinylidene chloride, tetrafluoroethylene, and methylacrylate are all forms of vinyl. Further polymerization of vinyl acetate yields polyvinyl acetate, which is used in shatterproof or safety glass. This same polyvinyl acetate is used to replace chicle (a rubbery substance from the sapodilla tree) in making chewing gums. If acrylonitrile is polymerized further, the product is polyacrylonitrile, which is commonly called Orlon®, Acrilan®, and Creslan®. These are employed in the manufacture of synthetic fabrics (e.g., the now well-known polyester).

Q. Why are some plastics very soft and pliable while others are extremely hard, such as the materials that safety hats or toy tricycles are made of?

A. The really durable plastics are polycarbonates. They are tough, hard plastics used to replace glass because of their transparency and shock resistance. Babies' bottles, plastic windows, display signs, the dials for rotary telephones, fireman's masks, motorcycle helmets, snowmobile bodies, binocular lenses, and eyeglass lenses are good examples. There have even been some fascinating break-throughs in the use of polycarbonates: an automobile engine with polycarbonate pistons and block seems to out perform conventional metal engines.

Pliable plastics such as those found in hoses, surgeon's gloves, food wraps, foams, and many others are prepared by decreasing the amount of bonding (recall that bonds are the forces that hold compounds together) which increases their flexibility. Let's use the carbon compounds of diamonds and graphite as examples. Both consist of 100 percent carbon, yet their hardness is quite different. This difference is due to the amount of bonding between the carbon atoms. In rather soft graphite, the carbon atoms are bonded together in sheets with no attraction between each sheet (that's why your carbon pencil wears out), but in a diamond each sheet of atoms is also bonded to each other sheet.

Q. What is polystyrene?

A. Polystyrene is an inexpensive, rigid plastic used for sturdy furniture, tables, and clear drinking glasses. When a gas is passed through liquid polystyrene, bubbly styrofoam is the product. Styrofoam forms are often used for thermal shock absorbers, egg cartons, disposable cups, and the infamous white packing pebbles.

Have you ever noticed that light fixture covers made of polystyrene turn yellow over time? This is because polystyrene degrades and absorbs this color. Ultraviolet radiation has enough energy to break apart and form radicals that degrade the polystyrene. Antioxidants are therefore mixed with the polystyrene to absorb the ultraviolet radiation (a sunscreen for plastics) and minimize the rate at which plastic degrades. Clear polystyrene products sparkle due to the refraction of light, and most products made with this plastic give a metallic ring when hit (e.g., milk jugs).

Q. Recently I had a water sprinkler installed in my lawn. What was the white plastic tubing made of?

A. Vinyl chloride when polymerized produces the fairly inert plastic polyvinylchloride (PVC). PVC is often used for water lines due to its excellent manufacturing properties and stability. Unfortunately, vinyl chloride is a carcinogenic gas, so it is not the material of choice when preparing PVC. Luckily, polyvinylchloride can also be made from polyethylene. The product, known as poly-vinylidene chloride, is best known as Saran® and is used in automobile seat covers. Unfortunately, when polymers containing chlorine burn they emit toxic and corrosive hydrochloric acid fumes.

Q. Oh, so is this the basic chemical from which plastic wrap is derived? Are plastic shopping bags (like the ones I get in the supermarket) and dry cleaning bags made from this same material?

A. Plastic bags are made from a variety of polymers such as polystyrene, Saran®, and polyethylene. The very thin, clear garment bags from dry cleaners are generally made from polyethylene. Polyethylene is very inexpensive but hard to color. Packaging manufacturers often use a variety of polymers such as polystyrene, polyvinyl chloride, and polyvinylidene chloride depending on their respective cost and the strength required for the item being manufactured.

Q. Is the Formica® used in making counter tops also a form of plastic?

A. Formica® is also known as Laminex®. When paper or cloth is impregnated with plastic and the sheets are then pressed and allowed to harden in an oven, the product is called Formica®.

USES OF PLASTICS

Source	Product	Use
Ethylene	Polyethylene	milk cartons, wire insulation, bread wrappers, toys, films, tubing, bottles
Vinyl chloride	Polyvinyl chloride	garden hoses, surgeons' gloves, raincoats, pool liners, shower curtains, credit cards, pipes, films, adhesives
Propylene	Polypropylene	similar to polyethylene
Vinyl acetate	Polyvinyl acetate	latex paints, adhesives
Vinylidene chloride	Polyvinylidene	freezer bags, clingy food wraps
Tetrafluoroethylene	Polychloride tetra-flouroethylene (PTFE)	nonstick pans, bearings, gaskets, insulation, chemically resistant films, raincoats
Styrene	Polystyrene	foams, molded objects, toys, electrical insulation, synthetic rubber, combs, bowls, appliance parts, packaging
Methyl methacrylate	Polymethyl methacrylate (PMMA)	safety glass, Plexiglass®, Lucite®
Acrylonitrile	Polyacryonitrile	Orlon®, textiles, fibers for rugs, high-impact plastics
Divinyl	Buna rubber	tires and hoses

ADHESIVES

Q. Is there a superior adhesive?

A. There are all kinds of adhesives formulated for every possible use. White glues are very good for cementing porous surfaces like wood. Epoxy resins form a hard and strong bond but take a while to set. They can also be irritating to the skin and their vapors are noxious. Adhesives like Superglue® bond quickly and form a firm contact to smooth surfaces. Contact cements set after the solvent evaporates and form a rather weak bond but they are convenient to use. Silicone cements form an airtight coating and can bond almost any surface. They also can tolerate very high pressure so they are used on such things as radiator hoses.

Q. I'm not sure I understand the various kinds of adhesives. Why are some glues better for one surface or for adhering one kind of object while others are not? Isn't glue just glue?

A. Glue is just glue if the pieces hold together. In reality there are many types of glue each with a different chemical composition. Adhesives attach to surfaces by a chemical interaction. Some glues (Elmer's® white glue, for example) permeate the surface of an object and then the glue hardens and joins the materials together. If this type of glue doesn't permeate the surfaces to be glued together, the bond will not be strong. Some glues form chemical bonds to the surfaces of objects. A common example of this type are cyanoacrylate glues (i.e., Superglue®).

Q. Why does Superglue® work so well?

A. Superglue® is really methyl cyanoacrylate. Cyanoacrylates react with water and alcohols. Surfaces of natural objects such as wood are made of compounds that have many alcohol groups. Superglue® forms chemical bonds with the alcohols. These new chemical bonds are what stick the pieces together. Metals as well as many other synthetic items have a layer of water and surface oxides that react with the cyanoacrylates to form strong chemical bonds.

Q. In discussions with others about the types of adhesives they use, some talk about working with epoxy. Can you tell me what kind of glue it is and what it's used for?

A. Epoxies are synthetic resins typically made from two components. One type of epoxy uses as one component a very reactive carbon-oxygen-containing compound called an oxirane, having two carbon atoms and an oxygen atom joined in a triangular configuration. Two points of the triangle are carbon atoms and the third is an oxygen atom. The term "epoxy" translates as "oxygen upon." The second component of the two-component epoxies are generally very reactive alcohols such as ethylene glycol or glycerine. These types of epoxies provide adhesion to many surfaces, are chemically resistant, stable at high temperatures, and provide insulation for electrical components. Other two-component epoxies are prepared by the reaction of unsaturated (double bond) carbon compounds with highly reactive carbon compounds that have structures similar to hydrogen peroxide. They are called organic peroxides. The term "two-component epoxy" simply means that it is made from resin and hardener.

Q. When I was a kid, we were always building models—airplanes, tanks, ships, cars, etc. Each new model would come with its own little tube of glue. Now we hear so much about the dangers of breathing the fumes from these glues. Is this really a problem? Why is the glue so harmful? Can't the manufacturers make the glue without the harmful element in it?

A. Many of the earlier glues contained a solvent for the resin used as the glue. A typical solvent is toluene. Toluene, also called toluol, is obtained from distilling coal. Toluene as well as chlorotoluene are vasodilators. These compounds expand blood vessels, are mildly toxic, as well as carcinogenic. Most of the time, model glues are not as toxic as the solvents used to make them fluid. Unfortunately, organic solvents like toluene are needed to help dissolve or soften the glues so they can be applied to the models.

PLASTER

Q. What is plaster?

A. Plaster is made from calcium sulfate and is used for such things as casts and molds. Calcium sulfate in its natural state has some water combined with it and is called gypsum. Gypsum is used for wallboards, tiles, and even a paint pigment. When preparing plaster, more than 18 percent by weight of water is added to the powdered gypsum. As the mixture dries, the crystals that form the basic chemical structure of gypsum interlock. If too little water is added, the plaster may tend to crack.

Under extreme pressure gypsum becomes even harder. This hardened material is called alabaster and is used as ornamental trim for buildings as well as carved for household decorations.

Q. Is this the same material that would be used to fix a hole or a large crack in a wall?

A. Yes. Plasters are generally mixed with other materials such as sand, glues, or plastic resins. These compounds give the plaster its texture and strength. Calcium sulfate is soluble in water and the glues or resins make a more durable product.

Q. Is there any difference between basic plaster (what you have called calcium sulfate) and "plaster of Paris"?

A. Gypsum typically has two molecules of water attached to each molecule of the calcium sulfate. Such calcined plaster is gypsum that has been heated to remove part of the water. Typically, plaster of Paris is calcined plaster having only one molecule of water for every two molecules of calcium sulfate.

Q. What is plaster board? Why isn't it as hard as objects made of plaster of Paris?

A. Plaster board is gypsum filled with about 15 percent by weight synthetic fibers. The fibers provide for a less brittle product. Plasterboards are used as fire-resistant materials for walls and ceilings. Normally the wall-boards for houses are coated on each side with special paper for further finishing.

Q. Which paints are better to use on plasters?

A. The surfaces of plasters are very porous and provide very good adhesion for paint layers. Water-based paints are often used for unfilled plasters. The porous surface of unfilled plasters soak up these water-based paints. The resins in some of the filled plasters used for wall-boards serve to attract the solvent-based paints.

Q. There is also a material called spackling paste that is widely used to fill holes and blemishes in walls and ceilings before painting. Is this a form of plaster?

A. Spackles are usually plasters filled with resins, glues, sand, and the like. Fillers provide strength to the plaster as well as a surface texture.

CEMENT AND CONCRETE

Q. What is cement? How does it differ, if at all, from what some call concrete?

A. First, let's clear up a misconception. Cement is not an organic material used in fastening materials together. Although some products use cement in their name, these are properly called glues and adhesives. Cements are used in construction for structural supports, flooring, roads, and so forth. Limestone (calcium carbonate), calcium oxide, clay, and shale are the main components of cements. Aluminum oxide (alumina), iron oxide (rust), and magnesium oxide (magnesia) are also components in cements. The color of the cement depends to a large extent on the amount of iron oxide in it and the type of sand used. As with plaster, the inorganic cement mixture absorbs water and forms a paste. Upon drying, the mixture "sets"; the material's strength is due to the crystals interlocking. Cement and concrete are very similar. We will discuss concrete shortly.

Q. What is white cement?

A. The white cements of France are generally higher in their percent of limestone and sand and lower in their percent of iron oxide. These cements are generally ground finer. The strength of the cement generally increases as the grind becomes finer (since there are many more crystaline bonds).

Q. I've noticed that some cements seem to become waterlogged very quickly and others appear to repel water. What is in the formula that repels water?

A. Finer-grained cements are more water repellent than the coarse-grained cements. However, water repellence is usually achieved with an additive or surface treatment.

Q. **I understand that cement paints are used to reduce water absorption, but isn't there a waterproof concrete that isn't coated with a paint?**

A. Waterproof concrete is made by adding mineral oil to the moistened mixture. You achieve water resistance but at a price: the time required to harden the cement increases by 50 percent and, unfortunately, its strength is slightly reduced. Water repellence is lost over time. Although mineral oil has a high boiling point, in hot weather the oil slowly evaporates.

Q. **What's the difference between cement and concrete?**

A. Concrete is usually cement to which sand, gravel, and crushed stone are added. Pure cements are expensive. Fillers such as crushed stone are inexpensive and provide strength to the cement. The volume of cement to sand and stone is typically in the ratio of 1:3:6—for every one part of cement, three parts of sand and six parts of stone are added.

Q. **Why does cement become warm when mixed with water?**

A. When water is added to the cement mixture it forms hydrates, which are molecules that have water as part of their crystalline structure. As the hydrates are formed, heat is given off and the mixture warms. Too much water makes the mixture porous and weak; too little water and the crystalline structure of the cement doesn't form completely resulting in the dried mixture being weakened.

Q. **How does concrete harden?**

A. As described above, water forms hydrates with the minerals in the concrete. However, hardening is a little more difficult to understand. In the moistened mixture the calcium, aluminum, and silicon salts interact and form new compounds called tricalcium aluminates and tricalcium silicates. This hardening process takes several days.

These inorganics form interlocking crystals that provide the cement with part of its strength. The strength of concrete is measured in terms of compression (the number of pounds it can hold per square inch) rather than tension (its ability to bend). For most structural purposes, concrete is designed to have a compressive strength of over 3,000 pounds per square inch.

Q. What is reinforced concrete?

A. Concrete tends to crack under tension. In areas where tension may be present and some flexibility is desired, concrete is reinforced with steel bars or steel mesh (e.g., buildings and roadways).

Q. Why should concrete and cement be kept wet for the first few days?

A. If the surface dries too quickly, the top becomes hard while the rest is still moist. Also, if the cement dries too quickly the crystals can't fully interlock and the material's strength is compromised. The hardening process ("curing") should continue for several days.

Q. Why does concrete crack?

A. The same process responsible for the erosion of rock is responsible for the cracking of concrete. Water is generally the culprit. Cements generally have microscopic cracks and crevices. Water soaks into these tiny openings and if it gets cold the water freezes and expands. The expansion of water as it freezes provides enough energy to cause the small crevices in the cement to widen, resulting in cracks. Concrete also changes in volume quite easily with shifts in temperature. It can expand and contract depending on weather conditions. Most concrete bridges and sidewalks have small gaps between sections to allow for the contraction and expansion as the temperature changes.

Q. What can I use to get rid of the oil stains on the cement floor of my garage?

A. Products sold for the removal of oil stains on cement floors are usually petroleum distillates. Solvent paint thinners may help for severely stained floors. Soaps and detergents will also help dissolve the oils with a little scrubbing. Here a little determination may be required. Unfortunately, uncoated cements are very porous and act like hard sponges. Oils seep into the cement and make cleaning difficult.

METALS

Q. I have purchased items made from brass, bronze, pewter, stainless steel, wrought iron, and others. What are these metals? How do they differ? How do I clean them?

A. Each of the types of metals you mention are made from a mixture of other metals—this mixture is called an *alloy*. Alloys give basic metals such as tin, copper, iron, silver, gold, and others different structural properties and their unique appearance. These need to be addressed individually. When cleaning metals always remember that many cleaners either contain abrasives to remove the surface metal or chemicals that dissolve the surface metal. Abrasives tend to scratch fine metals such as silver and gold: removing the surface metal is not desirable.

Q. What is brass?

A. There are many types of brasses, but they are mainly alloys of copper and zinc. The amount of zinc in these types of alloys is typically less than 40 percent. Copper oxidizes very quickly in the presence of moisture and oxygen. As zinc is added, the copper's resistance to corrosion increases.

   The hardness of brass is increased by *annealing,* a procedure in which hot metals are cooled very quickly by quenching in water. If allowed to cool slowly, metals form a highly organized network of crystals. As the cooling process increases, the metal's atoms can't organize into a discreet crystal pattern. As other metals are added to the brass alloy the properties significantly change. Tin increases hardness but reduces *ductility* (the ability to mold). Some obvious examples of brass objects would be door knobs and handles, door knockers, ash trays, etc.

   Often, brass is coated with a clear paint called a lacquer, which prevents corrosion. To determine if your brass is coated, lightly scratch an inconspicuous spot with a very sharp knife or razor blade. If a plastic comes off, then the object is coated brass.

Uncoated brass objects (e.g., figurines and other decorative pieces) should be cleaned with a vinegar and salt solution to remove surface discolorations. The solution should consist of two parts vinegar, one-quarter part salt, and two parts water. Soaking is generally required. However, this solution must then be quickly washed off with water prior to air drying to prevent corrosion. If the brass you buy is coated with lacquer (a nitrocellulose plastic), wiping it with a light mineral oil will also slow down surface oxidation. Abrasives remove the surface layers of brass and may be needed for severely pitted pieces.

Q. What is bronze?

A. Bronzes and brasses are nearly the same. Bronze is a type of brass, an alloy of copper and zinc often with other metals such as tin. For example, commercial bronze has about 10 percent zinc, jewelry bronze has about 13 percent zinc, and yellow bronze has about 35 percent zinc. Jewelry bronze has nearly the same color as 14-karat gold. Brass in which lead has been added is called hardware bronze. Adding lead to the bronze makes it easier to mold into usable products. Tin and manganese are often added to reduce corrosion. Bronze is often prized for the rich colors it obtains when weathered and aged. Abrasives will remove the surface oxidation of bronzes but many months to years may be required before the richness of surface colors return. Natural elements of oxygen, water, and salt will generally form green copper oxides. Sulfur and sulfur oxides produced from tobacco products and the cooking of foods will generally form surfaces rich in reddish browns.

Q. What is pewter?

A. Old pewter is an alloy of tin and lead. Originally the Romans used an alloy of about 70 percent lead. More recently the amount of lead has decreased. As the amount of lead decreases, the hardness of the metal increases and the metal lightens in color. Antimony (a brittle, bluish-white, metallic element) is often added in small amounts to make the alloy polishable. Unfortunately, antimony is not recommended for pewter designed to hold food. Antimony is poisonous by nature, and acidic foods might remove some of the antimony as well as some of the lead.

Efforts to clean pewter to a polished finish depend on the pewter alloy used. Abrasives remove the surface layers. However, a wool cloth and a little rubbing should bring the luster back. Oatmeal or wheat bran may be used as a mild abrasive if cleaning has been infrequent.

Q. What is cast iron?

A. Cast iron is an alloy of iron that contains large quantities of carbon. Under intense temperatures iron carbides are formed that result in a product having great material strength and capable of being processed into many useful items. Unfortunately, cast iron rusts very quickly.

Rust can be removed from cast iron with a wire brush. Painting the surface will generally prolong the life of cast iron as will periodic wiping with mineral oil, or vegetable oil for cast iron cooking utensils. The oil prevents oxidation.

Q. While we are talking about different metals, why are foods more likely to burn in some of my pots and pans and not in others?

A. When choosing from the variety of pots and pans available there are two basic principles to keep in mind: the thickness of the metals used and the type. Gas or electric burners supply a lot of heat to the bottom of your pots and pans. The better as well as more expensive pots and pans usually have a very thick bottom to distribute the heat evenly. Thin pans (the less expensive ones) don't distribute heat evenly, which allows some areas to get hotter, thus increasing the likelihood that foods will burn.

Aluminum, although lightweight and inexpensive to produce, is notorious for uneven heat distribution. You'll recall when we discussed chemistry in the kitchen we mentioned that aluminum is also not recommended for cooking acidic foods. Tomatoes and citrus fruits, as well as many other foods, will dissolve the surface oxides found on aluminum.

Copper is one of the best metals to cook with but should only be used when the cooking surface is coated with another metal. Copper like aluminum is mildly toxic and can be dissolved by acids found in foods such as tomatoes.

Stainless steel, although not quite as good as copper at distributing heat, is relatively inexpensive to mass produce and is not usually affected by acids found in foods. Cast iron pans are usually very thick and distribute heat evenly. However, as we've pointed out, this metal tends to rust easily. After cooking with cast iron, always lightly coat pans with a thin layer of vegetable oil to prevent rust.

Q. I know stainless steel is made from iron. Why doesn't it rust as easily as iron?

A. Stainless steel is mainly an alloy of iron and chromium. If the amount of chromium is above 12 percent, part of the chromium migrates to the surface of the metal and forms a thin chromium oxide layer, which helps protect the iron against rusting. Nickel and other metals added to the stainless steel alloys tend to form microscopic grains of the added metals. These grain boundaries increase the strength of the alloys.

Q. My son asked me to pick up some 316 stainless steel tubing for a college project he was working on. What does the 316 stand for?

A. The American Iron and Steel Institute (AISI) has standardized grades of stainless steel. Stainless steel with the number 316 is highly corrosion resistant and contains about 16 percent chromium, 10 percent nickel, 2 percent manganese, 2 percent molybdenum, and 1 percent silicon. Stainless steel used in medical instruments is generally number 304. Medical-grade stainless steel is slightly higher in chromium (18 percent) but lower in nickel (about 8 percent) than the 316 stainless steel. Because of its greater strength, 304 stainless steel is ideal for the manufacture of lightweight medical instruments.

Q. What is wrought iron?

A. Commercial wrought iron is formed by oxidizing the surface of pure melted white iron with an oxidizing flame.* The metal is cooled and then rolled into a sheet. Wrought iron usually contains other metals along with silicon and manganese to increase its resistance to corrosion and to give it greater strength.

Q. I know that pure gold is 24-karat. But what is a carat and why can't I find 24-karat gold jewelry?

A. Gold is a very chemically resistant metal that is also very soft: for example, it can be pounded into tissue-thin sheets. A gram of gold (1/454 of a pound) can be made into a six-square-foot sheet or into a wire over a mile in length. Gold jewelry is usually alloyed with copper and silver. The copper and silver provide the alloy with strength for durability and add different shadings to the gold. Jewelry gold is usually between 14 and 18 karats.

   Pure gold is 24 karats. A karat is an arbitrary unit of measure indicating the number of units of pure gold in an alloy. Pure gold is very soft; it bends and deforms easily. For these reasons, it would be impractical to use it in making jewelry. Fourteen karat gold is 14 parts gold, 8.25 parts silver, and 1.75 part copper (a total of 24 parts). Gold that is 18 karat is 18 parts gold and 6 parts silver (18 + 6 = 24).

   Gold jewelry may be cleaned by soaking it in a mild detergent and gently rubbing the surface coating. Be careful not to use this procedure with gold jewelry containing opals. Opals will begin to discolor and start to dissolve.

Q. How do I clean silver?

---

*A flame that is air-rich, fuel-lean, and burns with an intense hot blue flame having a distinctive clear interior cone is called an oxidizing flame because oxygen is added. (Remember oxidizing agents?) Yellow-orange flames occur because of incomplete oxidation from having a fuel-rich and clean-air combustion. They are appreciably cooler than oxidizing flames. A properly adjusted gas range or space heater will give a hot blue flame. Gas and all fuel space heaters that use an improper air/fuel ratio give a yellow-orange flame that is not only inefficient and a waste of fuel, but it will also produce deadly carbon monoxide gas. Blue flames produce carbon dioxide gas, which is safe.

A. Silver tarnish is generally a silver sulfide. Silver can be cleaned without much rubbing, though many silver cleaners contain abrasives and are expensive (they also remove the surface layer of silver). A home remedy for cleaning silver has been around for a hundred years or more. Heat some water in an aluminum pan and dissolve some tartaric acid (cream of tartar). A few tablespoons of the acid should be sufficient per quart of water used. The silver sulfide tarnish is removed without silver loss by dipping the silver piece into the aluminum pan. When silver touches aluminum a simple battery is created. In the presence of salt and water, electricity flows, and in this situation the silver tarnish is removed. This procedure is better for ornate patterns versus mirror finishes; it's inexpensive, and doesn't require hand polishing.

Q. Why doesn't aluminum rust?

A. Pure aluminum is an extremely malleable metal that is highly resistant to corrosion. Actually the surface contains a very thin oxide layer. The surface oxide layer is quite dense and prevents further oxidation of the metal. The strongest of the aluminum alloys is made with small amounts of magnesium. As the alloying metals increase in proportion to the aluminum, the corrosion resistance decreases. Alloys for cast aluminum products—melted aluminum that is mixed with additives and then poured into molds to be cooled—are made with a high concentration of silicon.

   Aluminum may be cleaned by using an ammonia glass cleaner and a little borax detergent. Rub a paste made from the detergent and ammonia glass cleaner on the aluminum. This should bring back the surface luster of the metal. For aluminum pots and pans, soaking in vinegar or rubbing with lemon juice followed by rinsing with water will remove surface discolorations. This process does take several hours, so soaking over night is usually recommended.

10

The Back Yard

In this section we will discuss soils, fertilizers, composting, pesticides, LD_{50}, natural insecticides, fungicides, herbicides, and the chemistry of maintaining a swimming pool. Various complex chemicals are used to protect lawns and gardens as well as for the pool. Unfortunately, most of the compounds used for these areas around the house have long chemical names. We will try not to delve too deeply into chemical nomenclature. Instead, we will present common chemical names where appropriate.

SOILS

Soil is a complex mixture of several things: organic material in various stages of decomposition, minerals, bacteria, and fungi. Regional soils have different colors, textures, and nutritional needs to support plant growth. For example, coastal soils tend to be sandy (containing silicon dioxide), whereas the clay soils of the South are dense and contain high percentages of minerals from the weathering of rocks. The red clays of the South and Southwest are rich in iron. However, the iron content of these soils is not accessible as a mineral supplement for plant growth. The black soils of the East are very rich in organic matter.

Plants in general don't require too much to sustain growth. Plants require air, minerals found in the soil, energy from the sun, and water. During photosynthesis plants use energy from the sun to convert water and carbon dioxide from air into the simple sugar known as glucose. Minerals and other elements are required as special catalysts the plants use to facilitate glucose formation. Large amounts of calcium, magnesium, nitrogen, phosphorous, potassium, and sulfur are required to form plant proteins and energy reserves. Some minerals are only required in small amounts: for example, chlorine, copper, iron, manganese, and zinc. Most minerals used by plants need to be present as water-soluble salts. Plants must be able to absorb these minerals through their root systems.

Nitrogen gas, although it makes up over 70 percent of our air, is not easily absorbed by most plants. Beans and peas do take up nitrogen but by a different route than most other plants. A bacteria near their roots converts nitrogen into a more usable form by combining it with hydrogen. Water-soluble salts of nitrogen made from ammonium ions are usually absorbed by plants to produce proteins and vitamins. These plants then provide humans and animals with a convenient source of nitrogen for protein synthesis. One of the least expensive forms of nitrogen for fertilizer is from nitrates and nitrites (commonly used as food preservatives).

Many compounds found in plants contain phosphorous in their molecular structure. Phosphates are partially used to help plants store energy. Phosphate-containing fertilizer additives are often made from calcium dihydrogen phosphate, which is water soluble and easily absorbed by plants.

Calcium and magnesium are also required for plant growth: calcium for the production of cell walls, and magnesium for the formation of chlorophyll. Few soils are deficient in magnesium, and calcium is also found in sufficient quantities in most soils. Sandy soils have difficulty holding onto many minerals: most plant minerals are water soluble and for that reason heavy rainfall can wash them out of these soils.

Potassium ions, from water-soluble potassium chloride, are also required by plants in large concentrations. Potassium is used in the formation of plant enzymes, maintaining cell structure, balancing the nutrients of sap, and is a determining factor in the strength and growth of plant stems. Plants as well as humans must maintain a strict balance between potassium and sodium ions: too much or too little of either ion creates cellular problems,* and, much like humans,

---

*plant stems can break, or the outer walls of some cells will thicken

plants must control their salt intake. Wood ash (potash or potassium hydroxide) dust, seaweed, and lime are good sources of potassium.

FERTILIZERS

Q. What minerals are present in commercial fertilizers? What do numbers such as "12-18-12" on fertilizers mean?

A. Most fertilizers provide a source of nitrogen, phosphorus, and potassium. Calcium, magnesium, and sulfur are often present but in small amounts. The three numbers listed on fertilizers are the percentages of nitrogen, phosphorus, and potassium respectively. A 12-18-12 fertilizer contains 12 percent nitrogen, 18 percent phosphorus, and 12 percent potassium. Different plants require different amounts of these three major components as well as other minerals. Fertilizers rich in phosphorous are required for fruits, and those rich in nitrogen are generally required by green plants and grasses.

Nitrogen is often in the form of nitrates. Phosphorous is usually listed as the percentage of phosphorous in diphosphorous pentoxide. Potassium is often listed as the percentage of potassium in potassium oxide (potash).

These synthetic fertilizers can present some environmental risks. For example, the number nitrogen-producing bacteria is often reduced when large quantities of fertilizers are used. Hence, more fertilizers may be required for future crops. Most soils contain a sufficient amount of iron. However, too much lime (calcium oxide) may interfere with the plants' absorption of iron.

Fertilizers leach out of the soil when it rains. The fertilizer is then carried to ponds and lakes and may promote algae growth. Phosphates from laundry detergents are the culprit of algae growth promotion and ultimately the death of many lakes, as we learned early in our discussion of the laundry room. Algae removes oxygen from the water and crowds out other aquatic plants and fish.

Boron and molybdenum are also among fertilizer ingredients. Boron is needed for calcium intake and molybdenum is required by legumes for nitrogen intake.

Q. I hear a lot about slow-releasing fertilizers that don't require as many applications. What are they? Are they worth the money?

A. Plants require water-soluble mineral supplements to replace what is removed from the soil during plant growth. Unfortunately, in areas of high rainfall these minerals are flushed from the soil. Fertilizers that release their nutrients slowly have less soluble forms of the minerals and other nutrients. Over time these products release soluble minerals as they decompose. In times of high rainfall these less soluble fertilizers are not leached as quickly as the inorganic fertilizers.

Bone and blood are slow-releasing fertilizers rich in complex phosphates. As these materials are decomposed, nutrients are added to the soil. Bone and blood fertilizers are rich sources of potassium, calcium, nitrogen, and iron. They are used for "organic gardening" and are quite expensive. Inorganic fertilizers are less expensive and just as good.

Plants remove minerals from soil. For lawns and permanent landscaping, nutrients need to be replaced periodically while at the same time maintaining the soil's pH level. (We will talk shortly about soil pH.) Nitrogen and phosphorous need to be added to create a lush green lawn. In areas of moderate to low rainfall, inorganic fertilizers are less expensive and should provide adequate nutrients. In areas of high rainfall or areas with sandy soils, slow-release fertilizers are recommended. The application of synthetic fertilizers provides the best results when added in the spring when rain can dissolve the minerals into the soil. We tend to use slow-releasing fertilizers to save time since fewer applications are generally needed. Always read labels and compare costs of fertilizers. Don't pay for a fertilizer rich in nitrogen, phosphorous, and potassium if your needs are for one richer in nitrogen.

Q. Why does my nursery recommend plant rotation for my garden?

A. During their growth, plants remove minerals and other nutrients from the soil. Different plants have different needs. For example, grasses remove a lot of nitrogen from soils. If grasses were planted year after year the nitrogen content of the soil would decrease and plant failure might arise. Other plants require more phosphorous and still others might require greater amounts of magnesium or calcium. Rotation allows for the replenishment of nutrients in soils by one plant to help the next plant.

Q. I saw my neighbor spraying what looked like a soap solution on his lawn and hedges. Is he crazy?

A. Maybe not. Phosphate detergents degrade slowly in the sun and release phosphorous into the soil. Dilute solutions of this type of detergent can also be effective as an insecticide against aphids. All that is needed for application is a drop or so of liquid phosphate detergent per gallon of water. Be forewarned: unfortunately, phosphates may also promote algae and fungus growth.

Q. I went shopping for some plant food at the grocery store. I found twenty or so different varieties. Which one should I have purchased?

A. Common household plant food should be high in nitrogen. Remember that of the three numbers listed on plant food labels, "20-10-10" for example, the first corresponds to nitrogen. When comparing pricing on household plant food, you must not only look at the ratio of nitrogen to phosphorous and potassium but also the percent and cost of these to the pound. For example, compare two types of plant food: one being a 20-10-10 fertilizer at $6.00 a pound and the other a 10-5-5 fertilizer at $4.00 a pound. First we look at the ratio of nitrogen and find that the first one is 20 percent per pound and the other is only 10 percent per pound. To apply the same amount of nitrogen we would have to add twice as much of the second fertilizer. This would effectively raise the cost of the second one from $4.00 a pound to $8.00 a pound in order to get the same amount of nitrogen. The first is more cost effective in this example.

    Let us compare a fertilizer listed as 20-10-10 at $6.00 a pound to one that is listed as a 10-10-10 fertilizer at $3.00 a pound. Here it would take twice as much of the second to get the same nitrogen as the first. Two pounds of the 10-10-10 would cost us $6.00. In the long run the second fertilizer is still a better buy, since it is less expensive. Yes, it is true that two pounds of the second fertilizer would 'cost us $6.00. This would give us the same nitrogen as one pound of the first fertilizer for $6.00.

However, each contains the same percent of phosphorous and potassium per pound. Yet we can buy two pounds of the second fertilizer for the $6.00.

Some plants—African violets, for example—need more phosphorous than other house plants. However, buying a plant food of 10-20-10 just for African violets and another for the rest of your plants may not be needed. Using one is generally acceptable, though the pH may still need to be adjusted for the optimum conditions of each plant.

Q. Why do some fertilizers require watering and others do not?

A. Mineral fertilizers containing nitrogen, phosphorous, and potassium need to be leached into the ground with water. Too much fertilizer near the roots and stems of plants destroys plant cells. This is often called *fertilizer burn.* Overfertilized lawns may start turning brown in the sun. Too much fertilizer has the same effect as insufficient watering. Too much water distributes the fertilizer further down into the soil and may then be completely leached out of the soil. Applying fertilizers in the spring is recommended because the plant roots need a light application of fertilizer for early growth. This should be followed in the summer by a high nitrogen fertilizer for stem growth. Depending on your area's climate, you might wish to fertilize in the fall as well.

Slow-releasing fertilizers are often not as harsh as inorganic fertilizers. The minerals in slow-releasing fertilizers are in the form of complex organic materials, which are released over time. Decomposition of the organic matter is required to release mineral and other food supplements gradually to plants. Be careful— some natural organic fertilizers are rich in nitrogen but in the form of ammonia. Manures, for example, may need to be mixed with other decaying plants to dilute them. Composting natural plants and mixing with manure can be a very effective fertilizer.

Q. Which is a better fertilizer, compost, or manure?

A. This is a complex question. Loose soils that are high in organic matter are generally preferred by most plants. Often, composted soils mixed with commercial fertilizers and sand produce the best mixtures for plants and gardens.

Composts are a method of speeding up the decomposition (rotting) of organic material. Moisture, microorganisms, and oxygen are usually required. Oxygen is required for the growth of microorganisms that speed the decomposition process. It is an environmentally sound procedure for producing a fertilizer rich in nutrients. Organic matter slowly releases nutrients into the soil as it decomposes. Composted materials are a form of slow-release fertilizer. Remember, the compost heap must be turned (the contents mixed about) to aerate them to assist in growth of microorganisms.

Compost heaps tend to warm up as heat escapes during decomposition. The heat generated may be high enough to ignite other organic matter. Initially, the temperature of compost heaps can rise to about 80 degrees Fahrenheit while the microbes are decomposing the organic matter. If the temperature rises much above 80 degrees, the microbes start dying off and the process slows down. As the compost heap cools, the process begins again. Cellulose from paper is a complex carbohydrate (complex sugars) and may also be composted.

Manure is very rich in nutrients. However, it is too rich in nitrogen in the form of ammonia. Manure needs to be mixed and composed with hay to reduce the strength of the manure. *Using pure manure will kill most plants.* Although inexpensive to produce, much of the cost of processed manure products is due to the expense of composting and the high cost of transportation.

Most inorganic fertilizers tend to compact soils over time. This ultimately reduces the soil's ability to absorb moisture and the ability of plants to take in nutrients from the soil. Gardens and flower beds generally perform better with loose soil. Loose soils are better aerated and tend to decompose organic matter quicker. Sand is often mixed into compact soils to loosen them.

Q. What is meant by soil pH?

A. As we have discussed earlier, pH registers the levels of acidity, in this case soil acidity. Different plants thrive in soils with specific pH levels. Some flowering bushes such as azaleas prefer slightly alkaline soils; corn and tomatoes prefer slightly acidic soils; and potatoes prefer very acidic soils. Most flower gardens and lawns need to be slightly acidic. (See page 24 for the pH scale of common acids and bases.)

Q. What compounds can I safely use to acidify my soil?

A. Gypsum (calcium sulfate) is an economical mineral source to acidify soils. Gypsum is used in plasters and wall boards. Natural gypsum from California has about 15 to 20 percent sulfur. Calcium sulfate is also cheaply converted to the more water-soluble forms of fertilizer. Ammonium salts as well as dihydrogen phosphates increase soil acidity by neutralizing alkaline components in the soil. Sulfur powder is also a very common soil additive for decreasing pH. The bacteria in soil convert sulfur into sulfuric acid.

The killing of many forests by acid rain is a prime example of overacidified soils. Oxides of sulfur are produced from the combustion of organic fuels (oil and gasoline products). Sulfur oxides react with water in the air to produce sulfuric acid.

Calcium carbonate may be added to soils that are too acidic. Carbonates react with protons as well a organic acids, and release carbon dioxide. Lime (calcium oxide) can also be used to make soils more alkaline.

Q. How can I test my soils for pH?

A. The pH level of soil can be tested quite easily. Take about four tablespoons of soil from a spot about four inches deep. Mix the soil with about two cups of distilled water and allow the soil to settle. Distilled water must be used since this type of water should be neutral (pH = 7). Any discoloration of the water is due to the presence of minerals. The water may now be tested with pH testing paper, litmus paper, or a pool pH kit.

Certain dyes change color depending upon the pH level they encounter. Testing papers are coated with these pH sensitive dyes. Litmus is a naturally occurring pH dye prepared from several varieties of lichen. Actually, fermentation of lichens by yeast produce the blue-colored pH dye. In the presence of acids the blue litmus turns red. When red litmus changes to blue the solution is alkaline. Papers used for testing pH are often available at pool supply stores. Pool pH kits are just liquid forms of other pH-sensitive dyes. If you test your soil frequently and if you happen to have a swimming pool, it would be cost effective to purchase a battery powered electrode to measure pH. (See the section of this chapter on pool chemistry.)

PESTICIDES AND HERBICIDES

In general, a pesticide is anything that repels or kills pests. This term is generic and describes a variety of products such as herbicides, insecticides, rodenticides, bactericides, fungicides, algaecides, and the like. Pesticides fall into two main groups: inorganic and organic. Ideally we would like to have a pesticide that is quick acting; nontoxic to humans, livestock, and pets; and one that breaks down into harmless chemicals and doesn't pose a long-term threat to the environment. Most products today can't meet all of these requirements.

Q. What are the common inorganic pesticides?

A. Inorganic pesticides are usually compounds containing heavy metals. The most common contain mercury, lead, arsenic, antimony, and zinc, but fluorides, sulfur borates, and polysulfides are also useful. These types of compounds are not widely used as pesticides for large areas. Heavy metal pesticides are not very specific and are highly toxic to humans and pets. Arsenic compounds, for example, are defoliants (removes leaves), insecticides, herbicides, and rodenticides (e.g., rat poison). Arsenic poisoning may cause nausa and vomiting and it may damage the liver, blood, and kidneys. Many arsenic-containing compounds are very carcinogenic. Arsenic has been recognized as a cancer-causing agent for the lungs, liver, mouth, and skin. Inorganic pesticides should not be used within easy access of children or pets.

Lead arsenate is insoluble in water and not absorbed by plants. Although it may be used as a pesticide it is usually washed away by rain and can contaminate rivers and streams as well as water supplies. Fluorides are not specific and should not be used around children and pets. Calcium arsenate, a stomach poison, and white arsenate are also useful in killing rodents.

In Texas, cockroaches are a problem. Sodium borate (Borax® or Boraxo®) is a slow-acting but very effective pesticide. It is the least expensive and most active cockroach pesticide sold today. Boric acid powder is available at supermarkets and pharmacies. It is much less expensive than other brand-name cockroach pesticides sold at garden shops. We mix a little boric acid with some bacon grease and place this in a paper cup under sinks. It is deadly for cockroaches but not very toxic to humans or pets.

Elemental sulfur is a poor insecticide but a rather effective fungicide and acaricide (mite killer). Another metal, copper, is used in a mixture called Bordeaux®, which consists of copper sulfate and lime. This mixture is also an effective fungicide. Paris Green® contains copper and arsenic, both of which are very poisonous to human beings. Bordeaux® and Paris Green® are inorganic insecticides that also destroy fungi (they are fungicides).

Q. Are there any natural insecticides?

A. Natural insecticides are all around us. Some products we see and use everyday contain natural insecticides. These are typically organic molecules. Garlic oils, oils removed from citrus fruit rinds, caffeine, and nicotene are all insecticides. Chrysanthemums also act as a barrier to insects.

Q. I've heard about this repellent effect of chrysanthemums. Does it really work?

A. Chrysanthemums have been used for thousands of years by the Chinese as an insecticide. The flowers of these plants are rich in compounds called *pyrethrums*. Natural pyrethrums are extracted from chrysanthemum flowers. Pyrethrums from plants are no more effective at killing insects than synthetic pyrethrums— and are much more expensive. A seventeen-ounce spray can of one of the top brands of ant and roach spray contains less than 1 percent by weight of pyrethrums. The rest are inert ingredients and aerosols! We end up paying more for manufacturing, packaging, and advertising and than for the actual ingredients.

Q. Are there really different types of household insecticides for different kinds of bugs, or is this just an advertising gimmick to sell more sprays?

A. Some insecticides can kill a broad spectrum of insects while others are more effective for certain species. Usually, only the insecticides that are less persistent (don't stay in the environment very long) and less toxic are used first to kill specific species. As the need arises to kill resistant insects (those which have developed immunity to other insecticides) then the more toxic chemicals are used. The indiscriminate use of powerful or "broad spectrum" pesticides when they are not needed gives rise to environmental hazards and resistant insect species (see Rachel Carson's *Silent Spring*). For an example of the use of specific rather than broad-spectrum insecticides consider naphthalene (mothballs) and diazinon. Naphthalene kills moth larva and silverfish and not much else. Diazinon kills moth larva, silverfish and cockroaches, fleas, ants, spiders and a lot more. Using diazinon just to kill silverfish is akin to using a canon to kill a bird in a tree. No bird, no tree. A sane philosophy for using insecticides is not to use stronger ones unless absolutely needed.

Q. **If citrus rinds contain insecticides, why don't they seem to affect fruit flies?**

A. Many plants and fruits can synthesize their own insecticides (pyrethrums, caffeine, nicotine, rotenone, garlic, and lemon oil). Unfortunately, nature has been unable to keep up with the genetic changes in insects, many of which have become resistant to our synthetic insecticides (e.g., medflies). As soon as we develop a new insecticide to kill the resistant mutant, another species evolves, and the tragic scenario occurs again. Another problem occurs when herbicides are used to kill weeds: the weeds become so resistant that chemical companies must develop "super herbicides" and then develop new strains of crops that can grow with the herbicide.

Q. **What about the organic insecticides?**

A. The United States uses over ten million pounds of insecticides annually. Over five hundred different organic compounds are used separately or mixed together to produce tens of thousands of insecticide formulations that are currently on the market. There are three main classes of insecticides: chlorinated hydrocarbons, carbamates, and organophosphates. Chlorinated hydrocarbons interfere with the transport of ions within and between the cells of the bugs. Organophosphates destroy nerve impulses, thus leading to paralysis. Carbamates also destroy nerve impulses.

Q. What are the benefits and limitations of these organic insecticides?

A. As with inorganic pesticides, the organic types have some limitations. Such chlorinated hydrocarbons as DDT®, Chlordane®, Lindane®, toxaphene, heptachlor, dieldrin, aldrin, aldicarb, methoxychlor, endrin, and benzene hexachloride are relatively nontoxic to humans and are low to moderately low in toxicity to animals. However, these compounds are not degraded very quickly (ten to fifteen years) into harmless compounds and tend to build up in concentration over time in the tissues of humans and other mammals. Water run off into streams and lakes carries these compounds into the food chain. Algae absorb these compounds, fish eat the algae, and then birds eat the fish. Over time the birds build up high concentrations of these chemicals in their tissues. The chemical DDT® has been banned since the early 1970s due in part to its impact on the thickness of the egg shells of birds.

Use caution with all pesticides. Lindane, an organochlorine insecticide is moderately toxic. For example, if a cow were to ingest one-tenth of a pound of Lindane®, it could be lethal. The lethal dose of Lindane® for humans is less than one scant teaspoon. This compound is a central nervous system stimulant that produces convulsions. Lindane® is even more toxic than DDT®.

Flea collars use plastics soaked in organic pesticides. The choice of pesticide is generally limited to those relatively nontoxic to humans. Plastics absorb the pesticide and slowly release them over time.

Organophosphates such as malathion, parathion, methylparathion, endothion, ethyl guthion, dimethyl dichlorovinyl phosphate (DDVP), dimethoate, and diazinon are very common nerve poison insecticides and fungicides. In high concentrations some are also very effective herbicides. Over time these compounds are readily broken down into harmless chemicals. But they are many times more toxic to humans than the chlorinated hydrocarbonds. Organophosphates should be used with caution around the home and around livestock and pets. Since these types of compounds break down in a few weeks to a few months, repeat applications are required. Other phosphate esters like Abate® and Temophos® are effective insecticides by inhibiting enzyme formation in the insects.

Carbamates are derived from carbamic acid, a nitrogen-containing organic acid. These are the types of chemicals used around the house to control lawn and garden pests. Carbamates such as Furadan® and Sevin® are relatively unselective insecticides but decompose readily (from a few days to a few weeks).

Some pesticides are actually diet pills. Antimetabolites stop the insects' desire to eat. Dimethyltirazinoacetanilide, rotenone, sulfur, and nicotine sulfate are common examples. These compounds are usually mixed in powdered form, 5 percent or less by weight, with caly limestone or sodium fluorosilicate.

Horticulturists at local nurseries can provide information on choosing pesticides for lawns and gardens and on their appropriate use. The needs of specific areas of the country will differ depending on the types of pests present, the temperature, the amount of rainfall, and local flora (plant life).

There are safer methods to reduce insect populations: lady bugs eat aphids; traps lure insects by smell, either from sugar or other nutrients; pheromones (sex attractants); and the recent introduction of sterile insects to reduce reproduction. All of these methods have limited use for specific pests. The use of biological agents is becoming increasingly important in areas like southern California for the control of some forms of fruit flies (medflies) that destroy fruit and vegetable crops. The introduction of sterile male screw worms in Texas has helped to prevent the loss of cotton crops.

In gardens many insects live on the underside of plants, away from the sun. If you have a small garden, just place a foil skirt around the base of your plants to reduce insect populations. Rodents don't seem to like the feel of the foil either.

Q. I was charged a considerable amount of money to get rid of some termites. What kind of chemicals do exterminators use?

A. Heptachlor (3-chloroclordene) was probably used. This is relatively close in structure to Chlordane.® The Environmental Protection Agency (EPA) has recalled the use of this pesticide except for injection into soil (subsurface insertion). In animals, heptachlor acts like a central nervous system stimulant accompanied by loss of appetite. Death of mammals can occur from consuming as little as 1/100 of a pound of heptachlor. Heptachlor has been replaced with other Chlordane® or dieldrin products for above-ground sprays for termites in wood flooring and framing.

Q. What are the best products for insect control around the house?

A. Most insecticide products—bombs, sprays, and powders—contain pyrethrum derivatives. When used in small quantities, these compounds are only mildly toxic to humans. But pyrethrums do take a while to kill the insects.

Sprays and bombs are generally only good as contact insecticides. In other words, the spray must actually come in contact with the insects. Areas behind walls and underneath cabinetry are hard to reach. With sprays, most of the cost of the product is in the packaging and advertising rather than in the insecticide. We suggest staying away from spray products; they are much too costly. Most pyrethrums are oils that slowly evaporate from surfaces; repeat sprayings are often required.

Powders are generally less expensive but are visible and may be unsightly around the house. Some traps and insect "motels" lure insects into them by smell; once inside, the insects can't find their way back out. (Why would anyone have something in the home that *attracts* bugs?) Other products use powders that are carried back into the nest but these are usually slow-acting insecticides. For roaches, boric acid is still probably the most cost-effective solution. Insects also crawl inside wall spaces and follow along electrical wiring between apartments. Other than removing sources of food, powders placed in obscure locations where the insects crawl is the least expensive method to remove pests where they breed. By placing some powder near or inside openings you may also help prevent infestation from outdoors.

Fly papers attract insects by smell. Although these are reasonably inexpensive to use, they are a mess to handle, not the most attractive decoration, and they are utterly useless outdoors. Local flies may be quickly trapped but others will be attracted by the smell. Liquid fly traps are nothing more than a bottle or bag containing sugar and water. Flies are attracted by the smell, then can't find their way out. Again, these are unsightly and not very good outdoors. Glass traps might be the solution here: they allow insects to fly in, but prevent them from leaving. A glass trap with a lump of wet manure inside is placed down wind of the outdoor area to be protected. We have seen hundreds of flies caught and killed in an hour.

Ants are generally attracted by foods high in sugars such as fruit and fruit juices, toothpaste, candy, and soda so clean up spills immediately. Keeping food areas clean will generally keep ants out. Once ants arrive, they are very persistant at finding new sources of food. Powders applied around the outside of the house have some effect at keeping ants from entering. Unfortunately, rain makes frequent applications necessary. Inside the house, we have great luck with a generic ammonia glass cleaner in a spray bottle. The glass cleaner is only a contact insecticide, relatively nontoxic and inexpensive. You can spray and clean the counter top in one step. After a few applications the ant infestation often stops.

Q. My doctor tells me that I'm allergic to mites, molds, and fungus living in dust. How can I get rid of them?

A. Fleas and mites as well as molds and fungus can live off of hair and skin that we shed every day. Frequent vacuuming and the application of insecticide dusting powders will reduce house infestations. Lawns, gardens, and play areas around the house may also need to be treated to prevent tracking fleas back inside the house.

A haven for these pests is in heating and cooling duct work—places where we tend to forget to clean. In the summer the damp cool air is a great breeding ground for mold, mildew, and mites. A professional cleaning is expensive and hard to do but may be necessary if you are extremely allergic. Some limited results can be obtained with circulating some ammonia cleaner through the duct work. Place a little ammonia water or other disinfectant near the fan source. As air is drawn over the cleaner it is evaporated and carried throughout the duct work.

The least expensive and most effective insect repellent is naphthalene (moth balls). N,N-diethyl-meta-toluamide (DEET) and dimethyl phthalate (DMP) are probably the most common insect repellents sold in the United States today.

Q. I know that most pesticides are mildly to extremely toxic. Some material I have read talks about LD_{50}. What is this?

A. LD_{50} refers to how toxic the chemical is. The LD_{50} of a compound is the dose required to kill half of the animals or insects used in the toxicity testing. The smaller the LD_{50}, the more toxic the substance is. Extremely toxic substances have an LD_{50} value of less than 1 mg/kg. This means that 1 milligram of the substance is required for every kilogram weight of test animal or insect used. Substances with LD_{50} values between 1 and 50 mg/kg are highly toxic; 50 to 500 mg/kg are moderately toxic; and over 500 mg/kg are considered mildly toxic.

Exposure limits are also listed for chemicals that can be readily absorbed through the skin. The Registry of Toxic Effects of Chemical Substances produced by the National Institute for Occupational Safety and Health Administration (OSHA), a part of the United States Department of Health and Human Services, Cincinnati, Ohio, contains information on most toxic substances.

Q. What are herbicides?

A. There are over two hundred types of herbicides (defoliants) currently in use in the United States. Herbicides are often mixtures of nitrogen containing organics, and organic phosphates. Organic nitrogen compounds such as triazines kill plants by interfering with photosynthesis. Dinitro-o-cresol, 2-methyl-4-chloro-2-methyl-phenoxy-acetic acid, Pichloram, chloro-opropham, paraquat, and diquat are some common examples. Defoliants are the quickest way to kill noxious plants, and normally the safest (except for Agent Orange). We could use chemicals to poison the roots but these leave excess chemicals in the soil.

Paraquat, diquat, and disodium 3,6-endoxohexahydrophthalate are ionic organic-nitrogen compounds that start to kill once they are in contact with the leaf. These nitrogen ions are like the organic ammonium ions used in cationic surfactant laundry detergents. You'll recall from chapter 2 that laundry detergents work by destroying the surface tension of water and by part of the detergent dissolving into the dirt so it can be carried away. If the same approach is taken with leaves, the plant will wither and die. Paraquat (methyl viologen) is used extensively to wipe out crops of marijuana. It is also very toxic to people who might smoke contaminated leaves.

Aminotriazoles are also used as herbicides but are often carcinogenic to humans. Some products such as Roundup® contain glycophosphates, which act as herbicides by inhibiting the plant's ability to synthesize amino acids.

Other herbicides, referred to as systemic herbicides, are absorbed by the plant's roots and cause extensive plant growth. The plants then can't get enough nutrients to sustain themselves. Systemic herbicides simulate plant hormones or growth stimulants like indoleactic acid.

Q. What about fungicides?

A. Many of the insecticides are useful fungicides as well. Zinc compounds are often added to paints and coatings to prevent growth of fungus. Fungicides either attack the fungus directly or are systemic.* Fungicides like hexachlorophene are used to protect stored seed. We recommend that you save yourself some money around the house: use bleach or hydrogen peroxide as cleaning agents. Diluted forms of these chemicals are very effective against fungus as well as killing mildews. *BUT DO NOT MIX BLEACH AND HYDROGEN PEROXIDE TOGETHER.* Hypochlorous acid and chlorine gas can result. Both are very corrosive to the mucous membraines of the lining of the lungs, mouth, and eyes.

Q. As a child I remember we burned candles of some kind to get rid of mosquitoes. Why did they work?

A. This was probably a device that contained citronella oil. Burning the candles allowed the oil to distill off. Mosquitoes as well as

---

*Systemic fungicides (or any pesticide) are absorbed by the plant and transferred to the leaves or fruit (not edible fruit!) where the fungi or other pests eat them and die.

many other insects don't like the smell. Citronella is obtained from grasses in Sri Lanka, Java, and India. This as well as other naturally occurring oils like garlic oil and caffeine are useful natural insect repellents.

HOME WATER TREATMENT

Most municipalities do a good job of treating tap water; consequently, the need to purchase purified water is rarely needed. Good tap water contains trace amounts of calcium, chloride, magnesium, sodium, and other minerals that are beneficial in appropriate amounts.

If your tap water gives off a rotten egg odor, it is usually due to the presence of sulfur. Your water may not smell very good but it is not dangerous. Water that has a foul smell and appears brown might be high in iron. Generally speaking, high iron content isn't dangerous either, but for those people who are sensitive to iron in the water, diarrhea often is one of the symptoms. Municipalities can easily remove smells and minerals from water, but less expensive methods are often used to save money. The result may be hard water that smells. Inexpensive water can be made available by your municipality. However, conversion of water treatment plants to better methods of processing can be costly.

Ozone and chlorine are antiseptics that remove most odors. Ozone is preferred, but more expensive than chlorine. It's not surprising, therefore, that many municipalities reduce their costs by using chlorine. Overchlorinated water has a definite smell and can damage or kill house plants.

If your water smells, a simple and inexpensive carbon filter at the sink can be used. There is usually no need to treat all the water coming into your house. Water used for gardening, washing, flushing, and the like doesn't normally need to be treated, so most people only need to use a unit in the kitchen or wherever water is used for consumption. When purchasing a carbon filter look at the total surface area of carbon. This should be stated on the label in terms of volume per unit weight (gallons of water per pound of carbon is an example). Another important feature of carbon filter units, besides cost, is the ease with which you can change the carbon element yourself. There is a huge disparity in price between carbon filter units. Some of the expensive units are impregnated with silver, a bactericide. Buy what you need. If your water has only a trace smell, buy a carbon filter for drinking water. In this situation, why buy a filter unit for the entire house? You might end up pouring the water and money down the drain.

Q. Will carbon filters do anything for hard water?

A. Hard water is another matter, since it is due to the presence of high concentrations of chlorine, calcium magnesium, or iron. Hard water is not harmful but it can be expensive to use. It can leave stains on sinks and toilets, clog hot water pipes, and build up in your iron. As we've seen, soaps and detergents don't work as well in hard water, which means more detergent may be needed to clean clothes successfully. Use of detergents in hard water can result in metal ions like calcium and magnesium (soap scum). Carbon filters are only useful at removing organics, not minerals.

Q. Can I do anything about hard water?

A. For a complete discussion of what you can do to remedy your hard water problems, see chapter 2, pages 27–28 where we explain ion exchange units and reverse osmosis units.

Q. My tap water has tiny particles that are barely visible. Should I be concerned?

A. Absolutely. Tap water should not contain any visible particles. Have your water tested, and try a carbon filter cartridge.

Q. I noticed that some carbon cartridges are made from coconut shell carbon. Are these cartridges better than generic carbon types?

A. The source or form of carbon is not as important as manufacturers of the units would have you believe. Don't be fooled! A carbon cartridge removes visible particles and removes odors, that's all it is supposed to do.

Q. I don't mind the taste of my tap water, but on special occasions, for friends and relatives, I like to buy bottled water at the grocery store. I can't taste the difference. What is in the packaged water?

A. Packaged or bottled water is sold with many different labels and names. Distilled water, purified water, natural water, effervescent water, carbonated water, and mineral water are the most common. A leading consumer magazine tested and tasted tap, bottled, and packaged water from many different areas across the country. One year, New York City tap water ranked first in taste and in safety and was found to be superior to such expensive and popular brands as Evian®, Perrier®, Ozarka®, Poulans®, Artesia®, Vittel®, and Utopic®.*

Purified water is often just a very good drinking water from a differing municipality. The term "natural water" has no legal definition: water *is* a natural substance. Effervescent or bubbly water is generally tap water that has carbon dioxide added to it; it's soda without the added flavors and colors. The term "mineral water" can mean almost anything, except that the water has been distilled or treated with reverse osmosis. Distilled water is relatively free from minerals and organics. Although good for plants, it tastes flat. Municipalities that use reverse osmosis often add minerals to the water to give it some taste. Remember, trace minerals naturally found in water are needed for proper nutrition.

Q. Can't we drink distilled water? Isn't it the safest form of water to drink?

A. Distilled water stored in glass containers is safe but lacks the natural minerals that give water a pleasant taste. As we've said, distilled water tastes bland. The trace minerals in most tap waters don't make the water *unsafe.*

SWIMMING POOL CHEMICALS

Keeping a swimming pool sparkling clean is not very hard. However, the uneducated use of swimming pool chemical additives can not

*"Bottled Water," *Consumer Reports,* January 1987.

only be expensive but dangerous as well. The chemistry is deceptively complex but the basic concepts are easy: a basic understanding of pH, oxidizing agents, buffers, algaecides, superchlorination, and testing methods.

The control of water pH is critical to all the chemical reactions that occur in pool water, since pH controls the formation of sodium hypochlorite from chlorine gas and the reverse reaction of converting hypochlorite into chlorine. Chlorine gas is dissolved in water and sold as a solution. The pungent smell sometimes noticed in an indoor pool is from the noxious chlorine gas. The optimum pH for pool chlorine is between 7 and 8. At a more acidic pH (less than 7), hypochlorite can form hypochlorous acid and chlorine gas, which may evaporate from the pool. At higher (less acidic and more basic) pH levels, the chlorine gas doesn't form hypochlorite as easily and chlorine gas does not escape from the water. A pH in the range of 7 to 8 also helps keep other reactions in check. Not keeping the pH range of your pool at recommended values wastes pool chemicals and is a safety hazard for swimmers and observers alike. Chlorine gas irritates the mucous linings of the nose, mouth, and lungs, and also can irritate the eyes. Don't be cavalier about chlorine gas! If it can bleach your swim suit and kill bacteria in your pool, imagine the permanent damage it could do to your body if present in higher than recommended amounts. Chlorine gas was used in World War I as a deadly weapon. Normally, there shouldn't be much, if any, free chlorine gas in your pool. The chlorine should be present as hypochlorite, chloride ion (a chlorine atom carrying an extra electron which gives a negative charge), or forms of unreactive chlorine (chloramines).

Sodium hypochlorite has a very high pH (about 10, which is a moderately high alkaline level); muriatic acid (hydrochloric acid) is then added to drop the pH of the water to its safe level of 7–8. Concentrated hydrochloric acid is a strong and dangerous acid and it should not be allowed to make contact with your skin. The very small amount of the acid used to decrease the pH in your pool becomes so diluted that it does not constitute a safety hazard. The pH of pool water changes because the sodium hypochlorite reacts with bodily secretions and natural debris. To replenish the supply of sodium hypochlorite, the chemicals in the pool "rearrange" to form more sodium hypochlorite. This "rearrangement" of chemicals is a reaction that causes the pH to decrease (become more acidic). Sodium carbonate (washing soda) is added to increase the pH to the optimum values for the production of hypochlorite in your pool. If the pool water is allowed to remain acidic, free chlorine gas is formed and can escape. Hypochlorite is a good oxidizing agent. That is, it can react with any organic matter (sweat, oil, urine, hair, bacteria, leaves, and other debris) to form carbon dioxide gas, which can escape.

Pool chemistry over the years has departed from the true reaction nomenclature that chemists use today. We refer to the alkalinity of pools in terms of pH. An alkaline pH is above 7. However, in pool chemistry it is used in a different sense: there it is defined as the ability of pool water to buffer or withstand large changes in pH. Sodium carbonate is a common and inexpensive buffering agent. Buffers resist the changes in pH. They react or tie up acids to prevent the pH from dropping, and they react with bases to prevent the pH from rising.

Oxidizing agents added to pools react with organic matter and break it down into an unreactive form. Oxidizing agents remove organic matter that could serve as food for algae. Sodium hypochlorite is the oxidizing agent that converts organic molecules into carbon dioxide gas. This oxidizer converts minute but solid carbon (organic) particles to a gas and then they escape from the pool, thus preventing algae from forming.

Superchlorination is sometimes called shock chlorination. This process is often used to start new pool water chemistry as well as revitalize old pool water. In superchlorination of old pools, hypochlorite is added to convert organic nitrogen compounds into chloramines. Often more sodium hypochlorite is added to destroy the chloramines. At this point the excess hypochlorite is free to destroy organic matter that has been added by bathers or the wind.

The biggest mistakes that pool owners make are in the measurement of pH, the amount of hypochlorite to use, and the dispensing of pool chemicals. The thought that if "a little is good, then a lot must be better" is often practiced. Unfortunately this doesn't work in chemistry. This practice for pools ends up costing the owner quite a bit of money, time, and patience. What many owners do is add more chlorine or sodium hypochlorite than they need. This in turn raises the pH of the pool too high. Then they have to lower the pH by adding muriatic acid. If too much muriatic acid is added, more chlorine is required or more buffering agents, and so on. In the end the pool becomes very salty. *The only way to remove excess sodium is to replace the water.*

Q. What is an accurate method of determining pool pH?

A. There are three easy techniques: pH test papers, liquid test dyes, or—the most accurate and simplest method—using a battery operated pH meter. Inexpensive meters are available. These may be more expensive than the pH papers but in the long run they will save time and money. Usually in a couple of years the cost of the meter is recovered in lower chemical cost.

Q. What about measuring the chlorine levels of pool water?

A. The measurement of pool chlorine is more difficult. There are two methods currently employed: one measures free chlorine and the other measures total pool chlorine. Chlorine can be bound to organic nitrogen compounds. Be sure that any test you purchase measures total chlorine. Both tests involve dyes that change color depending on the level of chlorine in the water. The total chlorine test adds a second step that converts the bound chlorine into free chlorine.

Q. You have mentioned chlorine and sodium hypochlorite to moderate the alkaline level of pool water. Which is better to use?

A. Chlorine gas in water is inexpensive but bulky to use; it also smells. Calcium hypochlorite is a solid and is generally supplied in tablet form for slow release of chlorine in the form of hypochlorite. This saves time since the hypochlorite is released over several days.

Sodium hypochlorite is unstable in the solid form so it is dispensed as a solution in water. It reacts quicker than calcium hypochlorite and is preferred by some pool owners. The least expensive, easiest, and most accurate supply of hypochlorite is to use an electrolysis unit (produces hypochlorite from crude, inexpensive rock salt with electricity) that pumps it directly into the pool. Over a two- or three-year period of use in mild climates, the unit will pay for itself.

Q. I would like to trim the border of my in-ground cement pool with paint. Is there a certain kind I should use?

A. Pool paints should be used and are available at local pool stores. These paints generally have a silicone binder for water resistance.

Q. I forgot to add chlorine and now I have algae. What do I do?

A. Algae are nothing more than plants that are growing in your pool. Chlorine and hypochlorite destroy algae. Use of commercial algaecides prevents the growth of algae. Get the chlorine level back up and the algae should die. Superchlorination may be required.

TOXICITY AND THE DISPOSAL OF HOUSEHOLD CHEMICALS

General disposal of household chemicals is one of the major contributors to landfill pollution in the United States. We throw away millions of tons of partially filled paint cans, household cleaners, batteries, plastic products such a disposable drink containers and disposable diapers every year. Many plastics take thousands of years to degrade, while such chemicals as paint solvents leach into river beds and pollute the environment. As the world's population grows we will need to take better care of our air, water, and land.

Every day we throw thousands of tons of recyclable materials into our landfills. Tires made from plastics float to the top of landfills over time. Advances in technology now enables used tires to be turned into durable road paving compounds at a reasonable cost. Paper products are now being recycled for further use, as are many types of glass and aluminum cans. The manufacture of these recycled products requires energy, fuel from electricity, and oil products, but only a fraction of the energy needed to produce the products anew from raw material.

Q. Where can I recycle paper, glass, aluminum, and plastics?

A. Many large cities provide local pick ups for recyclable materials such as glass, plastic, and paper products. Many states require deposits on soft drink and other beverage containers, which can be returned for cash at supermarkets. Numerous states require various types of bottles and cans to be recycled, and they provide the receptacles for this purpose. If you are new to an area, call the city manager or the local dump and ask about recycling facilities in your area.

Q. What about household chemicals?

A. Industrial waste is highly regulated and costly. Industrial dumping of hazardous materials is often thought of as the major cause of landfill pollution, especially when stories of toxic waste dumps and their impact on human life and the environment are highly publicized. However, household disposal of hazardous materials is really the major cause of landfill pollution.

Paints, petroleum products, pesticides, insecticides, and the like should never be thrown out in your trash for the local dumps. Always call your landfill or city utilities department for instructions on how to dispose of your hazardous materials. In many localities, household products are collected for disposal by the city several times a year. Each state has its own regulations on the disposal of household products. Although households are allowed to throw away many toxic items, laws are always changing to protect the environment.

Q. Besides pesticides, insecticides, and the like, which products around the house are toxic materials?

A. Strong alkalis are present in many cleaning products such as liquid and dry chemical drain cleaners. These chemicals cause severe tissue damage when they come in contact with your skin, the mucous membranes of your eyes or mouth, and your gastrointestinal tract. These chemicals are designed so that they may be flushed down the sink or toilets.

If you accidentally ingest any of these, call your local poison control center then the operator or 911 immediately and *do not induce vomiting unless instructed to do so by a medical professional.* For skin or eye contact, flush with lots of water and seek medical attention. Most household products will tell you what to do in the event they are swallowed. If you are in doubt, always seek medical attention.

Many products around the house are either irritants, toxic, corrosive, or produce noxious fumes when mixed. Know the products around your house and don't mix chemicals together to make a "better" product or to dispose of them. For example, never mix household bleach with any acids (such as vinegar) because the fumes generated are very corrosive. A partial listing of some toxic chemicals found in the home is provided below.

COMMON TOXIC CHEMICALS IN THE HOUSE

Chemical Name	Use	Result of Contact, Inhalation, or Ingestion
Acetone	Nail polish remover	Dryness, headache, fatigue. and possible narcosis
Bleach	Laundry aide	Disinfectant, strong irritant
Caustics	Drain cleaners	Strong irritant, attacks mucous membranes
Dichlorobenzene	Mothballs	Irritant, damage to liver
Insect sprays	Insecticides	Headaches, nausea, vomiting, internal organ damage, and possible death
Iodine	Antiseptic	Ingesting a large does may cause circulatory failure, nausea, diarrhea
Isopropanol	Rubbing alcohol	Headaches, dizziness, coma, fatal if ingested in large quantities
Lead	Lead-based paints	Kidney damage, damage to red blood cells, liver and nervous system disorder
Methanol (wood alcohol)	Paint thinner	Headaches, fatigue, blindness, death
Mercury	Thermometers	Long-term exposure to vapor causes kidney damage
Petroleum distillates	Solvent	Fire hazard, emits bitter fumes when heated, possible carcinogens (benzene)
Toluene	Solvent	Acts as a narcotic in high concentrations

SAFETY IN USING POISONS AROUND THE HOUSE

Since there are many types of poisons, we limit our discussion to the common ones found in your home and yard. Just about any compound could be lethal if taken in large enough quantity. We therefore reserve the term "poison" for any compound that causes death or tissue damage when small quantities are consumed or have made contact with the body. They work by blocking normal life process or destroying tissue on contact. The latter are called *corrosive poisons*. Strong bases, strong acids, and oxidizing compounds destroy tissue on contact.

SOME COMMON CORROSIVE POISONS

Bases

Ammonia	Cleaning solutions
Sodium hydroxide	Lye, drain cleaners
Sodium carbonate	Washing soda
Sodium perborate	Laundry builder

Acids

Hydrochloric acid	Toilet bowl, brick, tile, and metal cleaners
Oxalic acid	Metal polish, ink remover
Sulfuric acid	Auto battery, drain cleaners

Oxidizing Agents

Hydrogen peroxide	Antiseptics, bleach
Ozone	Electric discharge
Sodium hypochlorite	Laundry bleach

Metabolic poisons interfere with normal metabolic processes and can cause death. Some examples are cyanide, carbon monoxide, fluorides, alcohols, and broad-spectrum pesticides. The latter are considered nerve toxins and are classified as neurotoxins. The tasteless, odorless, and colorless gas carbon monoxide is produced when combustion occurs in a fuel rich (or low oxygen) burning situation. Tobacco smoke, auto emissions, tunnels, auto garages, and gas or charcoal grills are outdoor sources, while steel mills and space heaters that use kerosene or natural gas are indoor sources. Carbon monoxide kills by converting the healthy oxyhemoglobin in aerated blood into carboxyhemoglobin, which cannot transfer oxygen from the lungs to the rest of the body—the body literally suffocates.

Cyanide gas is formed when metal cyanides contact any acid. It is a colorless gas with a strong, bitter-almond odor, which is formed in gas chambers by adding hydrochloric acid to sodium cyanide tablets. The reaction is over in a few seconds. Cyanide then attacks an enzyme in the human body that helps metabolism. This stops cells from using oxygen, so the victim dies a painful death in about fifteen minutes.

Fluorides in high concentration react with calcium needed for ion transport and become unreactive calcium fluoride. The loss of soluble calcium causes muscle spasms, depressed breathing, irregular heartbeat, and can cause death.

Alcohols such as methanol (methyl alcohol or wood alcohol), isopropyl alcohol (rubbing alcohol) and other alcohols are converted by oxidation in the body to poisonous formaldehyde and oxalic acid or ethylene glycol. One antidote for alcohol poisoning is to administer ethanol (ethyl alcohol, drinking alcohol). Ethanol provides a safer route in the metabolism of other alcohols. *Be cautioned: drinking large quantities of ethanol can depress the central nervous system and can cause coma.*

Neurotoxins are poisons that disrupt the flow of nerve impulses to and from nerve cells. These poisons include: nerve gases (phosgene, used by Iraq against the Kurds), most organophosphate and carbamate insecticides, snake venom, strychnine, curare, nicotine, mushroom toxins, the chemical that causes Red Tide (the red pigmented secretions from minute organisms in the sea that indiscriminately kill millions of fish) and the botulism bacterium (Clostridium botulinum). Less than one millionth of a gram of this toxin can kill a person.

Broad spectrum insecticides are generally organophosphates such as malathion and Dursban®, carbamates such as Sevin®, or chlorinated hydrocarbons—Chlordane®, Lindane®, dieldrin, aldrin, or heptachlor. The reader should be aware that we are using the terms *insecticide* (kills insects), *pesticide* (kills pests) and *fungicide* (kills fungi) quite loosely to mean any chemical that kills undesirable pests whether they be insect, fungi, rodents (*rodenticide*) and weeds (*herbicides*). The best first aid for *any* swallowed poison is to administer one to two table-spoons of activated carbon (also called activated charcoal) dissolved in water or juice. Activated carbon is very porous and can absorb poisons and render them harmless (they pass through intestines unreacted). **ALWAYS CALL FOR PROFESSIONAL HELP FIRST. DO NOT ATTEMPT TO GIVE THIS OR ANY OTHER ANTIDOTE WITH-OUT CONTACTING MEDICAL PROFESSIONALS FIRST.**

Toxic metals count among their more harmful types arsenic, cadmium, lead, mercury, beryllium, and antimony. Historically, metal poisons were used to kill fungi, insects, and rodents. Hatters at one time used mercury salts on their hats as a fungicide and also to tan leather. Painters often used lead, cadmium, and other heavy metals as pigments for their paints. Van Gogh also drank the liqueur absinthe which also contained heavy metal salts.* Absinthe is a green liquer made from wormwood, and while it once contained many heavy metals, the absinthe sold today has none. Since lead utensils and dishware were not sealed (glazed sufficiently to prevent metals from leaching out), most of the chronic lead poisoning (ingesting low levels of the poison over an extended period of time) came from drinking acidic liquids (wine). Most of the wealthy Romans drank wine from this unprotected lead dishware while the poor drank from clay pottery. Poverty actually saved lives!

---

*The heavy metals are usually cadmium, mercury, bismuth, thallium, and lead. Some chemists call arsenic a heavy metal, though technically it is a metalloid (part metal and part nonmetal).

11

Conclusion

We believe that the information provided here will serve as a valuable reference source for you. Chemicals have been and always will be around us in our everyday lives. It is vital that readers know a bit more about them. As we become more familiar with chemical terminology and how various processes of chemistry impact our daily existence, the mystery that surrounds the average person's awareness of chemistry will fade away. In recent years we have begun to talk more openly with our doctors about our health. We have also become more interested in the food we eat as well as in keeping the world clean. By understanding about the nature and properties of the chemicals in ordinary products we are far more likely to become better consumers.

During the last hundred years we have been deluged with new discoveries. Technological advances have helped us to live longer, acquire information faster, and, for the most part, make our lives easier. But as we advance we are faced with an ever-growing and potentially confusing body of information. Each new day brings more household cleaners, over-the-counter drugs, and personal care items. Now, when faced with new products on the market you will be better able to understand their basic composition and make intelligent decisions about their intended uses.

Prior to embarking on our discussion of household chemicals, no doubt many of you had difficulty when purchasing products for home use. When going shopping how did you choose between the many different ant and roach killers? How were you expected to distinguish between forty to sixty different types of laundry detergents, hand soaps, or shampoos. With all the manufacturers' claims and counterclaims, the task probably seemed beyond your comprehension. What ever happened to the days when a bar of soap was just a bar of soap? With all the additives and ingredients in these products—fragrances, preservatives, antibacterial agents, dyes, pH adjusters, and so on—the average consumer is at a loss to decide among them on anything other than a trial-and-error basis or on the strength of claims each manufacturer makes in this or that advertisement. But now that you know more about the chemical composition of the products you use, a careful look at ingredient listings will show that most of the same types of products from different manufacturers have the same basic chemical content. Remember that often the only way to make money is with advertising. "New and improved" seems to be everywhere. But now you understand that "new and improved" may mean only a slight change in chemical formulation.

Words like "new and improved," "longer lasting," "more cleaning power," "value priced," and "new economy size" are just a few of the slogans that are designed to catch our eye and influence us to buy specific products. With the information we have presented in this book, it is our hope that thoughtful consideration will replace susceptibility to powerful advertising campaigns.

When faced with the purchase of an automobile, a gas or electric range, or a washer and dryer, you recognize the expense involved, which prompts you to ask a lot of questions and read advertising literature in the hope of making the most economical purchase given the quality desired. But stop and think. How much do you spend *every week* for household products? Over the course of a year, this can add up to hundreds of dollars. You can now apply the same determination you may have for car purchases to many other items you must buy. Until now, some of you bought and used products without ever really knowing what they contained. You didn't have the information you needed to make these important choices. Throughout this book we have tried to show you that this decision-making process is actually much simpler than it may have first appeared.

Now you know that there are relatively simple answers to the questions you had about household chemistry. We have provided you with an understanding of common household products without delving too deeply into the complex chemistry involved. For most of you this is all you will ever really need. You now understand household chemistry in simple terms and will be able to make better decisions. We have provided you with information and relevant terminology used to describe the contents of a variety of consumer goods, how to buy the right products for you, and how to use them safely.

As informed consumers you are now positioned to appreciate trends in many of the formulations of products used in household cleaning and personal care products. By reading labels, you find that most soaps, detergents, hair care products, shaving cream, cosmetics, and general health care products are not very different from brand to brand. Shaving cream labels are very similar. Some creams contain different types of skin conditioners and fragrances, but most of the differences appear to be in the packaging and presentation.

Now that you know the essential differences between soaps and detergents, antiperspirants and deodorants, and many other types of products, use what you have learned about their ingredients to help you choose the best product. In this sense, "best" means a product that performs the required task at a reasonable price.

Consider the packaging you select and how the product is dispensed. Remember, fancy packaging is often used to make a product stand out, to increase sales. Aerosol sprays may be easy to use but they tend to waste the product and your money. Pump dispensers of liquid soap may be fashionable, but if you just want to wash your hands bar soap is much cheaper to buy and it cleans just as well.

It is our hope that after reading this book all of you will never buy a product without carefully reading the label. As we have said time and time again, product labels are *very* important. They are especially useful when considering over-the-counter drugs, many of which contain the same types of ingredients. Now you can judge for yourself the relevant merits of acetaminophen, aspirin, and ibuprofen. In addition, you now know that there are really only a few expectorants and cough suppressants on the market even though there are dozens of products to choose from.

Cosmetics are produced by a variety of well-known manufacturers. Here, as in the clothing trade, advertising plays a big role in the marketing of a new product. Glamorous ads tend to increase sales by luring the uninformed. But you are now positioned to make intelligent choices. Although specific formulations are closely guarded trade secrets, you are able to distinguish between colognes, perfumes, and toilet waters, or the various skin creams on the market. You can choose less expensive products that look, feel, smell, and perform like costlier brands. Fortunately, most of the products that are applied to the skin undergo extensive testing and are closely monitored for safety by the Food and Drug Administration.

When making a purchase we hope that you will remember to check unit pricing. Over the years it has been impressed into our minds that buying larger sizes saves money. Remember, as we have shown, this is not always the case. Besides, if you can't possibly use all of the product in the larger size, why buy it!

In recent years consumers have become more and more aware of food products and what they contain. The terminology used on food labels may seem complex but don't be concerned. We have made reading labels much easier.

Fat grams, calories, and daily allowance of vitamins and minerals are placed on most food items for dietary planning. Unfortunately, as fat grams are lowered or removed, taste is often compromised. As we have shown, to revive the taste of these foods, spices, sometimes even sugar, are added to perk up the flavor. Adding sugar to bran muffins is the easiest way to make bran taste better. You have become familiar with food terminology, cooking methods, preservatives, and food additives. With this information in hand, you should be able to shop more effectively to purchase the foods you want while getting more value for your money and meeting your nutritional needs.

Plastics seem to be everywhere. Remember that plastics are used in packaging, in furniture and appliances, in cooking utensils, in clothing, and in many other items you use around the house. Plastics are nothing more than very large molecules made up of much smaller molecules. Polymers are also used on the surface of wood furniture. These coatings provide protection against weathering and sometimes add to the color as well. Looking back we find that waxes, stains and varnishes are also made from these polymers. Recently, while looking over a textbook on polymer chemistry, we found references to over six hundred different types of polymer brand names.*

In today's society an automobile is a necessity, but most of us

*Raymond B. Seymour and Charles E. Carraher, Jr., *Polymer Chemistry: An Introduction* (New York: Marcel Dekker, 1981).

are not mechanically inclined. Instead, we rely heavily on word of mouth and on the recommendations of our favorite car dealers and mechanics for advice on how to keep our cars looking good and running at peak efficiency. It seems that everybody has a different opinion on types of motor oils to use or even what polishes to buy. After discussing various car-care products, we hope you understand better the chemicals and terminology of these products and can recognize the value in the various products you purchase. Remember, expensive polishes and waxes contain many of the same ingredients as the less expensive brands. Gas, oil, and oil additives have complex formulations, but knowing the basics of what they are and what they do will help to keep your car running efficiently and cost effectively. This is one of the best ways that you can help to keep our environment clean.

As your awareness of household chemicals increases, we hope your concern for safety will improve as well. For example, we mentioned that you should not mix bleach with ammonia: to do so would produce toxic fumes. We also learned to be careful about disposing of waste products. Many storm drains empty directly into rivers, lakes, and oceans. Improper disposal of chemicals can have long-lasting negative results for our surroundings. The choices we make about the chemicals we use will impact plant and animal life as well as the foods we eat, the water we drink, and the air we breathe.

The use of commercial pesticides for home use are strictly regulated. As you know, pesticides of many types are on the market. Earlier we mentioned that in one supermarket we found over thirty different insecticides for use in and around the house. Now these products will no longer baffle and bewilder you. By checking the labels you can find that most of these products contain basically the same types of chemicals. The differences among them may aid you in deciding which is best for your particular needs.

Chemicals don't have to be scary or mysterious. Now you have some basic knowledge to build upon. Your curiosity will do the rest. Ask questions. Call the toll-free customer telephone numbers listed on product packaging to get more answers. Persistence and the background knowledge you now have are great tools to make your life easier and better.

Now what will you do? To look for more information about the topics you are interested in check the many reports issued each year by consumer awareness groups. We also recommend the books in our bibliography. You know that your environment is effected by the products you use and how you use them. Your local municipal water authority will be able to provide you with more information on the water you drink, pesticides, soil erosion, and so on. Contact your county's environmental management agency, your local university cooperative extension programs, your health department, and your sanitation district, the numbers for which should be listed in your telephone directory. These sources can provide information on a variety of topics you may be interested in. If the agency doesn't know the answers to your questions, it should be able to refer you to one that does.

We hope that you now feel less intimidated by chemistry in general and household chemicals in particular. The terms may be awkward but the basic functions of these chemicals can be understood and appreciated by anyone who wants to learn more about them and about how chemistry continues to change the way we live, work, and play.

Appendix 1

The Chemical Elements and Their Symbols (1995)

Some of the symbols for elements seem to have no relationship to their names. This is due to the fact that these elements were originally named in Latin, German, or Norwegian languages. The symbol for the element gold is Au because the Latin name for gold is *aurium*. The same is true for lead (Pb), which is derived from the Latin *plumbium,* and Fe stands for *ferium,* the Latin name for iron. The Latin term for the element silver (Ag) is *argentium.* The symbol for the element tungsten is W primarily because in Germany and some other European countries the element is still called Wolfram. (Many inexpensive light bulbs sold in the United States are produced in Hungary. Perhaps you have noted "Wolfram" printed on the bulbs.)

Symbol	Name	Symbol	Name
Ac	Actinium	Be	Beryllium
Ag	Silver	Bi	Bismuth
Al	Aluminum	Bk	Berkelium
Am	Americium	Br	Bromine
Ar	Argon	C	Carbon
As	Arsenic	Ca	Calcium
At	Astatine	Cd	Cadmium
Au	Gold	Ce	Cerium
B	Boron	Cf	Californium
Ba	Barium	Cl	Chlorine

Symbol	Name	Symbol	Name
Cm	Curium	No	Nobelium
Co	Cobalt	Np	Neptunium
Cr	Chromium	O	Oxygen
Cs	Cesium	Os	Osmium
Cu	Copper	P	Phosphorus
Dy	Dysprosium	Pa	Protactinium
Er	Erbium	Pb	Lead
Es	Einsteinium	Pd	Palladium
Eu	Europium	Pm	Promethium
F	Fluorine	Po	Polonium
Fe	Iron	Pr	Praseodymium
Fm	Fermium	Pt	Platinum
Fr	Francium	Pu	Plutonium
Ga	Gallium	Ra	Radium
Gd	Gadolinium	Rb	Rubidium
Ge	Germanium	Re	Rhenium
H	Hydrogen	Rh	Rhodium
He	Helium	Rn	Radon
Hf	Hafnium	Ru	Ruthenium
Hg	Mercury	S	Sulfur
Ho	Holmium	Sb	Antimony
I	Iodine	Sc	Scandium
In	Indium	Se	Selenium
Ir	Iridium	Si	Silicon
K	Potassium	Sm	Samarium
Kr	Krypton	Sn	Tin
La	Lanthanum	Sr	Strontium
Li	Lithium	Ta	Tantalum
Lr	Lawrencium	Tb	Terbium
Lu	Lutetium	Tc	Technetium
Md	Mendelevium	Te	Tellurium
Mg	Magnesium	Th	Thorium
Mn	Manganese	Ti	Titanium
Mo	Molybdenum	Tl	Thallium
N	Nitrogen	Tm	Thulium
Na	Sodium	U	Uranium
Nb	Niobium	Une	Unnilennium
Nd	Neodymium	Unh	Unnihexium
Ne	Neon	Unp	Unnilpentium
Ni	Nickel	Unq	Unnilquadium

Symbol	Name
Uns	Unnilseptium
V	Vanadium
W	Tungsten
Xe	Xenon
Y	Yttrium
Yb	Ytterbium
Zn	Zinc
Zr	Zirconium

Appendix 2

Metric Equivalents and Conversions

LINEAR MEASURE

1 centimeter (cm)	0.394 inch (in.)
1 in.	2.54 cm
1 millimeter (mm)	0.094 in.
1 decimeter (dm)	3.937 in. or 0.328 feet (ft.)
1 foot (ft.)	3.048 dm
1 meter (m)	39.37 in. or 1.0936 yards (yd.)
1 dekameter (da)	1.9884 rd
1 rod (rd.)	0.5029 da
1 kilometer (km)	0.621 mi.
1 mile (mi.)	1.609 km

SQUARE MEASURE

1 square (sq.) cm	0.155 sq. in.
1 sq. in.	6.452 sq. cm
1 sq. dm	0.1076 sq. ft.
1 sq. ft.	9.2903 sq. dm
1 sq. m	1.196 sq. yd.

1 sq. yd.	0.8361 sq. m
1 acre (a.)	0.4047 h
1 hectare (h)	2.47 a.
1 sq. km	0.386 sq. mi.
1 sq. mi.	2.59 sq. km

MEASURE OF VOLUME

1 cubic (cu) cm	0.061 cu in.
1 cu in.	13.39 cu cm
1 cu dm	0.0353 cu ft.
1 cu ft.	28.316 cu dm
1 cu m	0.308 cu yd.
1 cu yd.	0.7646 cu m
1 stere	0.2759 cord
1 cord	3.624 steres
1 liter (l)	0.906 qt. dry (0.264 gallon [gal.]) or 1.0567 qt. liquid
1 quart (qt.) dry	1.101 l
1 qt. liquid	0.9463 l
1 dekaliter	2.642 gal.
1 bushel	03524 hektoliter

WEIGHTS

1 gram (g)	0.03527 ounces (oz.)
1 oz.	28.35 g
1 kilogram (kg)	2.2046 pounds (lbs.)
1 lb.	0.4536 kg

1 metric ton	0.98421 English ton
1 English ton	1.016 metric ton
1 metric carat	0.2 g. or 3.09 grain (gr.)
1 tonne (t.)	1000 kg. or 1.1023 short tons

TEMPERATURE

To convert temperatures in Celsius (°C) to their equivalents in Fahrenheit (°F), simply multiply the temperature in Celsius by 1.8 and then add 32.

$$°F = 1.8°C + 32$$

For example, if the temperature outside in Toronto, Canada, is 28°C, the Fahrenheit temperature equivalent would be:

$$°F = 1.8 (28) + 32 = 82.4°C$$

If you wish to convert from Fahrenheit degrees to Celsius degrees, subtract 32 from the Fahrenheit temperature *first,* then divide by 1.8.

$$°C = \frac{°F - 32}{1.8}$$

In frozen Moosemouth, Minnesota, a temperature of 5°F is equivalent to:

$$°C = \frac{5 - 32}{1.8} = \frac{-27}{1.8} = -15× F$$

Use the table below to convert from one temperature reading to another for quick conversions, but the results are only accurate to plus or minus 0.1 degree. The center column in boldface is used for the temperature you wish to convert, whether you wish to convert it to Fahrenheit or Celsius. First find the temperature in the center column. Now, the correct Celsius temperature reading is obtained by locating the adjacent temperature in the right or Celsius column.

To convert from Celsius to Fahrenheit degrees, note the temperature in the center, but this time read the value off the left or Fahrenheit column. Example, 90°F is found in the center column and the equivalent Celsius temperature of 32.2 degrees is found on the right column. Likewise, –4.0°F = –20°C and the boiling point of water is either 212°F or 100°C.

°F	Temperature to be converted	°C
+ 14	– 10	– 2.3
+ 21	– 6	–21.1
+ 25	– 4	–20.0
+ 32	0	–17.8
+ 39	+ 4	–15.6
+ 50	+ 10	–12.1
+ 59	+ 16	– 9.4
+ 68	+ 20	– 6.7
+ 77	+ 25	– 3.9
+ 86	+ 30	– 1.1
+ 95	+ 35	+ 1.7
+104	+ 40	+ 4.4
+113	+ 45	+ 7.2
+122	+ 50	+10.0
+131	+ 55	+12.8
+140	+ 60	+15.6
+149	+ 65	+18.3
+158	+ 70	+21.1
+167	+ 75	+23.9
+176	+ 80	+26.7
+185	+ 85	+29.4
+194	+ 90	+32.2
+203	+ 95	+35.0
+212	+100	+37.8
+221	+105	+40.6
+230	+110	+43.3
+239	+115	+46.1
+248	+120	+48.9
+257	+125	+51.7
+266	+130	+54.4

AMERICAN UNITS

Length

1 in.	2.54 cm
1 ft.	12 in. or 0.3048 m
1 yd.	3 ft. or 0.9144 m
1 mi.	1760 yd. or 1.852 km
1 nautical mile	1.852 km or 2025 yd.

Area

1 sq. in.	645 sq. mm
1 sq. yd.	9 sq. ft. or 0.836 sq. m
1 sq. mi.	640 a. or 2.6 sq. km

Volume/Capacity

1 cu ft.	1728 cu in. or 28 cu dm
1 cu yd.	27 cu ft. or 0.77 cu m
1 dry pint (pt.) (USA)	0.5506 l.
1 bushel (USA)	1.25 cu ft. or 35 l.
1 liquid pt. (USA)	0.4732 l.
1 gal. (USA)	8 liquid pt. (USA) or 3.78 l.
1 fluid oz. (USA)	29.67 cu cm

Weight

1 gr.	64.80 mg
1 oz.	28.35 mg or 437 gr
1 lb.	16 oz. or 0.454 kg
1 short hundred weight (cwt.)	100 lb. or 45.36 kg
1 long hundred weight (cwt.)	112 lb. or 50.80 kg
1 short ton (tn.)	20 short cwt. or 907 kg
1 long tn.	20 long cwt. or 1016 kg

OTHER COMMONLY USED UNITS

1 tablespoon (tbsp.)	¹/₁₆ cup
3 teaspons (tsp.)	1 tbsp.
4 cups liquid	1 qt. or 2 pt.
2 cups dry	1 lb.
1 cup butter	½ lb.
1 tbsp. powder	½ oz.
1 pinch	⅛ tsp.
60 drops	1 tsp.
2 tbsp. (liquid)	1 fluid oz.
5 medium eggs	1 cup
2 tbsp. (dry)	1 oz.
Juice of 1 lemon	3 tbsp.
Juice of 1 orange	6 tbsp.
1 lb. meat	454 g or 0.454 kg
12 drops	1 ml
1.06 qt.	1 liter (l)
1 qt.	0.943 l
1 dash	not defined
350 gr. (aspirin)	22.4 g
1 mi.	1.609 km
20 miles/hour	32 km/hour
60 miles/hour	96 km/hour
100 miles/hour	161 km/hour

There are other units employed in the United Kingdom and elsewhere in the world which are not given here because they are seldom encountered.

Appendix 3

Knowing the Risks and Taking Precautions

A. COMMON HOUSEHOLD CHEMICALS AND THEIR TOXICITY LEVELS

This abbreviated list was prepared from *Clinical Toxicology of Commercial Products—Acute Poisoning* by Gleason, Gooselin, Hodge, and Smith (Baltimore, Md.: The Williams and Wilkins Publishers, 1984). Most (about 85 percent) of the toxicity ratings were taken from this text, while the other 15 percent were taken from the references in the text; but the common uses and explanations are ours. In an effort to keep this list to a manageable length, we eliminated pharmaceuticals (over-the-counter or prescription), chemicals used only in industry, and those chemicals seldom encountered in the home. The reader should be aware that *any chemical*—even those not on this list—should be treated as toxic, dangerous to the skin or lungs, unless stated otherwise in the literature (first aid books, safety texts, chemical safety sheets, etc.). Many innocuous (otherwise safe and harmless) compounds have been omitted, such as cinnamon, because we felt the average layperson would recognize them as being safe compounds. We have included several common compounds, which are normally thought to be safe but are toxic if taken in large quantities. The toxicity of each compound in the list is identified by a scale of 1 to 6. This scale is based on the toxic reactions that will occur when a specified amount of the compound is taken orally. The rationale for this approach is based on the fact that a small amount of a very toxic compound will be as harmful as a relatively large amount of a safer compound. The toxicity of each compound was not always

279

determined by clinical evidence for humans, since the use of chemicals on humans is not always feasible. Small animal toxicity (LD$_{50}$) studies were extrapolated to humans and these results were used.

Although corrosive chemicals such as battery acid, bleaches, bases, and the like are generally lethal if consumed, their toxicity is not listed. These corrosive compounds cause death by tissue injury, toxemia, shock, infection, hemorrhage, and obstruction. Where possible we have listed skin damage along with the toxicity rating because we feel that the nontoxic compounds are irritating to the skin. *The reader should be aware that there are many toxic chemicals that were not placed on this list. Neither the authors nor the publisher are responsible for the uses to which this list may be put; it is presented only for informational use.* Readers should contact their local Poison Control Center for more detailed information or for the toxicity levels of chemicals that are not listed, and for advice on first aid.

TOXICITY RATING CHART

Toxicity Rating	Probable Lethal Dose (humans) for 150 lb Male
6 Supertoxic	A taste (less than 7 drops)
5 Extremely Toxic	Between 7 drops and a teaspoon
4 Very Toxic	Between one teaspoon and one ounce
3 Moderately Toxic	Between one ounce and one pint (or pound)
2 Slightly Toxic	Between one pint and one quart
1 Practically Nontoxic	More than one quart

Some special terms used: *Fungicide,* kills fungus; *agaricide,* kills fungus also; *parasiticide,* kills parasites; *humectant,* absorbs water and keeps items soft; *topical,* refers to application on the skin; *herbicide,* kills weeds; *astringents,* close-up pores on skin.

Chemical	Normal Use	Toxicity
Acetal	Solvent in perfumes	3 (hypnotic)
Acetaldehyde	Solvent	3
Acetic acid	Corrosive acid	not rated

Chemical	Normal Use	Toxicity
Acetone	Solvent	3 (flammable)
Acetophenone	Perfume	3 (hypnotic)
Acifluorofen	Herbicide	4 (irritant)
Agar	Food thickener	1 (laxative)
Alcohol, Ethyl	Solvent, beverage	1
Aluminum Chloride	Antiperspirant	3 (skin irritant)
Aluminum Hydroxide	Antacid	1 (constipation)
Aluminum Potassium Sulfate, (Alum)	Astringent	3 (skin irritant)
Ammonia (in water)	Many uses	3 (skin irritant)
Ammonium Bisulfide	Preservative	2 (allergic)
Antimony Pentoxide	Fire retardant	5 (vomiting, death)
All antimony salts		5
Aspartame	Nonnutritive sweetener	1
Barium Carbonate	Rat poison	3-6
Barium Sulfite	Depilatory	3-6
Soluble barium salts		6
Insoluble barium salts		2
Bayberry Bark	Emetic	2 (dehydration)
Belladonna Leaf	Deadly Nightshade plant	4
Bentonite	Plaster base	1
Benzene	Solvent	4
Benzoic Acid	Food preservative	3
Bismuth Salts	Soluble or insoluble	3
Bismuth Subgallate	Stomach coating	2

Chemical	Normal Use	Toxicity
Boric Acid	Antiseptic, kills insects	4
Bromelain	Meat tenderizer	2
Brucine	Denaturant in alcohol	5
Butyl Acetate	Gas additive	3
Butyl Alcohol	Gas octane booster	3
Butylparaben	Food preservative	1
Cadmium Salts	Soluble or insoluble	5
Caffeine	Stimulant (in its 99 percent pure form)	4
	In coffee, tea, and cola	1
Calcium Carbonate	Antacid	1
Calcium Cyclamate	Nonnutritive sweetener	1 Banned in the United States
Calcium DiEDTA	Food preservative	1
Calcium Fluoride	For water	1 (mottling of teeth)
Calcium Formate	Food preservative	1
Calcium Lactate	Food preservative	1
Calcium Nitrate	Fertilizer	1 (gastric upset)
Calcium Nitrite	Corrosion inhibitor—concrete	1 (gastric upset)
Calcium Oxide	Plasters, mortars	1 (blisters skin)
Calcium Sulfate	Plaster casts	1
Calcium Sulfite	Juice preservative	1 (gastric upset)
Camphor	Vasodilator	4
Capsicum	Chemical in hot, spicy foods	3 (irritant)
Carbitol	Solvent	3 (irritant)

Chemical	Normal Use	Toxicity
Carbon Disulfide	Solvent	3
Carbon Tetrachloride	Solvent	4
Carbowax	Wax for cars, etc.	1
Cetyl Alcohol	Emollient, antiseptic	4
Chloramine—T	Oxiding agent	3
Chlordane	Pesticide	4
Chloroform	Solvent	3 (CNS depressant)
Chromate Salts	Many uses	4 (also corrosive)
Cinnamyl Antranitrate	Food flavoring	1
Cobalt Salts	Many uses	4
Collagen	Food casing	1
Copper salts (all) Name is, cupric or cuprous	Herbicide, pesticide	5
Cottonseed Oil	In soaps, detergents	1
Coumarin	Rat poison	5
Creosote	Kills parasites	4
Cupric Phosphate	Herbicide	4
Cuprous Sulfite	Fungicide	4
DDT	Herbicide, banned	Not rated
Dextromethorphan	Antitussive, in cough syrup	4
Diazinon	Insecticide	4
Dimethyl Sulfoxide	Anti-inflammatory	4
Dithianone	Fungicide	4
EDTA	Metal scavenger	1 (bone loss)

Chemical	Normal Use	Toxicity
Econazole	Antifungal	4
Eosine Black	Dye	2
Eosine Yellowish	Nail polish coloring	2
Ethylene Glycol	Permanent antifreeze	3
Fuel Oil	Home heating oil	3
Fructose	Fruit sugar	1
Gasoline	Fuel, solvent	3
Glucose	Blood sugar	1
Glycerol	Humectant (moisturizer)	1
Hexachlorophene	Antibacterial	4
Hydrocortisone	Topical anti-inflammatory	1 (Steroid)
Hydrochloric Acid	Many uses	5 (Corrosive acid)
Hydrogen Peroxide	Antiseptic	1 (at 3 percent solution)
Hydroquinone	Removes pigment in skin	4
Iodine	Topical antiseptic	5 (Nausea, vomiting)
Iodophor	Topical antiseptic	2
Iron salts	Dietary supplement	1
Isoamyl Acetate	Artificial flavoring	3
Isolan	Insecticide	5 (convulsions)
Isopropyl Alcohol	Antiseptic	3
Kerosene	Degreaser, fuel	3
Lactose	Milk sugar	1

Chemical	Normal Use	Toxicity
Lanolin	Base for ointments	1
Lead Antimony	Yellow paint pigment	3 or 4
Lead Salts	All soluble lead salts	3 or 4
Lindane	Acaricide	4
Linseed Oil	Drying Oil	1
Litmus	Acid-base indicator	2
Lye	Corrosive alkali	Not rated
Magnesium Hydroxide	Antacid	3
Magnesium Oxide	Antacid (milk of magnesia)	3 (Any magnesium salt may cause diarrhea)
Malathion	Insecticide	4
Menthol	Antiseptic	4
Methyl Alcohol	Octane booster, solvent	3
Methyl Cellusolve	Solvent	3
Methyl Parathion	Insecticide	5
Monosodium Glutamate	Flavor enhancer	1
Methyl Salicylate	Counterirritant—skin	4
Naphtha	Solvent	3
Naphthalene	Mothballs	2
Neatsfoot Oil	Leather softener	1
Nickel Salts	All nickel salts	4
Nicotine	Fungicide, insecticide (when 99 percent pure)	4
Nitric Acid	Corrosive	Not rated
Nimidane	Acaricide	4

Chemical	Normal Use	Toxicity
Oil of Citronella	Insect repellant	3
Oil of Cloves	Local anesthetic (esp. teeth)	1
Oil of Eucalyptus	Expectorant	2
Oil of Sassafras	Topical anti-infective	5
Olive Oil	(Used as Emollient)	1
Oxalic Acid	Rust remover	4
Papain	Protein digesting aid	1
Paraformaldehyde	Disinfectant	4
Parathion	Insecticide	6
Paraquat	Herbicide	5
Pepsin	Digestive enzyme	1
Petrolatum	Lubricant	3
Phenol	Disinfectant	4
Pine Tar Oil	Antieczematic	3
Plaster of Paris	Calcium sulfate	1
Polyethylene Glycol	Ointment	1
Potassium Bicarbonate	Effervescent salts	1
Potassium Oleate	Detergent	2
Propylparaben	Antifungal agent	3
Pryolan	Insecticide	5
Pumice	Skin abrasive	1
Pyrethrums	Insecticide	3
Quaternary Ammonium Salts	Detergent	3-4
Quinine	Antimalarial agent	4
	In tonic water	1

Chemical	Normal Use	Toxicity
Rapeseed Oil	Lubricant	3
Resorcinol	Topical antibacterial	4
Rosin	In varnishes and adhesives	1
Saccharin	Nonnutritive sweetener	2 (may be a carcinogen)
Salicylic Acid	Topical antiseptic, vasodilator	4
Scopolamine	Reduces motion sickness	6
Selenium Sulfide	Controls seborrhea and eczemas	1
Sepia	Polishing agent	2
Silicone	Lubricant and sealant	1 (tissue damage)
Silver Nitrate	Antiseptic	4
Insoluble silver salts (all)		1
Sodium Arsenate	Many uses	5 to 6
Sodium Ascorbate	Vitamin C source	1
Sodium Bisulfite	Preservative and a bleach for foods	1
Sodium Fluoride	Insecticide and a fluoride source	4 (mottled teeth)
Sodium Hypochlorite	Laundry bleach	Corrosive Alkali
Sodium Lauryl Sulfate	Detergent	3
Sodium Metabisulfite	Antioxidant	1
Sodium Nitrate	Fertilizer	3 (may be a carcinogen)
Sodium Perborate	Dry bleach, in mouthwashes	4 (skin irritant)

Chemical	Normal Use	Toxicity
Sodium Sulfite	Meat preservative	3
Stannic Oxide	Tin salts	1
Stearic Acid	Soaps, many other uses	1
Strychnine	Rodenticide	6
Sucrose	Sugar	1
Sulfur Elemental	Kills parasites	1
Sulfuric Acid	Battery acid, many other uses	Corrosive acid*
Sulphenone	Acaricide	5
Talc	Dusting powder	1
Tannic Acid	Astrigent	3
Terpin Hydrate	Expectorant	3
Tertrasodium Pyrophospate	Rust remover	4
Theobomoa oil	Chocolates, massage oil	1 (stimulant)
Thymol	Prevents mildew, colds also	4
Titanium Dioxide	White pigment in paints	1
Tobacco Extract	Insecticide	4
Tolnaftate	Antifungal agent	3
Trichlorobenzene	Termite insecticide	4
Trifluralin	Herbicide	5
Tung Oil	Quick drying enamels	3
Turpentine	Solvent for many uses	3
Undecylenic Acid	Topical antifungal	3
Urea	Fertilizer	2

*Concentrated sulfuric acid dehydrates skin and destroys tissue!

Chemical	Normal Use	Toxicity
Vanillin	Flavoring agent	1
Vitamin C	Antioxidant	1
Warfarin	Rat poison	4
Wheat Germ Oil	Source of vitamin E	1
Witch Hazel	Mild astringent	2
Xanthan Gum	Thickener	1
Xylene	Solvent	4
Zinc Acetate	Antiseptic, astringent	4
Zinc Chloride	Astringent	4
Zinc Oxide	Calamine lotion, Sunblock	3
Zinc Phosphate	Dental Cement	1
Zinc Stearate	Waterproofing cement, dusting	3

B. PRECAUTIONS: SOME CHEMICALS DO NOT MIX!

There are certain over-the-counter medicines that definitely do not mix. The proper term for this failure to mix is *synergism* of chemicals. Being *synergistic* simply means that the effect of two or more medicines is greater than the sum total of the effects of the medicines taken independently. Alcohol and barbiturates can produce a deadly synergistic effect. *Some synergistic effects are much less serious or do not occur in most people.* We have listed some common over-the-counter preparations that have synergistic effects. NOTE: We have omitted prescription medications as much as possible. The interactive effects of these are best left to your pharmacist and/or physician. We advise you to contact your physician or pharmacist if you have any concerns about the potential interactions of medications you may be taking.

Acetaminophen

Tylenol® and Datril® are two brand names for acetaminophen, a popular pain reliever. It can be dangerous—most particularly it can harm the liver—if taken for extended periods during which alcohol is consumed or barbiturates are also being taken. Acetaminophen can enhance the effects of diazepam, a tranquilizer with the brand name Valium®, and anticoagulants (blood-thinning medications). Its action is easily blocked by antacids and coricosteroids, which reduce inflammation, and enhanced by cimetidine (Tagamet®), which reduces hyperactivity in the stomach.

Acne Preparations

Mixing two or more acne preparations can cause dryness or irritation.

Antacids

Bismuth subsalicylate, best known as Pepto Bismol®, can block the action of the family of antibiotics named tetracyclines. Aluminum-containing antacids can block the action of fluoride. You only need to read the label to determine if an antacid contains aluminum, magnesium, or any other element or compound. Magnesium antacids are dangerous for those who must have their blood cleansed with dialysis. Calcium antacids destroy the action of prescribed medications called "beta blockers." Other antacids or mixtures of the three main types can *sometimes* cause the effects of a number of medicines to be blocked including: aspirin, tetracyclines, digoxin (a digitalis preparation that corrects irregular heart beat and strengthens the heart), antifungal agents, diazepam, cimetidine, Zantac, pseudoepinephrine, and many others.

Antihistamines

They should not be taken with alcohol or cimetidine.

Decongestants

Pseudoepinephrine (Sudafed®) can cause headaches and increased blood pressure. Oddly, a different decongestant named oxymetazoline (Afrin) can lower blood pressure.

Diet Pills

Many such preparations contain phenylpropanolamine, which can increase blood pressure; change the heart rhythm; and cause seizures, strokes, and heart attacks. They are especially dangerous when taken with substances containing caffeine, which, oddly enough, is also a common ingredient in diet pills. Phenylpropanolamine and caffeine are a safe combination in some over-the-counter diet pills if the diet-control product is *taken according to instructions*. The amount of these chemicals permitted in diet pills is quite small; however, the abuse of dieting aides can result in the complications noted.

Ibuprofen

This popular analgesic can block the action of certain diuretics and can cause some people to retain too much potassium. Blood clotting is also hindered by ibuprofen. Motrin®, Advil®, and Nuprin® are common brand names.

Mineral Oil

This innocuous compound can decrease the absorption of vitamins A, D, K, and E. These vitamins are soluble in fats and oils; therefore they dissolve in the mineral oil and are passed through the gastro-intestinal system without being absorbed by the body.

Mineral Supplements

Calcium, iron, and zinc can block the action of tetracyclines, and excessive intake of calcium alone can cause kidney damage.

Paraaminobenzoic Acid—PABA

PABA, histamines, and other related compounds can cause allergic reactions.

Topical Anesthetics

Benzocaine used in high concentrations or too frequently may produce an allergic reaction when mixed with other topical anesthetics. Lodocaine may disturb heart rhythms.

Appendix 4

How to Reach Manufacturers

A. TOLL-FREE TELEPHONE NUMBERS FOR SELECTED MANUFACTURERS

This is only a partial list of toll-free telephone numbers through which you can receive product information from manufacturers. To obtain more numbers either use an 800 directory or read the toll-free numbers on the label of the specific products you have questions about. Alternatively, you can call the 800 directory service from your long-distance carrier just as you would for any number in a given area code. You will be charged for the directory assistance call.

Some companies, such as the Gillette, do not provide a toll-free number but instead list an address for their consumer representative. Some brand names (e.g., Minute Maid®) are not listed because they are owned by a larger company (Minute Maid® is owned by Coca-Cola). Brands that do have their own customer representative office (e.g., Nabisco) but are owned by a larger company (Nabisco is owned by R. J. Reynolds) are included in our list. Some of the toll-free numbers are for a particular product and not for the company that makes it nor for other products manufactured by the same company.

Alcon Laboratories	1-800-451-3937
Arm and Hammer Co.	1-800-624-2889
Alpo Co.	1-800-366-6033

293

Beecham Products	1-800-245-1040
Becton Dickson Consumer Products	1-800-237-4554
Bristol-Meyers *Squibb*	1-800-468-7746
Burroughs and Welcome	1-800-334-2413
Cheesebrough Ponds	1-800-243-5804
Chlorox Co.	1-800-292-2200
Citrus Hill	1-800-462-4162
Clairol	1-800-223-5800
Coca-Cola	1-800-962-6531
Colgate Palmolive	1-800-221-4607
Dannon Co.	1-800-321-2174
Del Monte Co.	1-800-543-3090
Dial Co.	1-800-528-0849
Dole Co.	1-800-232-8888
Drackett Products Co.	1-800-558-5252
Equal Co.(Nutrasweet)	1-800-323-5316
Faberge Co.	1-800-243-5804
Ford Motor Co.	1-800-392-3673
Frito Lay Co.	1-800-352-4477
General Foods (Maxwell House)	1-800-431-1000 or 432-6333
General Mills	1-800-328-1144
General Motors	1-800-213-8688
Hershey Chocolate USA	1-800-468-1718
Hunt-Wesson Co.	1-800-732-2431
Jello (see Kraft)	

Johnson and Johnson	1-800-526-3967
S. C. Johnson	1-800-558-5566
Kodak	1-800-242-2424
Kraft Inc.	1-800-431-1001 or 235-3235
Lakeside Pharmaceuticals	1-800-453-4865
Land O Lakes	1-800-328-4155
Lederle	1-800-282-8805
Lever Brothers	1-800-451-6679
Marion Merrel Dow	1-800-453-4865
McCormick Co.	1-800-632-5847
McNiel Consumer Division	1-800-843-2828
Miles, Division of Ames	1-800-348-8100
Nabisco	1-800-622-4726 or 622-4720
Neutragena	1-800-421-6857
Nestle Co.	1-800-637-8537
Noxelle Co. (Noxzema)	1-800-638-6204
Parke Davis Co.	1-800-323-8683
Pillsbury Co.	1-800-767-4466
Procter and Gamble Co. (foods)	1-800-262-1637 or 543-7276
Purina	1-800-345-5678
Reckitt and Coleman Products	1-800-444-7599
R. J. Reynolds Co.	1-800-252-3500 or 433-4000
Richardson-Vicks	1-800-843-9657
A. H. Robins	1-800-762-4672
Rorer Pharmaceuticals	1-800-548-3708

Sandoz Pharmaceuticals	1-800-327-4450
Shulton	1-800-932-2273
Smith Kline (see Beecham)	
Sterling Drugs	1-800-223-5511
Texize Co.	1-800-428-4795
Upjohn Co.	1-800-253-8600
Van Den Bergh Foods	1-800-735-3554
Warner Lambert	1-800-223-0182
Whitehall Laboratories	1-800-322-3129
Yoplait	1-800-967-5248

B. CONTACTING MAJOR PHARMACEUTICAL COMPANIES

The following list contains the addresses of most of the major pharmaceutical companies in the United States. Altogether, these companies produce most of the prescription medicine used in America, and account for a significant share of world-wide sales. Don't be surprised if you are unable to find some of our larger pharmaceutical companies on the list: firms such as Johnson and Johnson Products or Norwich-Eaton Pharmaceuticals sell primarily over-the-counter products.

Each company has one or more specialists to answer your phone calls and letters. These companies want to provide you and your physician with the latest information concerning use, side effects, and any other new developments relevant to their products. Do not hesitate to contact them, since they genuinely need your input on any problems or concerns you might have while taking their medicines. To write them simply mail a letter to the Consumer Affairs Office (or Consumer's Representative) for the company. To call them we suggest that you try to obtain their toll-free number first through

800 information and ask to speak to someone in the offices we just mentioned. We have tried to include as many phone numbers* as possible.

You may never have heard of some of these companies, because they are actually subsidiaries of a huge chemical conglomerate. For example, Butron, Parsons and Co. is a subsidiary of Alcon Laboratories; Dista Products Inc., is owned by Eli Lily Co.; Endo Pharmaceuticals is a subsidiary of the DuPont Co.; Hoyt Laboratories is a subsidiary of the Colgate-Palmolive Co.; and so on.

Abbott Pharmaceuticals: Abbott Park, P.O. Box 68, North Chicago, IL 60064. (312) 937-3806

Alcon Laboratories: P.O. Box 1959, Fort Worth, TX 76134. (817) 293-0450

Allergan Pharmaceuticals: 2525 Dupont Dr., Irvine, CA 92713. (714) 752-4500

American Critical Care: Division of American Hospital Supply Corp.: McGaw Park, IL 60085. (312) 473-3000

Armour Pharmaceutical Co.: 303 S. Broadway, Tarryton, NY 10591. (914) 631-8888

Astra Pharmaceutical Products: 7 Neponset St., Worchester, MA 01606. (617) 852-6351

Ayerst Laboratories: Division of American Home Products Inc., 685 Third Ave., New York, NY 10017. (212) 878-5900

Beecham Laboratories: Bristol, TN 37620. (615) 764-5141

Berlex Laboratories: Cedar Knolls, NJ 07927. (201) 540-8700

Boehringer Ingelheim Ltd.: 90 East Ridge, P.O. Box 368, Ridgefield, CT 06877. (203) 438-0311

Boots Pharmaceuticals: 6540 Line Ave., Shreveport, LA 71106. (318) 869-3551

---

*Please note that these numbers are not toll-free.

Breon Laboratories: 90 Park Avenue, New York, NY 10016. (212) 907-2705

Bristol Laboratories: Div. of Bristol-Meyers Co., Thompson Rd., Syracuse NY 13201. (315) 432-2000

Burroughs Wellcome Co.: 3030 Cornwallis Rd., Research Triangle Park, NC 27709. (919) 541-9090

Burton, Parsons & Co.: Div. of Alcon Laboratories, 6201 S. Freeway, Fort Worth, TX 76134. (817) 293-0450

Carnrick Laboratories: 65 Horse Hills Rd., Cedar Knolls, NJ 07927. (201) 267-2670

CIBA Pharmaceuticals: 556 Morris Ave., Summit, NJ 07901. (212) 267-6615

Coopervision Pharmaceuticals: Medical Dept., Moutain View, CA 94043. (800) 227-8313

Dermik Laboratories: 1777 Walton Rd., Blue Bell, PA 19422. (215) 641-1962

Dista Products: Div. of Eli Lily Co., Medical Dept., 307 E. McCarty St., Indianapolis, IN 46285. (317) 261-4000

Dorsey Pharmaceuticals: Div. of Sandoz Pharmaceuticals, Inc., Medical Dept., Route 10, E. Hanover, NJ 07936. (201) 386-7500

Endo Pharmaceuticals: Subsidiary of the DuPont Co., One Rodney Square, Wilmington, DE 19898. (302) 773-3652

Ex-Lax Pharmaceuticals: Div. of Sandoz Pharmaceuticals, Inc., New York, NY 10158. (302) 773-3652

Flint Laboratories: Div. of Travenol Labs, Deerfield, IL 60015. (312) 940-5211

Geigy Pharmaceuticals: Medical Services Dept., Ardsley, NY 10502. (201) 277-5000

Glaxo Inc.: 1900 West Commercial Blvd., Fort Lauderdale, FL 33309. (305) 776-5300

Hoechst-Roussel Pharmaceuticals: Route 202-206, N. Somerville, NJ 08876. (201) 231-2000

Hoyt Laboratories: Div. of Colgate-Palmolive Co., 575 University Ave., Norwood, MA 02062. (617) 769-6850

Ives Laboratories: 685 Third Ave., New York, NY 10017. (212) 878-5125

Janssen Pharmaceuticals: 501 George St., New Brunswick, NJ 08903. (201) 524-0400

Key Pharmaceuticals: 18425 NW 2nd Ave., Miami, FL 33169. (305) 653-2276

Knoll Pharmaceuticals: 30 N. Jefferson Rd., Whippany, NJ 07981. (201) 887-8300

Kremers-Urban Co.: P.O. Box 2038, Milwakee, WI 53201. (414) 354-4300

Lederle Laboratories: Div. of American Cyanamid, One Cyanamid Plaza, Wayne, NJ 07470. (914) 735-5000

Eli Lilly Co.: Medical Dept., 307 E. McCarty, St., Indianapolis, IN 46285. (317) 261-2000

Marion Laboratories: Pharmaceutical Div., Marion Industrial Park, 10236 Bunker Ridge Rd., Kansas City, MO 64137. (816) 761-2500

McNeil Pharmaceuticals: McNeilab Inc., Spring House, PA 19477. (215) 628-5000

Mead Johnson Pharmaceutical Division: 2404 W. Pennsylvania St., Evansville, IN 47721. (812) 426-6000

Merck Sharpe and Dohme: Div. of Merck and Co., West Point, PA 19486. (215) 661-5000

Merrell-Dow Pharmaceuticals: Subsidiary of the Dow Chemical Co., Cincinnati, OH 45214. (513) 948-9111

Miles Pharmaceuticals: 400 Morgan Lane, West Haven, CT 06516. (203) 934-9221

Norwich-Eaton Pharmaceuticals: Medical Dept., Norwich, NY 13815. (607) 335-2565

Ortho Pharmaceuticals: Medical Research Dept., Raritan, NJ 08869. (201) 524-0400

Parke-Davis: Div. Warner-Lambert Co., 201 Tabor Rd., Morris Plains, NJ 07950. (201) 540-2000

Pennwalt Pharmaceutical Division: Pennwalt Co., 755 Jefferson Rd., Rochester, NY 14623. (716) 475-9000

Pfizer Laboratories: 235 42nd St., New York, NY 10017. (212) 573-2422

Pharmacia Laboratories: 800 Centennial Ave., Piscataway, NJ 08854. (201) 457-8162

The Purdue Fredrick Co.: 100 Connecticut, Norwalk, CT 06854. (203) 853-0123

Reed & Carnrick Co.: 1 New England Ave., Piscataway, NJ 08854. (201) 272-6600

Riker Laboratories: Subsidiary of 3M Company, 19901 Nordhoff St., Northridge, CA 91324. (213) 709-3137

A. H. Robins Company: Pharamaceutical Division, 1407 Cummings Dr., Richmond, VA 23220. (804) 257-2000

Roche Laboratories: Division of Hoffman-La Roche Co., Nutley, NJ 07110. (201) 235-5000

Roerig Co.: Div. of Pfizer Pharmaceuticals, 235 E. 42nd St., New York, NY 10017. (212) 573-2187

William H. Rorer Co.: 500 Virginia Drive, Fort Washington, PA 19034. (215) 628-6492

Ross Laboratories: Division of Abbott Laboratories, Columbus, OH 43216. (614) 227-3383

Sandoz Pharmaceuticals: Route 10, East Hanover, NJ 07936. (201) 386-7500

Schering Corporation: Galloping Hill Rd., Kenilworth, NJ 07033. (201) 558-4000

Searle & Company: Medical Communications Dept., Box 5110, Chicago, IL 60680. (800) 323-4397

SmithKline and French Laboratories: Div. of SmithKline Beecham Corporation, 1500 Spring Garden St., P.O. Box 7929, Philadelphia, PA 19101. (215) 751-4000

E. R. Squibb & Sons Inc.: P.O. Box 4000, Princeton, NJ 08540. (609) 921-4000

Stuart Pharmaceuticals: Division of ICI Americas Co., Wilmington, DE 19897. (302) 575-2231

Syntex Pharmaceuticals: 3401 Hillview Ave., Palo Alto, CA 94304. (415) 855-5050

USV Pharmaceuticals: 1 Scarsdale Road, Tuckahoe, NY 10707. (914) 631-8500

The Upjohn Company: 7000 Portage Rd., Kalamazoo, MI 49001. (616) 323-4000

Wallace Laboratories: P.O. Box 1, Cranbury, NJ 08512. (609) 655-6000

Webcon Pharmaceuticals: Division of Alcon Inc., P.O. Box 1629, Fort Worth, TX 76101. (817) 293-0450

Westwood Pharmaceuticals: 468 Dewitt St., Buffalo, NY 14213. (716) 887-3773

Winthrop Laboratories: 90 Park Ave., New York, NY 10016. (212) 907-2000

Wyeth Laboratories: Div. of American Home Products, P.O. Box 8299, Philadelphia, PA 19101. (215) 688-4400

Glossary

Acaridicide (a-car'-id-i-cide). A substance that kills mites or ticks.

Acetaldehyde (a-ce-tal'-de-hyde). A poison sometimes formed when alcohol is distilled.

Acetaminophen (a-cet-a-mi'-no-phen). Aspirin-free pain reliever. See *analgesic* and *antipyretic*.

Acetic acid (a-ce'-tic). A weak acid found in vinegar and spoiled wines.

Acetone (ac'-e-tone). A solvent for many uses (including toy cement and nail polish remover). **Hazardous if inhaled.**

Acetone-free. In nail polish removers, ethyl acetate replaces acetone as the solvent.

Acetylsalicylic acid (ac'-e-tyl-sal-i-cyl'-ic). The generic name for aspirin. See *analgesic*.

Acid. Reacts with metals, neutralizes bases, tastes sour, gives off hydrogen ions, and turns blue litmus red. See *base (basic)* and *litmus*.

Acidulant (a-cid'-u-lant). Substance added to foods and juices to make them more tart or acidic.

Acrilan® (ac'-ri-lan). A synthetic fiber possessing "wool-like" properties.

Acrylic (a-cryl'-ic). A glassy thermoplastic used for molded parts or as coatings or adhesives.

Adobe (a-do'-be). Sun-dried, unburned brick of clay and straw.

Aerobic (aer-o'-bic). A chemical process that requires oxygen.

Alcohol (al'-co-hol). See *denatured alcohol, ethyl alcohol, isopropyl alcohol,* and *methyl alcohol*.

Alkaline (al'-ka-line). See *basic*.

Alkaline battery. A battery made from manganese dioxide, zinc, and potassium hydroxide. Replaces the toxic mercury battery.

Alkyd (al'kyd). A thermoplastic or thermosetting resin used for molded parts or as coatings or adhesives.

Alkyd Sulfonate (sul'-fo-nate). A detergent, a surfactant. See *surfactant*.

Allergen (al'-er-gen). A substance (usually proteins) that causes an allergic reaction.

Aluminum chlorohydrate (chlor-o-hy'-drate). An antiperspirant. See *antiperspirant*.

Aluminum Oxide (ox'-ide). Used as an abrasive in toothpaste, also as a pigment.

Aluminum Hydroxide (hy-drox'-ide). An antacid. Also coats stomach ulcers.

Ammonium lauryl sulfonate (a-mo'-ni-um; laur-yl). A detergent used in shampoos.

Analgesic (an-al-ge-sic). A pain-relieving agent (which may or may not be an antipyretic or an anti-inflammatory medication (reduces inflammation around joints). See *antipyretic*.

Anerobic (an-er-o'-bic) [also spelled anaerobic]. A chemical process that occurs without the presence of oxygen.

Anesthetic (an-es-thet'-ic). A compound that numbs the skin and/ or tissues. The names of such compounds often end in "caine" or "cain."

Anion (an'-i-on). A positively charged atom or molecule.

Annotto (an-ot'-to). A yellow coloring agent used in the making of butter.

Anticholinergic (an-ti-cho'-lin-er-gic). Prevents the breakdown of acetylcholine, which causes irregular heart beat and over-stimulation.

Antidiarrheal (an-ti-di-arrh-e'-al). Any substance that reduces the severity of diarrhea: *psyllium* provides bulk fiber that reduces the amount of water, Pepto Bismol® coats the affected bowel, and a *laperamide* reduces spasms.

Antiemetic (an-ti-em-et'-ic). Substances such as phosphates and sugars mixed together (e.g., cola syrup) that prevent nausea and vomiting.

Antifungal (an-ti-fun-gal). Prevents the growth of fungus.

Antihistamine (an-ti-his'-ta-mine). Deactivates histamine, which causes allergic reactions. See *histamine*.

Antioxidant (an-ti-ox'-i-dant). A substance that inhibits the presence of oxygen. Such substances in foodstuffs prevent spoilage.

Antiperspirant (an-ti-pers'-pir-ant). Compounds that prevent sweat from forming by closing sweat glands. Most common compounds include aluminum chlorohydrate or aluminum chloride.

Antipyretic (an-ti-py-ret'-ic). Any substance that reduces fever.

Antiredeposition agent (an-ti-re-de-po-si'-tion). A compound in detergent that prevents dirt from collecting (redepositing) onto cloths or surfaces.

Antiseptic (an-ti-sep'-tic). A substance that checks the growth or action of microorganisms.

Antitussive (an-ti-tuss-ive). A decongestant in cold remedies; aids in curbing the cough reflex.

Arteriosclerosis (ar-ter'-i-o-scler-o'-sis). Hardening of the arteries.

Ascorbic acid (as-cor'-bic). A source of vitamin C.

Aspartame (as'-par-tame). An amino acid used as a nonnutritive sweetener.

Aspirin (as'-pir-in). Acetylsalicylic acid. An analgesic.

Bakelite (bake-lite). A hard, durable plastic used for old photograph records.

Baking powder. A mixture of a weak acid with sodium bicarbonate to produce carbon dioxide gas for leavening in dough.

Baking soda. Sodium bicarbonate, a weak base.

Basic (also known as alkaline). A caustic substance having an excess of hydroxide ions and a high pH. Often used to neutralize acids, basics are slippery to the touch and have a bitter taste. They turn red litmus paper blue.

Benzene (ben'-zene). A poisonous solvent used in the preparation of aromatic hydrocarbons.

Benzocaine (ben'-zo-caine). A topical anesthetic; numbs the skin and gums. See *anesthetic* and *topical*.

Benzoyl peroxide (benz-oyl per-ox-ide). A compound commonly used to treat acne.

Beer. See *ethyl alcohol*.

Beta blocker. Slows down the heart rate and decreases blood pressure. E.g., Propanolol (Inderal®).

Betacarotene (be'-ta-car'-o-tene). A compound that the body uses to make vitamin A.

BHA—Butylhydroxyanisole (bu'-tyl-hy-drox'-y-an-i-sole'). A preservative used in foods and soaps. See *antioxidant*.

BHT—Butylhydroxytoluene (bu'-tyl-hy-drox'-y-tol'-u-lene). A preservative used in foods and soaps. See *antioxidant*.

Bisacodyl (bi-sa-co'-dyl). A stool softening agent.

Biodegradable (bi-o-de-grad-able). A substance that decays in the presence of water, air, and sunlight.

Bismuth subgallate (bis'-muth sub'-gall-ate). A stomach-coating and antidiarrheal agent. (One typical brand: Pepto Bismol®.)

Blueing. Removes the yellow from white clothing.

Borax (bor'-ax). Sodium tetraborate. A water softener.

Brandy. An alcoholic beverage made by distilling the alcohol in wine.

Buffer. A substance that prevents substantial changes in the acidity or alkalinity of a solution.

Builder. A substance that adds surfactants in cleaning.

Butyric acid (bu-tyr'-ic). An acid produced by the decomposition of fat (e.g., in butter). It has a pronounced foul odor.

Calamine lotion (cal'-a-mine). A pinkish lotion prepared from 98 percent zinc oxide and 0.5 percent iron oxide (responsible for pink color). Soothes and protects skin irritations.

Calcium carbonate (car'-bon-ate). A weak base used as an antacid. Sample brand name, Tums®.

Calcium cyclamate (cy'-cla-mate). Artificial sweetner, currently banned only in United States.

Calcium hydroxide (hy-drox'-ide). Lime; strong, insoluble base; decomposes organic matter. (Also known as calcium oxide.)

Calcium hypochlorite (hy-po-chlor'-ite). A disinfectant, similar to sodium hypochlorite (laundry bleach), except it is a solid and reacts slower. *Caution: It burns skin on contact!*

Camphor (cam'-phor). Used as a heating agent for the skin, an insect repellent, and as a stimulant.

Capsaicin (cap-sai'-cin). A peppery, reddish-brown liquid obtained from hot spices.

Carbamide peroxide (car'-ba-mide). This antiseptic forms hydrogen peroxide upon contact with moisture in the mouth or throat. Used to mechanically remove pus and debris. See *antiseptic*.

Carbohydrate (car-bo-hy'-drate). A compound consisting of carbon, hydrogen, and oxygen: especially sugars and starches. Carbohydrates serve as a source of energy in the body.

Carbonated water (car'-bon-ated). Water that has been bottled with carbon dioxide gas.

Carboxymetacellulose (car-box-y-met-a-cell-u-lose). A thickening agent used in foods; also absorbs water and provides bulk in the colon. Serves as an antiredeposition agent in detergents. See *antiredeposition agent.*

Carcinogen (car-cin'-ogen). A substance capable of causing cancer.

Caries. Tooth decay.

Carotene. (car'-o-tene). Yellow-red natural food dye.

Castile (cas-tile). A fine, colorless soap made with olive oil.

Castor oil. A pale yellow oil from castor beans; used as a laxative.

Casua flour (cas'-u-a). A thickening agent used in cosmetics.

Catalyst (cat-a-lyst). An agent that speeds up chemical reactions without being used up in the process. E.g. enzymes.

Cation (cat'-i-on). A negatively charged atom or molecule.

Caustic (cau'-stic). A very alkaline substance capable of dissolving fat.

Cellophane (cell'-o-phane). Regenerated cellulose in transparent sheets.

Cellulose (cell'-u-lose). A polysaccharide that constitutes the chief part of the cell walls of plants. See *polysaccharide.*

Cetylpyridinium chloride (ce-tyl-py-ri-din-i'-um). Antiseptic used for the mouth and throat.

Chloroflurocarbons (chlor'-o-flur'-o-car-bons). Compounds used in refrigerants and in aerosol propellants. Studies have determined that their use deteriorates the protective ozone layer of the earth's atmosphere. See *freon.*

Cholesterol (cho-les'-ter-ol). A fat-like compound produced in the body and capable of causing hardening of the arteries.

Chromium oxide (chro-mi-um). The artificial green color used in toothpastes, paints, and soaps.

Cinnamon. A spice from the lourerii tree of Asia.

Citric acid Ascorbic source, source of vitamin C.

Clarified butter. Butter that has all suspended matter removed.

Coal tar. A mixture of chemicals obtained from converting coal to charcoal. It has therapeutic value for skin and hair.

Cocoa butter. A pale vegetable fat obtained from cocoa beans. Used to smooth skin.

Collagen (col-la-gen). The fibrous connective tissue of bones and cartilage.

Cologne. Diluted perfume. Sometimes termed eau de toilet.

Composting. The process of converting a mixture that consists largely of decaying matter for fertilizer.

Compound. Consists of two or more atoms of different elements.

Congener (con-gen'-er). In the manufacturing of alcoholic beverages, this is the liquid portion of the distillate that contains the characteristic flavor and aroma of gin, bourbon, scotch, and etc.

Cough suppressor. See *antitussive.*

Counterirritant. An agent taht causes irritation or even mild skin inflammation in order to relieve a more serious pain.

CPD—Cost per dose. Obtained by dividing the cost of a medication by the weight or volume of the product.

Cream of tartar. A baking powder from tartaric acid and sodium bicarbonate.

Cyanide (cy'-an-ide). A toxic gas, sometimes found in fruit pits.

Cyclamate (cy'-cla-mate). A nonnutritive artificial sweetener. Banned in the United States.

Dacron®. A polyester synthetic fiber formed from a polyacrylamide monomer. Commonly used in clothing mixed with other synthetic fibers or natural fibers to produce "permanent press" clothing.

DeLaney Amendment. A 1958 amendment to the Food and Drug Administration Act: it automatically bans from distribution and sale of any chemical shown to produce cancer in laboratory animals.

Demulcent (dem-ul'-cent). An oily substance that soothes or protects the mucous membranes of the respiratory system.

Denatured. The addition of a substance to ethyl alcohol to make it poisonous.

Denatured alcohol. Ethyl alcohol mixed with a chemical such as benzene to make it unsuitable for drinking. See *benzene* and *ethyl alcohol.*

Deodorant. Masks body odors, kills bacteria, and has perfume.

Depilatory (de-pil'-a-tory). Chemically removes unwanted body hair by breaking the hair down into smaller pieces.

Dextrose (dex'-trose). Same as table sugar. See *glucose.*

Dioctyl sulfosuccinate (di-oc-tyl sul-fo-suc-ci-nate). A stool softener.

Disinfectant. Kills most bacteria or viruses on contact.

Distillation (dis-till-a-tion). A purification process in which a liquid is converted to gaseous state, captured, and then the pure liquid is collected at room temperature.

Distilled water. Water that has been purified by distillation. It has no taste or odor and is freed of nearly all substances.

Disulfide bond (di-sul'-fide). The force holding hair in desired shapes—for example, permed hair.

Diphenhydramine (di'-phen-hy'-dra-mine). An antihistamine used in over-the-counter sleeping aids. Sample product: Sominex®.

DMSO—Dimethylsulfoxide (di-meth'-yl-sul-fox'-ide). A horse liniment sometimes used to increase warmth to aching joints and muscles. A powerful industrial solvent. Not recommended for humans.

Double bond. A chemical bond is a force holding atoms together in a compound. In a double bond some atoms are held together twice.

Doxylamine succinate (dox-yl-a-mine suc-cin-ate). An antihistamine used as a sleeping aid. Sample product: Unisom®.

EDTA—Ethylenediaminetetraacetic acid (eth'-yl-ene-di'-a-mine-te-t-ra-a-ce-tic). A food preservative. Removes trace metals from food. Also disodium EDTA.

Effervescent water. Same as carbonated water.

Electrolysis (e-lec-trol-y-sis). Splitting of compounds (in this case, human hair) into smaller units by passing electricity through the compound.

Emollient (e-moll'-ient). Any softening agent, especially ones that soften and smoothe the skin.

Emulsion (e-mul-sion). A liquid dispersed or suspended in a second liquid: for example, mayonnaise.

Endorphins (en-dor'-phins). Naturally occurring compounds in the body which bind to the nerve receptor sites in the brain and act as opiates. Endorphins are the body's natural pain relievers.

Enkephalins (en-keph'-a-lins). Morphine-like substances produced by the body.

Enteric (en-ter'-ic). A medicine that dissolves in the intestine rather than in the stomach.

Enzyme. A biological agent that catalyzes (speeds up) reactions in the body. See *catalyst*.

Ephedrine (eph'-e-drine). A very common antihistamine used in cold remedies. See *antihistamine* and *histamine*.

Epoxy resin. A cement prepared from a polymeric resin and a catalytic hardener. See *polymer*.

Essential amino acids. Eight vital amino acids that cannot be prepared in the body and must be supplied by diet.

Ethyl acetate (eth'-yl). A volatile compound used to substitute for acetone in nail polish remover.

Ethyl alcohol. A euphoric liquid obtained by the fermentation of carbohydrates. Found in beers, wines, liqueurs, and spirits. Generally speaking, it is safe (nontoxic) for consumption, though it can produce side effects such as dizziness, blurred vision, slurred speech, memory loss, and even unconsciousness if consumed in significant quantities. Drinking substantial quantities over a short period of time can result in alcohol poisoning, which could be lethal. Also, as the United States Surgeon General has determined, alcohol consumption during pregnancy can seriously effect the fetus. Alcohol can be either a stimulant or a depressant, depending on the individual. Also known as *ethanol*.

Ethylene glycol (eth'-y-lene gly'-col). A commercial permanent antifreeze.

Eugenol (eu-gen-ol). A liquid phenol obtained from clove oil. Relieves dental pain. See *phenols*.

Exfoliant (ex-fol'-i-ant). Causes the surface layer of skin cells to die so they can be washed away.

Expectorant. That which promotes discharge of mucous from the lungs.

Fatty acid. An organic acid that contains 4 to 20 or more carbon atoms in a long chain. Also called fat. Fatty acids with little unsaturation are solids obtained from animal fat. Fatty acids with more unsaturation are liquids obtained from plants. See *unsaturation*.

FDA. Federal Drug Administration.

Fiber. Insoluble cellulose or indigestible material. See *cellulose*.

Filler. Added to laundry detergents to increase the volume or weight and to aid in pouring or scooping: e.g., sodium sulfate.

Fluorapatite (fluor-ap'-a-tite). Tooth enamel that has some of the calcium replaced with fluorine. The surface is extremely hard.

Formaldehyde (for-mal'-de-hyde). An embalming fluid. Also used in the synthesis of some plastics.

Freon. Chloroflurocarbons used in refrigeration units. See *chloroflurocarbons.*

Fructose. Fruit sugar.

Fungicide (fun'-gi-cide). Any compound that kills fungus.

Galvanized metal. The addition of a protective metal on another metal by electrolysis. For example, galvanized steel has a protective zinc coating.

Generic. A product not protected by trademark registration.

Gin. An alcoholic beverage made from carbohydrates and juniper berry.

Glucose. A simple sugar. Also know as dextrose, grape sugar, blood sugar.

Glycerol [glycerine] (glyc'-er-ol). A substance that absorbs water and is a lubricant.

GRAS. Generally Regarded as Safe. This acronym is frequently used in reference to list of approved food additives.

Guar. A drought-resistant legume. Also a thickener in foods.

Hard cider. An alcohol beverage obtained from fermented apple cider or juice.

Hard water. Water that contains calcium, magnesium, or iron.

Herbicide. Any substance that kills plants.

Histamine (his'-ta-mine). A compound released in the body responsible for swelling sinues and other allergic reactions.

Hops. The dried ripe flowers of the hop tree. Used in brewing beer.

Humectant (hu-mec'-tant). Any substance that absorbs water, especially in foods.

Hydrated silicate (hy'-drat-ed sil'-i-cate). An abrasive in toothpaste, used for grinding debris off teeth.

Hydrochloric acid (hy-dro-chlor'-ic). Sometimes called muriatic acid. A very strong acid capable of attacking metals.

Hydrocortizone (hy-dro-cor'-ti-zone). Used to reduce inflammation as well as treating blood disorders and asthma.

Hydrogen peroxide. An antiseptic and a good oxidizing agent. See *antiseptic* and *oxidizing agent.*

Hydrogenated (hy-dro'-gen-at-ed). The addition of hydrogen gas to a liquid oil. This produces a solid margarine or shortening.

Hydroquione (hy-dro-quin'-one). A cosmetic that bleaches skin.

Hydroxyapatite (hy-drox'-y-ap-a-tite). Tooth enamel.

Hydroxymagnesium aluminate (hy-drox'-y-mag-ne'-si-um a-lu-min-ate). The active ingredient in some antacids such as Mylanta® or Rolaids®.

Hygroscopic (hy'-gro-scop-ic). Materials that absorb moisture from air.

Ibuprofen (i-bu-pro-fen). An analgesic used for deep muscle pain. See *analgesic* and *antipyretic.*

Inhibit. Slows down a chemical reaction by blocking a pathway.

Invert sugar. A fifty-fifty mixture of glucose and fructose. See *fructose* and *glucose.*

Iodine number. Related to the degree of unsaturation in an oil. Oils that have high iodine numbers are usually high in saturated fat.

Iodochlorhydroxyquin (i-o'-do-chlor'-hy-drox'-y-quin). Topical antiseptic.

Iodophor (i-o'-do-phor). Compounds that release iodine slowly. An antiseptic.

Ion exchange. A process by which harmful minerals are removed from water by trapping them in plastic resins.

Iron fumarate (fum-ar'-ate). Physiologically similar to iron gluconate.

Iron gluconate (glu'-con-ate). A dietary supplement of iron. It's not as irritating as iron sulfate.

Iron salts. Soluble iron compounds used to treat anemia.

Iron sulfate. The most common dietary iron supplement. It is not absorbed as easily as other iron supplements, and is more irritating for some people.

Isopropyl alcohol. (i'-so-pro'-pyl). Rubbing alcohol. A topical antiseptic. Also known as isopropanol. See *antiseptic.*

Kaolin (ka'-o-lin). Highly absorbent clay used to absorb fluids. Often used in medications for controlling diarrhea.

Kevlar (kev'-lar). A very strong, bulletproof plastic.

Keratin (ker'-a-tin). A protein obtained from hair, wool, horns, nails, and hoofs; used as a hair conditioner and as a coating on enteric capsules. Also used in white glues.

Keratolytic agent (ker'-a-to-lit'-ic). An exfoliant that causes infected or damaged skin to peel off, as in treatment of acne. See *exfoliant*.

KY Jelly®. A semi-solid liquid similar to petrolatum jelly, but less viscous and can be removed easily with water. Often used as a lubricant.

Lachrymator (lach'-re-ma-tor). Any substance that causes the eyes to tear.

Lacquer. Spirit varnishes such as shellac that dry to form a film with the evaporation of solvent.

Lactase (lac'-tase). The enzyme the body needs to digest lactose in milk and milk products. See *lactose*.

Lactic acid (lac'-tic). A moisture-attracting substance produced in the muscles by exertion. Also in milk.

Lactose (lac'-tose). A simple sugar molecule formed from glucose and galactose molecules. Also known as milk sugar.

Lager. A type of German beer. It has little hops and is aged for six weeks to six months.

Lanolin (lan'-o-lin). Sheep grease, frequently refined for use in cosmetics or ointments.

Latex (la'-tex). A water emulsion of rubber or plastics; used in coatings, paints, and adhesives.

Lauric acid (laur-ic). A crystalline fatty acid used to make soaps. It is obtained from coconut oil.

LD$_{50}$. The dose of a chemical needed to kill fifty percent of the test sample. An index of toxicity.

Leavening agent. Produces carbon dioxide gas in bread or pastry dough, thus allowing the dough to rise.

Legume. A pod-bearing plant, such as beans or peas, that is rich in protein.

Lichens (li'-chens). Plants found growing on rocks in northern seas. A main source of litmus. See *litmus*.

Lime. The common name for calcium hydroxide or calcium oxide. See *calcium hydroxide*.

Linoleic acid (lin'-o-le'-ic). An essential amino acid.

Lipids. Trigylcerides (soluble fats) in the blood.

Lithium battery (lith'-i-um). A high-output battery with extreme ruggedness.

Litmus. Extracted from lichens as a dye that indicates pH. Blue litmus turns red in the presence of acids, while red litmus turns blue in the presence of bases. See *lichens.*

Lye. Common name for potassium hydroxide or sodium hydroxide. See *sodium hydroxide.*

Magnesium carbonate (mag-ne′-si-um). An antacid and laxative.

Magnesium hydroxide. An antacid and laxative. Also known as Milk of Magnesia®.

Magnesium stearate (ste′-a-rate). Magnesium salt or stearic acid. See *stearic acid.*

Magnesium sulfate. Epsom salts. A drawing agent; sometimes used in laxatives.

Malting. The processing of grain into malt prior to use in beers.

Mannitol (mann′-it-ol). A natural sweetening agent with few calories. Also known as milk sugar. Also used as a softening agent in foods.

Methanol [methyl alcohol] (meth′-a-nol). The simplist form of alcohol. Sometimes called wood alcohol. Poisonous.

Methyl methacrylate (meth-ac′-ryl-ate). A thermoplastic material used in Plexiglass®, high-quality transparent objects, latex paints, contact lenses, and other items.

Methyl salicylate (sal-i′-cyl-ate). A topical counterirritant that offers relief from muscule soreness. See *counterirritant.*

Miconazole (mi-con′-a-zol). A topical antifungal. See *antifungal.*

Mineral oil. An emulsion of simple hydrocarbons and water. Used for lubrication of the intestines when constipation occurs.

Monosaturated fatty acid (sat-u-rated). Having mostly one (mono) unsaturated site. Shown to lower cholesterol. E.g., olive oil and cannola oil.

Monosodium glutamate (mon-o-so′-di-um glu′-ta-mate). Enhances the natural flavor of some foods.

Myrsil proionate (myr-sil pro-pi-on-ate). An emolient in cold creams.

Napalm (na′-palm). A gel containing incendiary polystyrene and gasoline. Used in warfare. See *polystyrene.*

Naproxen (na-prox′-en). One of the newest over-the-counter analgesics and antipyretics. Similar to ibuprofen in structure. See *analgesic* and *antipyretic.*

Natural. A meaningless term. See *organic.*

Natural water. Generally speaking, a meaningless term. It may indicate that the water has not been treated.

Nickel-Cadmium battery. Commonly called Ni-Cad. Rechargeable.

Nicotine. An extract of tobacco. Also used as an insecticide.

Nitrate (ni'-trate). An oxidizing agent, used in fertilizers and explosives. It is banned in the United States as a food preservative. Carcinogenic.

Nitrite (ni'-trite). A food preservative used in pork products. It can be carcinogenic when used in high concentrations.

Nitrocellulose (ni-tro-cell'-u-lose). A resin used in nail polish and explosives.

Notes. In perfumes this term indicates the permanence of odors. The top note evaporates quickly; the middle note persists for a few hours; and the bottom note requires several hours to disappear. This is why colognes have an intense odor when first applied but then soften throughout the day.

Nylon. A strong synthetic fiber used in making clothing.

Octane rating. An arbitrary scale used to compare the antiknock properties of gasolines.

Oil of cloves. Active ingredient is eugenol, a nerve-deadening agent used for dental pain.

Optical brightener. A compound that absorbs the invisible ultraviolet component of sunlight and re-emits it as visible light.

Organic. A compound containing carbon. When used in relationship to foods, the term means that fertilizers or insecticides have not been used in growing or harvesting the food item. Misuse of the term is widespread: for example, some vitamins are erroneously described as "organic."

Oxalic acid (ox-al'-ic). A poisonous, organic compound used in cleaning automobile radiators and other metals.

Oxidation (ox-i-da'-tion). The reaction of an atom or molecule with oxygen.

Oxidizing agent (ox'-i-diz-ing). Combines with oxygen to increase the positive charge of an element or compound. Destroys pigments.

Palm oil. Derived from palm fruit: a lubricant used in the preparation of soap and candles.

Palmitic acid (pal-mit'-ic). Derived from palm oil; used in the preparation of soaps.

Papain (pa-pain'). An enzyme from the papaya tree that dissolves protein.

Para-aminobenzoic acid (par-a-a-mi'-no-benz-o-ic). A sunscreen that absorbs ultraviolet light. Can be irritating to some people.

Petrolatum jelly (pe-tro-la'-tum). Often referred to as petroleum jelly. A semi-solid liquid of saturated hydrocarbons.

pH. A term used to indicate acidity or alkalinity (base). Values between 1 and 7 pH are acidic. A pH of 7 is neutral. Values of from 7 to 14 are basic (alkaline).

Phenolphthlein (phe-nolph-thal'-ein). A laxative. For example, Ex Lax®. Sometimes used as a dye to measure pH.

Phenols (phe'-nols). A very strong oxidizing agent and an antiseptic in cough medicines.

Phenylopropanolamine (phe'-nyl-pro-pa-nol'-a-mine). An over-the-counter decongestant in cold remedies.

Plaque. A thin film consisting of mucous and microorganisms on the dental surface and at the gum line. Also refers to the material deposited on artery walls, thus preventing proper circulation of blood to the heart.

Plexiglas®. Safety glass that doesn't shatter. A layer of methyl acrylate or polyvinylacetate plastic between two glass layers.

Polycarbonate (pol-y-car'-bon-ate). A clear, hard plastic used for helmets.

Polyester. The most commonly used synthetic fiber in clothes. See *Dacron®*.

Polyethylene (pol'-y-eth'-y-lene). A plastic having many uses. Low-density polyethylene is used in making trash bags and in coating electic wires. High-density polyethylene is used for plastic containers, shipping drums, and many children's toys.

Polyhydric alcohols (pol-y-hy'-dric). Drying agents used in shaving creams and speciality soaps.

Polymer (pol'-y-mer). A long chain of hydrocarbons made from the joining of monomers (small units). Can be found in plastics, silicates, and varnishes.

Polysaccharide (pol'-y-sac'-char-ide). Containing many sugars.

Polystyrene (pol'-y-sty'-rene). A plastic foam used for heat and shock resistance. Commonly found in disposable coffee cups and packaging.

Polyunsaturated (pol'-y-un-sat'-u-ra-ted). Indicates a fatty acid is liquid rather than solid; the molecule has more than one unsaturated site.

Polyvinyl chloride (pol-y-ví'-nyl). A plastic used for floor tile, raincoats, and phonograph records.

Polyvinylpyrroldone (pol-y-vi'-nyl-py-rol-done [PVP]). A resin in most hair sprays.

Porter [Porter's beer]. A weak stout containing 4 percent alcohol. See *stout.*

Portland cement. Contains calcium, iron, aluminum, silicon, and oxygen. Resembles glass in structure.

Potash (pot'-ash). Potassium hydroxide, usually from wood ashes.

Potassium pyrophosphate (po-tass-i-um py-ro-phos'-phate). Inhibits the conversion of plaque to tartar in the mouth. An ingredient in toothpastes and in some mouthwashes.

PPM. Parts per million or 0.0001 percent.

Precipitate (pre-cip'-i-tate). A compound that is insoluble in water and removed with filtration.

Precursor (pre-cur'-sor). An intermediate stage in some chemical reactions. For example, betacarotene (precursor) is converted to vitamin A in the body.

Proof. A term used to indicate alcohol content. Two proof equals one percent alcohol.

Propylene glycol (pro'-py-lene gly'-col). A commercial permanent antifreeze. Poisonous.

Protease (pro'-tease). Enzymes increase the speed of reactions; protease is an enzyme in the class that breaks down protein.

Provo-iodine. An antiseptic that supplies a slow, constant supply of iodine when placed on the skin.

Pseudoephedrine (pseu'-do-eph'-e-drine). A nonsedating form of the antihistamine ephedrine. One brand is Sudafed®.

Psyllium (psyl'-i-um). A natural polysaccharide that absorbs water in the colon and is an alternative to laxatives. See *polysaccharide.*

Psychotropic (psy'-cho-trop-ic). Drugs that affect the mind.

Purified water. Water that has been treated to remove impurities by some manner that is not obvious.

Pyrethrum (py-re'-thrum). Insecticide originally derived from chrysanthemums.

Pyretic (py-re'-tic). Of or relating to fever.

Quaternary ammonium hydroxide (qua'-ter-na-ry). A disinfectant and surfactant. Also used in shampoos and liquid soaps. See *ammonium hydroxide.*

Quinine (qui'-nine). Extracted from Cinchona bark and used as an antimalarial agent. Found in quinine water.

Rapeseed oil. A lubricant used in the manufacture of soft soap and margarine.

Reduction. Reverse of oxidation. Removal of oxygen.

Resorcinol (re-sor'-ci-nol). An antiseptic and antipruritic (relieves itching).

Reverse osmosis (os-mo'-sis). A process used to purify water by passing an electrical current through a membrane that removes most dissolved compounds as they migrate (move) out.

Reyes Syndrome. An uncommon but serious allergic reaction to aspirin.

Rubbing alcohol. Also known as isopropyl alcohol or isopropanol. Poisonous.

Rye. An alcoholic beverage obtained from the fermentation of rye meal.

Saccharin (sac'-char-in). A nonnutritive, artificial sweetener.

Safflower petals. A source for "natural" rouge color in some foods.

Sake (sak'-e). A Japanese wine made from rice.

Sal soda. Also known as washing soda, sodiuum carbonate. Poisonous.

Salicylic acid (sal-i-cyl'-ic). A topically applied substance used in the relief of rheumatism. Also a keratolytic agent (peels damaged skin off) for acne.

Salt. Sodium chloride. Low-sodium "salt" or "sodium free" salt means that sodium chloride has been replaced with potassium chloride.

Saponify (sa-pon'-i-fy). Making soap by heating fat and a strong base.

Saturated hydrocarbon. A compound of only carbon and hydrogen, having only single bonds.

Selenium (se-len'-i-um). A poisonous metal.

Selenium sulfide. Used in shampoos for antidandruff activity.

Senna. A natural extract used as a strong laxative.

Sequestering agent (se-ques'-ter-ing). A compound that can remove trace metals in foods. For example, EDTA or citric acid.

Serotonin (ser'-o-to'-nin). A drug that controls sensory perception and mood. It is also a powerful vasoconstrictor (narrows blood vessels).

Shellac (she-llac'). Purified lac used primarily as a wood finish and filler.

Silicon dioxide (sil'-i-con). Sand. An anticaking agent in some dry spices.

Simethicone (si-meth'-i-cone). An antibloating agent for gas in the stomach.

Single bond. The attractive force holding atoms together in a molecule. A single bond indicates only one bond holds atoms together. Saturated fats have mostly single bonds.

Smoke point. The temperature at which oil or solid fats break down and smoke when heated.

Sodium alkyd benzene sulfonate. A detergent that is biodegradable.

Sodium benzoate (ben'-zo-ate). A food preservative and an antioxidant. See *antioxidant.*

Sodium borate. A food preservative.

Sodium carbonate. Also known as washing soda or Sal soda; used in laundry soaps and detergents as a builder to increase pH, and as a water softener.

Sodium chloride. Table salt, rock salt.

Sodium cocoglyceryl sulfonate. (co-co-gly'-cer-yl). A surfactant in detergent bars for personal hygiene (e.g. Zest®).

Sodium hydroxide. A strong base used to neutralize acids and to react to fats to form soap.

Sodium hypochlorite (hy-po-chlor'-ite). Liquid laundry bleach, chlorine bleach. A disinfectant.

Sodium lauryl sulfate (laur'-yl). The first detergent. Still used in shampoos, toothpastes, and cosmetics.

Sodium perborate (per-bor'-ate). The ingredient of dry bleaches, oxygen bleach.

Sodium phosphate. Also known as trisodium phosphate. A wetting agent found in floor, wall, and title cleaners.

Sodium propionate (pro'-pi-on-ate). A food preservative and antioxidant.

Sodium stearate (stear'-ate). Sodium salt of stearic acid. Used in soap. See *stearic acid.*

Sodium sulfate. An inert substance added to solid detergents to aid in pouring.

Sodium tallowate (tall-ow-ate). A sodium salt of tallow (beef or mutton fat) used in bar soaps. It contains oleic, palmitic, stearic, myristic, and linoleic fatty acids.

Solute. The thing being dissolved. In sugar-water, sugar is the solute and water is the solvent. Together they form a sugar-water solution.

Solvent. That into which something dissolves.

Sorbitol (sor'-bi-tol). A humectant, drawing water into food and tobacco. Also a sweetener.

SPF. Sun protection factor. It indicates the amount of skin protection a sunscreen provides. The higher the SPF, more protection is offered.

Spandex®. A synthetic fiber made from polyurethane. It mixes well with other fibers in small amounts.

Sparkling wine. A wine containing dissolved carbon dioxide gas.

Starch. A complex carbohydrate used as an adhesive and in sizing.

Stearic acid (stear'-ic). A fatty acid in beef tallow. Used to make soaps.

Stout. A heavy, viscous form of beer with a remarkably strong taste. Stronger and sweeter than porter. See *porter* and *viscosity*.

Sublime (sub-lime'). The conversion of a solid directly to a gas. Normally no liquid state exists for the element or compound. For example, carbon dioxide as "dry ice."

Sucrose (su'-crose). Common table sugar made from sugar beets or sugar cane.

Sulfuric acid (sul-fur'-ic). A very strong acid that absorbs water. Used in car batteries and drain cleaners. It can destroy human tissue.

Superchlorination. Shock chlorination. An excess of chlorine is used to start up new pools and revitalize old ones.

Surface tension. The attractive forces in a liquid that prevent "wetting" (the absorption of a liquid).

Surfactant (sur-fac'-tant). A surface-active agent that can destroy the surface tension of liquid resulting in greater "wetting" ability, such as a detergent.

Synergistic effect (syn-er-gis'-tic). An effect much greater than expected from just the sum of the expected effects, such as when alcohol and barbiturates are mixed in the stomach.

Talc. Basic magnesium silicate used as body powder.

Tallow. Fats derived from heating beef, pork, and lamb.

Tartar. (tar'-tar). An encrustment on the teeth which is hard to remove.

Tartaric acid (tar-tar'-ic). Obtained from wine. An acidulant used in soft drinks, baking, and confectionary products. Also used in tanning leather. See *acidulant.*

Teflon®. An inert plastic made of carbon, hydrogen, and fluorine.

Thermosetting. The reaction of monomers to produce polymers upon heating. The structure is then rigid.

Tincture (tinc'-ture). Any solution that uses alcohol as the solvent.

Titanium dioxide (ti-ta'-ni-um). Sunblock, a white pigment in paints.

Tolnaftate (tol-naf'-tate). An antifungal agent. See *antifungal.*

Topical. Applied to the surface of the skin.

Total chlorine. A test for chlorine in swimming pools that includes all types of chlorine.

Thio-. A preface indicating that sulfur has replaced oxygen in a molecule. For example, sodium thiosulfate, thiogylcolic acid.

Thiogylcolic acid (thi'-o-gly'-col-ic). A depilatory. Removes hair chemically.

Trade mark. Word(s) registered to distinguish one product from all others. Coke® is a trade name. Coca and cola are not.

Triclocarban (tri'-clo-car-ban). An antibacterial used in many soaps and detergent bars.

Triethanolamine (tri-eth-a-nol'-a-mine). A surfactant used in shampoos.

Triethylene glycol (tri-eth'-yl-ene). Used in the manufacturing of plastics to increase pliability. Also air disinfectant.

Triple bond. An attractive force holding atoms together in a molecule. A triple bond indicates there are three bonds between two atoms.

Trisodium phosphate (tri-so'-di-um). A strong, basic compound used to cleaning floors and tiles (Spic 'n' Span®).

Tryptophan (tryp-to-phan). An essential amino acid.

Turpentine. A solvent extracted from pine oil.

Unsaturation. A hydrocarbon having a double or triple bond.

Urea. A soluble, weak basic solution found in urine. Also used in the synthesis of plastics and other polymers.

U.S.R.D.A. A list of the United States required daily allowance of vitamins and minerals.

Vanillin. The chief fragrant component of vanilla; used in flavoring and perfumes.

Varnish. A resin from the vernox or the Japanese sumac tree. A liquid that dries to a translucent, hard finish.

Viscosity (vis-cos'-i-ty). Resistance of a liquid to flow easily.

Vodka. An alcoholic beverage from any source and then filtered with activated carbon.

Volatile (vol'-a-tile). Readily forming a gas. For example, gasoline.

Vulcanized (vul'-can-ized). Rubber treated with sulfur to give it superior properties.

Water softener. Compounds that tie up or remove the metals that cause hard water (e.g., calcium, iron, magnesium).

Whitewash. A paint made from lime, egg whites, and water.

Wort. A dilute solution of sugars obtained from malt and fermented to form beer.

Zinc oxide. An astringent. Provides a protective coating. Can serve as a sunblock. See *astringent* and *sunblock*.

Zinc pyrithizone (pyr-i'-thi-zone). An antidandruff agent in shampoos.

Zirconium chlorohydrate (zir-co'-ni-um chlor-o-hy'-drate). The active ingredient in many antiperspirants.

Suggested Readings

Much of the literature on consumer chemistry is written at a level that most laypersons can understand. We have marked the more challenging works with an asterisk, but please don't ignore them just because they are a little more difficult.

Atkins, P. W. *Molecules.* New York: Freeman Publishers, 1990. (One of the best 190 pages on chemicals for the layperson. It is vibrantly written and illustrated with the quality of the noted *Scientific American* magazine. This book requires no previous knowledge of chemistry and can be read cover to cover, or special focus can be given to any of its self-contained chapters.)

Block, E. "The Chemistry of Garlic and Onions." *Scientific American,* March 1985.

Brown, T. *Energy and the Environment.* C lumbus, Ohio: Charles Merrill Publishers, 1971.

Carson, R. *Silent Spring.* New York: Houghton-Mifflin, 1962.

Elaine, S. "The Glue Revolution." *Popular Science,* August 1980.

Gabler, R. *Is Your Water Safe?* Mt. Vernon, N.Y.: Consumer Reports Books, 1988.

Griffith, H. *The Complete Guide to Prescription and Nonprescription Drugs.* New York: Body Press/Perigee Publishers (A Division of the Putnum Publishing Group), 1991.

Hill, J. *Chemistry for Changing Times,* 6th ed. New York, Macmillan, 1994. (A good source for the nonscientist.)

Holmes, A. "The Role of Food Additives." *Chemistry and Industry,* February 6, 1989.

"Kerosene Heaters." *Consumer Reports* February 1985.

Kosikowski, F. *Cheese and Fermented Milk Products.* Ann Arbor, Mich.: Edwards Brothers, 1977.

Lee, F. *Basic Food Chemistry.* Westport, Conn.: Avi Publishers, 1975.

Levie, A. *The Meat Handbook.* Westport, Conn.: Avi Publishers,, 1979.

The Merck Index, 11th ed. Rahway, N.J.: Merck and Company Publishers, 1989.

Miller, G. *Living in the Environment,* 6th ed. Belmont, Calif.: Wadsworth Publishers, 1990.

"Purifying Water, Cleaning Air." *ChemEcology,* March 1982.

Saadith, N. "The Chemistry of Sunscreens." *Cosmetics and Toiletries,* March 1986.

Sanders, H. "Herbicides." *Chemical and Engineering News* August 1981.

Schaffer, J. "Designer Drugs." *Science News,* March 1985.

*Sellinger, B. *Chemistry in the Marketplace,* 4th ed. Australia: Harcourt, Brace, Jovanovich, Pty. Limited, 1989. (One of the most comprehensive books on consumer chemistry. Most readers will benefit from the nonscientific sections.)

Seymour, R. "Polymers Are Everywhere." *Journal of Chemical Education,* April 1988.

Snyder, C. *The Extraordinary Chemistry of Ordinary Things.* New York: Wiley, 1992. (A thorough and often funny book.)

Snyder, S. *Drugs and the Brain.* San Francisco, Calif.: Freeman Publishers, 1987.

Ward, W. "Pesticides." *Chemical and Engineering News,* July 23, 1987.

Wood, G. and J. Failes. *Prescription Drugs Encyclopedia.* Peachtree, Ga.: F. C. & A. Publishers, 1988.

Zimmerman, D. *The Essential Guide to Nonprescription Drugs.* New York: Harper and Row Publishers, 1984.